THE ECONOMY OF CITIES

The ECONOMY of CITIES

JANE JACOBS

Vintage Books
A Division of Random House
New York

Vintage Books Edition, February 1970
Copyright © 1969 by Jane Jacobs
All rights reserved under International
and Pan-American Copyright Conventions.
Published in the United States by
Random House, Inc., New York
and simultaneously in Canada by Random House
of Canada Limited, Toronto.
Originally published by Random House, Inc.
Library of Congress Catalog Card Number: 69-16413
Manufactured in the United States of America
456789C

To
Betty, John, Jim
& our mother & father

"I will [tell] the story as I go along of small cities no less than of great. Most of those which were great once are small today; and those which in my own lifetime have grown to greatness, were small enough in the old days."

—HERODOTUS

Acknowledgments

The most valuable of a writer's materials is uninterrupted time in which to write, and I am grateful beyond measure to my husband, Robert Hyde Jacobs, Jr., and my children, James, Edward and Mary, for their gifts to me of time and their cheerful protection of it against incursions. I am grateful also to Rachele Wall, Martin Berger and Arthur Stoliar for adding to their own burdens much of my share of the work on two civic efforts dear to me; and to Leticia Kent, Erik Wensberg, Richard Barnett and my lawyer, Charles Rembar, for the exuberance with which they have defended my liberty in a contretemps with the authorities, and thus have permitted this book to be completed.

For assistance with the work itself, I am again indebted to my family for many criticisms and ideas; to Jason Epstein, my editor and publisher, whose advice and faith have both been indispensable; to Erik Wensberg and Alice Mayhew for their skillful and sensitive editing; to Roderick Gittens, Mariam Slater, Ole Thomassen, W. Lain Guthrie and P. Sargant Florence for information and to John Decker Butzner, Jr., Martha Barnett, and Hans Blumenfeld for comment and criticism (although none of these is responsible for the use I have made of his knowledge); to Howard Bentley for his preparation of the index; and to the New York Public Library for the use of its Frederick Lewis Allen Room.

August, 1968   J.J.

Contents

Appendix

THE ECONOMY OF CITIES

1

Cities First—
Rural Development Later

This book is an outcome of my curiosity about why some cities grow and why others stagnate and decay. I have relied greatly and gratefully upon the findings—reliable, as far as I am able to judge—of many scholars; historians and archeologists in particular. But I have not necessarily adopted their views about the meanings of their findings in my effort to develop a theory of city economic growth.

One of many surprises I found in the course of this work was especially unsettling because it ran counter to so much I had always taken for granted. Superficially, it seemed to run counter to common sense and yet there it was: work that we usually consider rural has originated not in the countryside, but in cities. Current theory in many fields—economics, history, anthropology—assumes that cities are built upon a rural economic base. If my observations and reasoning are correct, the reverse is true: that is, rural economies, including agricultural work, are directly built upon city economies and city work.

So thoroughly does the theory (in my view, the dogma) of agricultural primacy saturate the conventional assumptions about cities that I propose to deal with it in this chapter as the first order of business. In the chapters that follow I shall then describe what I have been able to learn about how cities grow, taking each part of the growth process separately. Thus this first chapter is a prologue.

We are all well aware from the history of science that ideas universally believed are not necessarily true. We are also aware that it is only after the untruth of such ideas has been exposed that it becomes apparent how pervasive and insidious their influence has been.

To take an example: for thousands of years otherwise intelligent men thought that those small animals found in rotting meat, cheese and still water took form and came to life without parents. Their environment, it was supposed, not only nourished them, it created them by a process called spontaneous generation. This theory seems to have gone unquestioned until the Renaissance, when a Florentine poet-physician demonstrated that maggots did not materialize in rotting meat if the meat had been screened from flies. He drew the proper inference that the new life arose from existing life. But just as his insight was gaining currency, the microscope was invented. Hitherto invisible bits of life now became visible. Their presence was promptly interpreted to be new proof of spontaneous generation and thus the dogma stood a full two centuries longer, buttressed, ironically, by the tools of science until it was demolished by Pasteur in the nineteenth century.

Pasteur repeated the Florentine experiment, using bacteria instead of flies as his experimental animals and wine instead of meat as his medium. His findings were savagely attacked by the most eminent biologists of his time because the new knowledge demolished so much that they knew about biology. For although the dogma of spontaneous generation ostensibly explained only the origins of tiny organisms, belief in it had subtly distorted much other biological observation and theory. It had simply closed off as "already explained" some very interesting questions, such as how single-celled animals really do multiply; hence had stultified the investigation and understanding of cells generally. For another thing, many biologists had invested their lives in rationalizing newly observed truths to conform with the traditional error; those biologists with the most eminent reputations had frequently been the authors of the most elaborate and arcane rationalizations.

In just such ways, I think, our understanding of cities, and also of economic development generally, has been distorted by the dogma of agricultural primacy. I plan to argue that this dogma is as quaint as the theory of spontaneous generation, being a vestige of pre-Darwinian intellectual history that has hung on past its time.

The dogma of agricultural primacy says: agriculture first, cities later. Behind the dogma lies the notion that in pre-Neolithic times hunting men lived only in small and economically self-sufficient groups, finding their own food, making their own weapons, tools and other manufactured goods. Not until some of these primitive groups learned to cultivate grain and raise livestock, it is thought, did settled and stable villages emerge, and not until after the villages were built did complex divisions of labor, large economic projects and intricate social organization become possible. These advances, coupled with a surplus of agricultural food, are supposed to have made cities possible.

One school of thought, the older, holds that cities evolved slowly, but directly, out of villages that were at first simple agricultural units but gradually grew both larger and more complex. Another school holds that cities were organized by non-agricultural warriors who put peasants to work for them, in return protecting the peasants from other warriors. In either version, the food produced by agricultural work and workers is presumed to have been an indispensable foundation for cities.

This sequence—first agricultural villages, then towns, then cities—ostensibly explains only the first cities. But the assumption has affected ideas of what cities are and what may be their place in the economic scheme of things now, as well as historically. If it is true that cities could not have been developed before agricultural settlements appeared, then it follows that development of agriculture, and of rural resources in general, is basic and that cities, since they are supported upon rural development, are secondary. Thus villages certainly, and probably towns, would seem to be more important to human life than cities. It follows also that cities would differ from lesser settlements primarily by being bigger and more complicated, or by being the seats of power.

All these logical sequels to the dogma of original agricultural primacy underlie—often as unspoken assumptions—modern, practical attempts at planned economic development. They are not merely academic notions. In both Marxist and capitalist countries these ideas are used as working assumptions.

Cities have long been acknowledged as primary organs of cultural development; that is, of the vast and intricate collections of ideas and institutions called civilization, and I have no intention of laboring that point.

Rather, my purpose now is to show that cities are also primary economic organs. To explain how this can be, I shall first touch upon modern and historical relationships between city and rural work; then conjecture what those relationships must have been in prehistoric times; and finally suggest why the conventional and contrary theory took hold.

Cities and Agricultural Productivity

It can readily be seen in the world today that agriculture is not even tolerably productive unless it incorporates many goods and services produced in cities or transplanted from cities. The most thoroughly rural countries exhibit the most unproductive agriculture. The most thoroughly urbanized countries, on the other hand, are precisely those that produce food most abundantly. A few years ago the United States and the European Common Market engaged in what was called a chicken war. Each was trying to push its surfeit of chickens off onto the other. But this does not mean that the industrialized and urban economies of the United States and Western Europe were built upon surfeits of chickens. They simply produced surfeits of chickens.

Surges in agricultural productivity follow the growth of cities. Japanese cities began their modern industrial and commercial growth in the latter part of the nineteenth century and by World War II Japan had become a highly urbanized country. During this time, although Japanese farmers were industrious and thrifty—the very models of those virtues—and although they used their land most carefully, neither they nor the city populations were well fed. Rice was the staff of life; for many Japanese there was little else except wild food—fish from the sea. Yet Japan did not raise enough rice for her own people and a full quarter of what they consumed had to be imported. It was the custom to ascribe this severe food deficit to Japan's small supply of arable soil.

But after the war and during the 1950s remarkable changes occurred in Japanese agriculture, changes that cannot be explained by catchwords like "reform"; indeed, the Japanese have made advances that have not been made in countries where reform of agriculture, land-holding and rural life have all been pursued more determinedly and heroically.

What happened in Japan was, although wonderfully effective, commonplace. The rural world began receiving in vast amounts, for the first time, fertilizers, machines, electric power, refrigeration equipment, the results of plant and animal research, and a host of other tangible goods and services developed in cities—the same cities where the richest food markets already lay.

Japanese agriculture rapidly achieved a degree of productivity that had been thought unattainable. In 1960, although the population was twenty-five percent larger than it had been before the war, and total consumption of rice had soared, Japanese farms were supplying all of Japan's rice; none was any longer imported. Even more interesting, the per capita consumption of rice had dropped a little, but not because of shortages. Like the steady, long-term drop in starch consumption in the United States, this drop was caused by the availability of more abundant and varied food. The farmers, in addition to supplying more rice, were producing so much more milk and other dairy products, fowls, eggs, meat, fruits and vegetables that the Japanese were not only eating more than before, they were eating better. Nowadays when Japan imports food and pays for it with industrial products, she imports meats, not rice.

If modern Japanese cities had waited to grow until a surplus of rural products could support that growth, they would be waiting still. Japan, reinventing its agriculture, has accomplished abruptly and rapidly what the United States did somewhat more gradually and Western Europe more gradually still. *It created rural productivity upon a foundation of city productivity*. There is no inherent reason why this cannot be done by other nations even more rapidly.

Modern productive agriculture has been reinvented by grace of hundreds of innovations that were exported from the cities to the countryside, transplanted to the countryside or imitated in the countryside. We are accustomed to think of these innovations in large, rather abstract groupings: chemical fertilizers, mechanical sowers, cultivators, harvesters, tractors and other substitutes for draft animals and hand labor; mechanical refrigeration; pipes, sprinklers, pumps and other modern irrigation equipment; laboratories for research into plant and animal diseases and their control; soil analyses and weather forecasting systems; new hybridized plants; marketing and transportation systems; canning, freezing and drying technologies; methods of spreading information. . . . The list is long.

To be sure, one can often find fertilizer factories, tractor plants, agricultural research stations, nurseries and electric power plants located in the rural world far from cities. But these activities were not created there. This is so not because farmers and other rural people are less creative than city dwellers. The difference lies in the contrasting natures of rural and city economies, for it is in cities that new goods and services are first created. Even innovations created specifically for farming depend directly upon earlier developments of city work. For example, McCormick's first horse-drawn reaper was a tremendous innovation for farm work; here was a machine that replaced hand implements and supple, complex hand movements. Although this idea and the device to carry it out were new to farm work, the same idea and devices similar in principle were already commonly used in industrial work. Nor could McCormick have manufactured the reaper if other industrial tools had not already been developed. The industrial revolution occurred first in cities and later in agriculture.

Electricity is now as necessary to modern farming and farm life as it is to city work and city life. Yet as late as 1935, fewer than five percent of American farms had electricity. First, electric power and a great variety of devices to use it were added to the economies of city after city, then rapidly to the economies of towns, but only belatedly to the economy of the countryside. It is all very well to say that the length of time this process took was the result of the reluctance of utility corporations to invest in rural electrification and also of their attempts to prevent anyone else from doing what they would not do themselves. But it is still true that these great innovations were added in cities and only after they had been developed and proved out there were they received into the agricultural world. This pattern is typical and it explains how agricultural productivity lags behind urban productivity; why, indeed, there is no way to increase rural productivity first and city productivity later.

There are numbers of instances which show how rural people by themselves are helpless to meet even their own food crises. Ireland affords a gruesome illustration. When the potato blight hit Ireland in the 1840s, the population had no resources to combat the famine, even though they were an agricultural people. Cecil Woodham-Smith in *The Great Hunger* describes the callous and fatuous policies of the English overlords of Ireland and their local puppets which failed to meet the crisis. But she also describes Ireland's inability to accept and use what relief was attempted. There were no ports to receive relief food in the areas where the need was greatest, and no interior means of transporting relief food once it could be landed. There were no mills for grinding relief grain. There were no mechanics or tools and equipment to build mills. There were no ovens for baking bread. There were no ways to spread information about how to grow crops other than potatoes. There was no way to distribute the seeds of other crops, nor to supply the farm tools that were indispensable for a change of crops, nor any way to make the tools. Potato culture in nineteenth-century Ireland was a much simpler type of agriculture than even prehistoric grain culture had been. What we think of as the most primitive agricultural arts and equipment, dating back some nine thousand years and more, had been lost in Ireland. And without the intervention of cities, there was no way for the rural people to retrieve old technologies, let alone employ new ones.

To be sure, the Irish had reached this pass because they were held in an iron economic and social subjection. But the very core of that subjection—and the reason why it was so effective and had rendered them so helpless—was the systematic suppression of city industry, the same suppression in principle that the English had unsuccessfully tried to enforce upon industry in the little cities of the American colonies.

The City Sources of Rural Work

It is one thing to notice that equipment to change and improve the productivity of already existing rural work arises in cities. But the full purport of this movement as a pattern of development is not apparent until we recognize that the same pattern also holds for the introduction of new work into the countryside. Let us drop agriculture for a moment; we shall get back to it. Let us consider a movement that we take as a matter of course, the transplanting of modern factory work from cities to the countryside.

When we see a factory out in the country, we do not automatically assume that the kind of work being done in the factory originated and developed in the country. The brassiere was invented by a New York seamstress, Mrs. Ida Rosenthal, who first manufactured brassieres in the 1920s in New York and then across the Hudson in Hoboken. As her company, Maidenform Brassieres, grew, she later transplanted much of the production work to rural areas where labor costs were lower. The Maidenform Brassiere factories in rural West Virginia employed local people who already knew how to sew and possibly even made their own underwear but this should not persuade us that therefore brassiere making developed from subsistence underwear making in West Virginia.

But we may not so readily realize that just such transplantations of city work were being made long ago. For example, it is conventional to call the country weaving of Europe a "cottage industry" and to imagine that it actually developed in the countryside. It developed there no more than brassiere manufacturing developed in the villages of West Virginia. In Europe, at the time the medieval cities began to form, the prevalent rural weaving was a degenerate and stagnated activity and its products were wretched. In time it disappeared. Between the eleventh and fifteenth centuries, European weaving was revolutionized in the cities. Indeed, for all practical purposes, it was almost re-created there. The looms, carding combs, dyes, methods of finishing cloth, the divisions of labor, the marketing—everything was changed. This is why the specialized crafts in the industry, and the guilds that institutionalized them—the Weavers, Burlers, Fullers, Shearmen, Carders, Beaters, Dyers, Drapers, and so on—were first formed as city organizations, not rural organizations. George Unwin, a British economic historian writing early in this century, notes in his *Studies in Economic History* that "For two generations before Shakespeare's time, the cloth manufacture had been rapidly spreading through the country districts, to the great alarm of the older urban centers of the industry. The town craftsmen complained bitterly of the competition. . . ." It was the city weaving, transplanted into rural Europe in late medieval and Renaissance times, that became a country industry, and in some instances a cottage industry because the spinners and weavers frequently worked in their homes.

In New York State today, apple coolers stand at numerous crossroads; apples are brought together from many farms and stored in carbon dioxide atmospheres until it is time for marketing them. These facilities are called "country storage." But this country storage is not a derivative of the old farm fruit cellars. Nor are the machines that control the temperatures of the coolers derivatives of the old rural icehouses. Just so, the large furniture-making industry in Virginia and North Carolina, employing farmers part-time, is not a derivative of the local farm carpentry, but city industry transplanted. It is easy to fall into the assumption that older rural forms of work evolved or developed into newer rural forms of work. This is a result of thinking abstractly about categories of work such as sewing, weaving, storing or cabinetmaking. It is like assuming that one course of a dinner somehow evolves or develops into the next course, and failing to notice that each new course is being brought in from the kitchen.

Because we are so used to thinking of farming as a rural activity, we are especially apt to overlook the fact that new kinds of farming come out of cities. The growing of hybrid corn was a revolutionary change in American agriculture; it amounted to a new kind of corn culture. The method was not developed on corn farms by farmers, but by scientists in plant laboratories in New Haven. It was explained, promoted and publicized by plant scientists and the editors of agricultural papers, and they had a hard time persuading farmers to try the unprepossessing-looking hybrid seeds. When the wheat farms of New York State changed to fruit farming, the change was promoted primarily from Rochester, by the proprietors of a nursery that first supplied the city people with frui trees, grape vines and berry bushes for their yards and gardens, and then showed farmers of the Gene-see Valley, who could no longer compete with wheat from the West, that orchards and vineyards were economic alternatives. The great fruit and vegetable growing industries of California did not "evolve" from that state's older wheat fields and animal pastures. Rather, the new California farming was organized in San Francisco, for the purpose of supplying fruits to preserving plants there and, later, vegetables to canneries.

But let us go back farther, to medieval Europe, where the cities seem to have re-created the "country industry" of agriculture, much as they later created a "country industry" of weaving.

After the fall of Rome, European agriculture had stagnated and then degenerated. Even the model monastery farms, in which Roman agricultural technologies and crops were preserved longest, stagnated and then degenerated. Charlemagne attempted to revitalize them but could not, and they continued to deteriorate during the tenth and most of the eleventh centuries, the period during which the medieval cities had begun to grow. At the start of the eleventh century, when bustling little Paris already had a population of thousands engaged in trade and craft manufacturing, this was the state of rural French agriculture as described by Duby and Mandrou in *A History of French Civilization*:

. . . the peasants of the year 1000 are half starved. The effects of chronic undernourishment are conspicuous in the skeletons exhumed from Merovingian cemeteries; the chafing of the teeth that indicates a grass-eating people, rickets, and an overwhelming preponderance of people who died young. . . . There is never enough food for subsistence, and periodically the lack of food grows worse. For a year or two there will be a great famine; the chroniclers describe the graphic and horrible episodes of this catastrophe, complacently and rather excessively conjuring up people who eat dirt and sell human skin. If stomachs are empty, and children are stricken by disease before adolescence, in spite of the enormous extent of cultivatable and undeveloped land, it is because the equipment enabling men to extract their nourishment from the soil is very primitive and inadequate. There is little or no metal; iron is reserved for weapons. In the most comprehensive and advanced monastic farms, maintaining some hundred head of beef in their stables, one may find a scythe or two, a shovel and an ax. Most of the tools are wooden—light swingplows, hoes with their points hardened by fire, unusable except in very loose ground and plowing that imperfectly.

The goods purchased by the little cities from the hungry countryside were largely materials that went into crafts: raw wool, hides, horn. The food of the little cities was, in large part, not agricultural produce but wild food: chiefly wild fowl and fish. Salt fish was as much the staff of life as bread; often more so. This, incidentally, is the reason why London's fishmongers were such important and prestigious merchants. Their wares, carried great distances from London, were helping to feed many other little trading cities, and manors out in the country too.

But the early medieval cities did depend in part on grain. Indeed, by using grain for bread, city people were also beginning the long process of reinventing the European diet; gruel and porridge, not bread, had become the customary European grain dishes in the centuries after Rome's fall. The mills and the bakeries of early medieval cities were not copies of village or manorial industry brought into the cities. They were, rather, the forerunners of village and manorial mills and bakeries.

Some of the grain of the little cities was probably gotten from the rural world. But much of it, likely most of it, the city people grew for themselves in the fields both within and without the walls; throughout Europe, such fields were standard facilities of early medieval cities. The medieval cities must have been their own first markets for the metal agricultural tools made by their smiths—the metal tools that were to become so important to rural Europe in the twelfth century and later.

In Europe of the eleventh century, it was still the general rural practice to use patches of land until the fertility was depleted and then to abandon those patches; or else to cultivate a field for several years, let it grow up to brush for another few years, then burn it over and plant again. Charlemagne had tried to reinstitute the old Roman system of alternating two crops, but his efforts were to little avail, if any, because not until the twelfth century was rotation widely adopted, and then it differed from the Roman practice.

In the medieval system, wheat or rye was planted on a given plot the first year, oats or barley (sometimes peas or beans) the second, and the land was allowed to lie fallow the third. Under the three-field system, as this scheme of crop rotation is called, three plots made a unit, each plot being at a different stage in the cycle, like a singer of a round. It was not a very efficient system of crop rotation but it was an enormous improvement, one of the chief changes in the complex collection of new rural practices and tools that historians call "the twelfth-century agricultural revolution."

Nobody knows just where the medieval three-field system began but this much is evident: it centered around cities. The rural areas that first adopted it were those near the cities and along the trade routes that lay between cities. Its further extension was rather slow. It took two centuries and more to reach the rural backwaters of Europe. The last places to adopt rotation were those most distant from cities and least touched by city trade and goods.

Early in the eighteenth century, a great improvement was made in crop rotation, a change so important that it is at the heart of what is called "the eighteenth-century agricultural revolution." In the former fallow year, crops not previously employed in the rural farming of Europe were planted: alfalfa, clover, and another fodder crop called sainfoin. The fodder crops did more than "give the land a rest." They replaced nitrogen used up by grain and at the same time supported cattle. The livestock provided nitrogen-rich manure. Fertility of the cropland and numbers of farm animals both increased at an extraordinary rate, making possible the abrupt European population increases that so alarmed Malthus.

Where did rural Europe get the fodder crops, along with the practice of fitting them into the rotation in place of the fallow year? Duby and Mandrou say the fodders were being grown in the city gardens of France for at least a century before they were adopted into rural farming, and that they were also grown in nearby fields to feed city draft animals. As in the case of the twelfth-century rotation, the new agriculture spread first near cities and along the trade routes, and it was adopted last in the rural areas most distant from cities and least touched by their trade and goods.

The idea that agriculture itself may have originated in cities, the thought to which I have been leading, may seem radical and disturbing. And yet even in our own time, agricultural practices do emerge from cities. A modern instance has been the American practice of fattening beef on corn before slaughter, the practice that has given us the corn-fed steak. This "farm work" did not begin on farms or cattle ranches, but in the city stock-yards of Kansas City and Chicago. It was a forerunner of such present farm work. The fattening pens are all but gone from the cities now because the work has been transplanted from cities to the rural world.

Meat-packing plants themselves are in process of moving from city to countryside To our descendants, it may seem almost incredible that the "country industry" of slaughtering and packing meat for city consumers, of saving pituitaries for laboratories, and of manufacturing toilet soap from animal fats were all formerly city work—as strange as it seems to us that growing alfalfa was once city work.

In very ancient times, too, cities were engaged in developing agriculture and animal husbandry. In the Egyptian cities of the Old Kingdom, for example, many experiments with animal domestication were tried; records of the efforts have been left in pictures. A zoologist engaged in modern attempts to domesticate wild African animals for meat, R. C. Bigalke of the McGregor Memorial Museum in Kimberley, notes that during early Old Kingdom times, "Hyenas were tied up and force-fed until fat enough for slaughter; pelicans were kept to lay eggs; mongooses were tamed to kill rats and mice in the granaries; and there is a suggestion that Dorcas gazelles were herded in flocks. Pictures also show ibex and two of the large kinds of antelope, addax and oryx, stabled and wearing collars." The ass and the common house cat were domesticated in the ancient cities of the Nile; they are "city animals," distributed into the rural world.

Both in the past and today, then, the separation commonly made, dividing city commerce and industry from rural agriculture, is artificial and imaginary. The two do not come down two different lines of descent. Rural work—whether that work is manufacturing brassieres or growing food—is city work transplanted.

A Theory of City Origins of the First Agriculture

The logical inference is that in prehistoric times, also, agriculture and animal husbandry arose in cities. But if this is so, then cities must have preceded agriculture. To imagine how this could occur, and how grain culture and domestication of animals could have emerged in pre-agricultural cities of hunters, let us try to imagine such a city. I am choosing to imagine for the purpose a city I shall call New Obsidian and I am pretending that it is the center of a large trade in obsidian, the tough, black, natural glass produced by some volcanoes. The city is located on the Anatolian plateau of Turkey.

There are two reasons for this choice. First, the ruins of a city, Çatal Hüyük, that might well have been the successor to my imaginary New Obsidian, have been found by a British archeologist, James Mellaart, and are beautifully described and illustrated in his book, *Çatal Hüyük*. Thus we have the advantage of seeing how our imaginary city developed later. To put it the other way around, the New Obsidian we are going to imagine is the precursor to a known ruin and so is less difficult to imagine than a city entirely made up. The second reason for my choice is that obsidian was the most important industrial material traded in the part of the world where scholars believe wheat and barley culture first arose, although it was by no means the only industrial material traded there. Thus a city in which obsidian trade centered is a logical choice as a pre-agricultural metropolis. To be sure, an equally logical choice might be a center of the copper industry in the Caucasus or the Carpathians during the same period, or a coast city that had developed a trade in its shells. But New Obsidian will serve as a suitable candidate to explain the principles.

While the city is imaginary, I shall be strict and unfanciful in describing its economy. I shall allow to New Obsidian only the same economic processes that I have found operating in cities of our own and historical times.

New Obsidian, although it thrives on obsidian trade, is not located at one of the several volcanoes on the Anatolian plateau from which the black glass comes. It is at least a score of miles away from the nearest volcano of the group, and probably farther. This is because the Upper Paleolithic hunting tribes who controlled the volcanoes when the trade began would not permit strangers near the seat of their splendid treasure. In the distant past, they themselves had wrested control of the obsidian-bearing territory from predecessors less wily than they. They did not risk a repetition of this conquest.

Thus, since at least 9,000 B.C., and possibly earlier, the trading of the local obsidian had taken place by custom in the territory of a neighboring hunting group who had become regular customers for the obsidian and subsequently, go-betweens in the trade with more distant hunting peoples. It is the settlement of this group that has become the little city of New Obsidian.

In 8,500 B.C., New Obsidian's population numbers about two thousand persons. It is an amalgam of the original people of the settlement and of the obsidian owning tribes, much of whose population is now settled within the city because of the trade and the various kinds of work connected with it. A small outlying population, to be sure, still works at the volcanoes and patrols the territory around them. Every day, parties from New Obsidian traverse the route between, bringing down treasure. The people of the city are wonderfully skilled at crafts and will become still more so because of the opportunity to specialize. The city has a peculiar religion because not one, but several, tribal deities are respected, officially celebrated and depended upon; these deities have become amalgamated like the population itself.

The system of trade that prevails runs this way: The initiative is taken by the people who want to buy something. Traveling salesmen have not yet appeared on the scene; the traders, rather, regard themselves, and are regarded as, traveling purchasing agents. Undoubtedly, they take trade goods of their own to the place of purchase, but this is used like money to buy whatever it is they came for. Thus, the traders who come to New Obsidian from greater and greater distances come there purposely to get obsidian, not to get rid of something else. For the most part, the barter goods they bring consist of the ordinary produce of their hunting territories. When the New Obsidian people want special treasures like copper, shells or pigments that they themselves do not find in their territory, parties of their own traders go forth to get these things from other settlements. With them they take obsidian, as if it were money.

In this way, settlements that possess unusual treasures —copper fine shells, pigments—have become minor trading centers for obsidian too. They exchange with nearby hunting tribes some of the obsidian that has been brought to them in barter and are paid in ordinary hunting produce. And New Obsidian, similarly, is a regional trading center for other rare goods besides obsidian.

New Obsidian, in this fashion, has become a "depot" settlement as well as a "production" settlement. It has two kinds of major export work, not one. Obsidian, of course, is one export. The other export is a service: the service of obtaining, handling and trading goods that are brought in from outside and are destined for secondary customers who also come from outside.

The economy of New Obsidian divides into an export-import economy on the one hand, and a local or internal economy on the other. But these two major divisions of the settlement's economy are not static. As time passes, New Obsidian adds many new exports to those first two, and all the new exports come out of the city's own local economy. For example, the excellently manufactured hide bags in which obsidian is carried down from its sources are sometimes bartered to hunters or traders from other settlements who have come to purchase obsidian but, after seeing the bags, wish to carry their obsidian back in one. Fine, finished obsidian knives, arrowheads, spearheads and mirrors of the kind that the workers in New Obsidian produce for their own people are also coveted by those who come for raw obsidian. The potent religion of prospering New Obsidian becomes an object of trade too; its common local talismans are bought. Trinkets of personal dress also go into the export trade.

A lot of copying goes on among the major trading settlements. For a while, New Obsidian sold quite a few of the hide bags, but then craftsmen in the copper- and pigment-trading settlements began copying them. Meanwhile, in New Obsidian, craftsmen began copying some of the imports that were popular there: strong, elegant little baskets occasionally imported from a settlement that traded red ocher, and carved wooden boxes from a settlement whose major trade was in fossil oyster shells. By the time the minor work of making hide bags for export had somewhat dropped off in New Obsidian, the little city had already developed a small, compensatory export trade in the imitated baskets and boxes.

The people of New Obsidian, the people of other major settlements, and the people of all the small and ordinary hunting settlements that lie between the major trade centers fiercely resent and try to repel encroachments upon their own hunting territories. Exceptions are made solely for trespass to reach trading centers. Thus the routes to New Obsidian from afar cross the territories of many, many hunting groups. These routes ran, at first, through the territories closest to the city and then extended outward as people farther away became customers, and then peoples beyond those. As the range of customers extended outward, so did the routes to New Obsidian. Linked to routes extended from other cities, the paths to New Obsidian help form a network that, by the time of Çatal Hüyük, will stretch almost two thousand miles from east to west.

A peace of the routes was early established. This was possible because trespass always ran through the territory of a group that was already being served by the trade. Any people that shut off the routes or that robbed and killed traders was itself denied obsidian, and moreover was fought by a coalition of warriors from the nearest city and from nearby hunting people who used the trade routes.

The resting and watering points used by trading parties along the routes have become traditional. They are spots of total sanctuary, protected powerfully under the city's religious code. These places always have a spring or other source of water and it is under the same protection. But there are no hotels. Traders eat sparsely on their journeys and carry their own food. They do not live off the land

on which they trespass. They travel swiftly without dawd-
ling, but they are usually hungry when they reach home.

In New Obsidian the buildings are made of timber
and adobe; later in the millennium there will also be buildings made of shaped mud bricks. The "center" or barter
space of the little city is physically on the edge where
the routes join and approach the settlement. As the city
has grown, this space has been kept clear. To its rear,
the city slowly grows larger. On the route side of the
barter square, the alien traders make their camps. These
have become permanent abodes although their residents
are transient. In the barter space, the two worlds meet.
The square is thus the only "open space" in the city itself,
left open originally because what has since become a
busy meeting and trading spot was at first a space of
separation, deliberately kept empty. The barter space,
or city square as it has become, is on the side of the
city that faces toward the volcanoes. The reason for its location is that in the beginning here was where the original New Obsidian people traded with the volcano owners.
When neighboring tribes began bartering at the settlement too, they used the already established barter point.
For obvious reasons, storehouses of treasure are not at
the barter square. But many workshops are squeezed
among the buildings around it, especially those using
materials of little intrinsic value.

To understand why New Obsidian has become a trading center of such importance, the goal of people from
great distances, it is necessary to understand the enormous
value of obsidian to hunters. Obsidian is not merely a substance that catches the eye or carries prestige; it is a vital
production material. Once possessed, it is regarded as a
necessity, both by the hunters in every little trading city
and by the rural hunting tribesmen. Obsidian makes the
sharpest cutting tools to be had. We get a hint of what
a material like this means to the Middle Eastern hunters

and craftsmen ten thousand years ago by considering a comment concerning modern knives in Peter Freuchen's *Book of the Eskimos*:

> In Committee Bay I have met Eskimos who had no knives. The only cutting instruments they had were made of old metal straps from barrels. For flensing they used sharp stones or knives made of bone. They were walrus hunters, and it would take them days to flense and cut up one single walrus. While they worked with their miserable tools hundreds of walrus would pass by their camp. If they had had steel knives, as they do now, the whole job could be done in half an hour and they could get out again while the hunting was still good and maybe get a whole winter's supply in a day or two.

Obsidian is not steel, but it is the nearest thing to it in the world of New Obsidian.

The food of New Obsidian is derived in two ways. Part of it comes from the old hunting and gathering territory—which is still hunted, foraged and patrolled as diligently as it formerly was when the people were solely hunters and gatherers—and from the territories of the volcano-owning groups whose headquarters are now also at New Obsidian. But a large proportion of the food is imported from foreign hunting territories. This is food that is traded at the barter square for obsidian and for other exports of the city. Food is the customary goods brought by customers who do not pay in copper, shells, pigments or other unusual treasures. Wild food of the right kind commands a good exchange. In effect, New Obsidian has thus enormously enlarged its hunting territory by drawing, through trade, upon the produce of scores of hunting territories.

The right kind of wild food to bring to the barter square is nonperishable. Except in times of great shortage and unusual hunger when anything is welcome, only nonperishable food is accepted. There are two reasons for this. First, unless the customers are from territories very nearby, nonperishable food stands the trip to the city best. Second and more important, the people of New Obsidian like to store the food and mete it out rationally rather than gorge upon it and perhaps go hungry later Thus the imported food consists overwhelmingly of live animals and hard seeds. In this New Obsidian resembles all pre-agricultural settlements that import wild food.

Because of New Obsidian's unusually voluminous and extensive trade, large quantities of live animals and seeds flow into the city. The animals are trussed up or carried in pole cages if they are dangerous. They are hobbled with fiber rope and alternately carried and driven on their own feet if they are not dangerous. Nonperishable plant food is easier to handle than animals, and traders carrying it can travel more swiftly. Thus, especially from the greater distances, beans, nuts and edible grass seeds pour into New Obsidian.

The imported food promptly enters New Obsidian's local economy and there it comes under the custody of local workers who specialize in its protection, storage and distribution. They are, in effect, stewards: stewards of wild animals and stewards of edible seeds. Consider, first, the duties of the animal stewards. In principle, their work is the not very difficult task of keeping the animals alive until it is time to slaughter them. This does, however, require judgment. The first animals chosen for slaughter are those that are either the hardest to feed or the most troublesome to manage, or both. Most carnivores fall into one or both of these categories and they are eaten very soon after their arrival in New Obsidian. The craftsmen get the pelts and other by-products. Animals that can live on grass are removed last from the natural refrigerator of life. And among the grass-eating animals, the females, being the less rambunctious, are kept longest. Sometimes they give birth to young before their time of slaughter comes; and when this happens there is, of course, extra wild meat and extra pelts The animal stewards of New Obsidian, with their unusually large supplies of meat to pick and choose among, make it a practice to save these docile breeders whenever they can. They have no conception of animal domestication, nor of categories of animals that can or cannot be domesticated. The stewards are intelligent men, and are fully capable of solving problems and of catching insights from experience. But experience has not provided them yet with any idea that can be called "trying to domesticate animals." They are simply trying to manage the city's wild food imports to the best of their abilities.

The only reason that second, third or fourth generation captives live long enough to breed yet another generation is that they happen to be the easiest to keep during times of plenty. Indeed, over and over, third and fourth generation captives are killed off without a qualm if the food is needed.

But the stewards make an effort to keep fresh meat always on hand, and, in particular, always to have some for the happy and exciting occasion when a party of New Obsidian traders returns from afar, weary, hungry and eager for welcome. And eventually, the stewards manage to keep fresh meat on hand permanently. They come in this way to possess, and to protect most carefully, what we would call breeding stock. But such animals mingle with imported wild stock that will not harm them, including different varieties of their own species. And among the offspring those that stand captivity best are, by definition, the best survivors and best meat producers on the forage at hand. Among these, the most docile are always kept by preference.

In New Obsidian, it so happens, the animal stewards concentrate especially upon saving and multiplying sheep —mainly because sheep meet the requirements of convenient maintenance and their meat is as well liked as any. Also, the craftsmen particularly value their pelts.

In another little city with which New Obsidian trades,

imported wild goats are being kept by preference because they thrive on poor provender. In still another, from which New Obsidian buys copper, wild cattle are being kept because the females are sufficiently docile and because the craftsmen regard the multiplication of horn to be especially desirable. Far in the western part of the trading belt, wild sows are being kept by preference because they can be pastured in forests and because they yield such splendidly large litters.

The seed stewards of New Obsidian have no reason to prefer saving one kind of barter seed over another, and they do not do so. The dry seeds taken in trade are all mingled together in storage and are also eaten as mixtures. Seeds of many, many different kinds of wild grasses flow into the city from wet soils and dry, from sandy soils and loamy, from highlands and from valleys, from riverbanks and from forest glades. They come from the territories of scores of tribes who do not harvest in one another's territories except during war and raids—when the raiders eat quickly what they have seized. But here in New Obsidian, the world's best market for edible wild seeds, the seeds flow together for storage.

Seeds that have never before been juxtaposed are tumbled into baskets and bins. Husked, pounded and cooked, they are often further jumbled with peas, lentils and nut meats.*

When seeds remain after the winter, they are used for wild patch sowing, a practice not productive of much food; it just makes gathering wild seeds more conven-

---

*We have today a distant equivalent of such food called by the trade name Pioneer Porridge, which I sometimes feed my family. It is a coarse mixture of half a dozen different whole grains, and the recipes on the bag recommend mixing the grains with beans and nuts; the barter seeds brought into New Obsidian would have been used for wild versions of just such dishes. It is food that sticks to your ribs, and it tastes good.

ient In and around the barter space, around the storage bins within the city, and in the yards where women husk and pound and carry seed to and from the household bins, some seeds spill. Whether spill sown, patch sown, or sown by little predators—rats, mice and birds— these plants cross in unprecedented combinations. It is no problem to get grain crosses in New Obsidian, or crossed beans and peas either. Quite the contrary; crosses cannot be avoided.

The crosses and hybrids do not go unobserved. They are seen, in fact, by people who are experts at recognizing the varieties and estimating the worth of barter seeds, and who are well aware that some of these city seeds are new. Mutations occur no more commonly than they would in the wild, but they are not unnoticed either, as they most likely would be in the wild; nor do occasional batches of mutant seeds brought in barter go unnoticed. But crosses, hybrids and the rare mutants are not deliberately put to use in selective breeding.

Barter-seed stewards do not have custody of locally grown seeds, no more than the stewards of imported animals have custody of meat killed by the hunters of New Obsidian itself. It is not the seed stewards who make the first selections of new grain plants. Some of the householders of New Obsidian take this step, and they do it at first inadvertently. Selection happens because some patches of sown seeds yield much more heavily than other patches do. The particular household bins filled from the lucky patches are, more often than not, the bins with seed left for sowing, in years when seed is saved for that purpose at all.

The unprecedented differentials in yields from New Obsidian's best and poorest seed patches lead to an arrangement formerly unheard of: some people *within* the city trade seeds to others. That is, they make a business of handing out seeds in return for trinkets. Possibly this

Cities First—Rural Development Later [29

trade is confined to the women. It is not as radical an arrangement as their ancestors would probably have
thought it, because the people inside the city who engage
in this practice are modeling their transactions upon the
barter that has long gone on in the city square.

Owing to this local dealing in seeds from patches that
yield most heavily, all the grain grown in New Obsidian
eventually yields heavily in comparison with wild grains.
The people of the city do not really know why their
grain is "the best," but they know that it is. And in the
second stage of the process, selection becomes deliberate
and conscious. The choices made now are purposeful,
and they are made among various strains of already cultivated crosses, and their crosses, mutants and hybrids.

It takes many generations—not just of wheat and barley but of people—to differentiate the New Obsidian seeds
into sophisticated cultivated grains. But it is only under
the following conditions that the thing could have happened at all:

1. Seeds that normally do not grow together must
come together nevertheless, frequently and consistently
over considerable periods of time.

2. In that same place, variants must consistently be
under the informed, close observation of people able to
act relevantly in response to what they see.

3. That same place must be well secured against food
shortages so that in time the seed grain can become
sacrosanct; otherwise the whole process of selective breeding will be repeatedly aborted before it can amount to anything. In short, prosperity is a prerequisite. Although
time is necessary, time by itself does not bestow cultivated
grains on New Obsidian.

Gradually, New Obsidian grows more and more of its
own meat and grain but it does not, as a consequence,
wallow in unwanted surpluses of imported food. First,
the very practice of growing foods in new ways requires

new tools and more industrial materials. The population of New Obsidian grows and so does the work to be done in New Obsidian.

The city's total food supply is made up of its own territorial yield of wild animals and plants, its imports of wild animals and seeds, and its new home-grown meats and grains. The total increases but the imports decrease as the new city-made food greatly increases. (The city's own traditional hunting territory probably yields about the same amount as in the past.) The city, in short, is now supplying itself with some of the goods that it formerly had to import. In principle, this is not much different from importing baskets and then manufacturing them locally so they need no longer be imported. Since New Obsidian had formerly imported so much wild food—in comparison to baskets or boxes, say—the substituted local production makes a big difference in the city's economy.

In place of unneeded food imports, New Obsidian can import other things—a lot of other things. The effect is as if the city's imports have increased enormously, although they have not. The city, instead, has shifted its imports from one kind of goods to other kinds. This change radically changes the economies of the people with whom New Obsidian trades. Now people from ordinary hunting tribes who come for obsidian find that ordinary industrial raw materials from their own territories —furs, hides, bundles of rushes, fibers and horn—are much welcomed in barter, while pouches of grass seeds and exhausted, scrawny live animals do not command the obsidian they once did.

Now too the traders of the city itself go forth ever more frequently to points ever more distant in search of exotic materials for the city's craftsmen. And the things that the craftsmen make of the new wealth of materials pouring in amount to an explosion of city wealth, an explosion of new kinds of work, an explosion of new exports, and an explosion in the very size of the city.

The work to be done and the population both increase rapidly—so rapidly that some people from outlying tribes become permanent residents of the city too. Their hands are needed. New Obsidian has experienced a momentous economic change peculiar to cities: explosive growth owing to local production of goods that were formerly imported and to a consequent shift of imports.

The traders of New Obsidian, when they go off on their trips, take along New Obsidian food to sustain themselves. Sometimes they bring back a strange animal, or a bit of promising foreign seed. And the traders of other little cities who come to New Obsidian sometimes take back food with them and tell what they have seen in the metropolis. Thus, the first spread of the new grains and animals is from city to city. The rural world is still a world in which wild food and other wild things are hunted and gathered. The cultivation of plants and animals is, as yet, only city work. It is duplicated, as yet, only by other city people, not by the hunters of ordinary settlements.

The Earliest City Yet Found

We need not merely imagine what a city like New Obsidian was like after it had replaced a major import and grown explosively, for Çatal Hüyük, the city found by Mellaart in Anatolia, had, I suspect, an economic history behind it like that of imaginary New Obsidian. Çatal Hüyük ("ancient mound at Çatal") was found while its discoverer, Mellaart, was actually looking for nothing more than a village. He had already unearthed a late Neolithic farming village that had been established in about 6,000 B.C., its culture already fully developed, upon the older site of a long abandoned pre-pottery settlement. Mellaart was seeking the parent culture of this farming village. He assumed it would be found in another village, older of course and more primitive. Among some two hundred possible mounds to explore, the most promising seemed one about two hundred miles east of the village he had already found: a weed- and thistle-covered hump rising gently fifty feet above a great, flat plain, beside what had once been a riverbank.

Digging, under Mellaart's direction, began in 1961. The results of three summers' work have been described in his book on the city.* Çatal Hüyük proved, as Mellaart had hoped, to be older than the farming village to the west, a good thousand years older. It spanned the period 7,000–6,000 B.C. Also, just as Mellaart had surmised, it was evidently the source from which the culture of the farming village derived. But, surprisingly, Çatal Hüyük was a more highly developed settlement, with a richer and more complex culture, than the younger farming village. Indeed, Çatal Hüyük was not a village at all. It was a city with remains "as urban as those of any site from the succeeding Bronze Age yet excavated in Turkey." Çatal Hüyük is both the earliest city yet found, and the earliest known settlement of any kind to possess agriculture. It is, up to this writing, the earliest known instance of Neolithic life.

Buildings of standardized mud bricks densely covered thirty-two acres at Çatal Hüyük. A dwelling for a good-sized household apparently consisted of one rather small all-purpose room, probably with a wooden veranda above. A population that must have run to many thousands was closely concentrated. Dwellings were entered by ladders leading down from "doorways" in the sheltered roofs.

It was a city of crafts, of artists, manufacturers and merchants. Mellaart has drawn up a catalog of the workers it must have contained:

. . . the weavers and basketmakers; the matmakers; the carpenters and joiners; the men who made the polished

*He has also summarized some of this material in an article in *Scientific American* of April, 1964. The quotations from Mellaart that I use are taken, for the sake of greater conciseness, from the condensed material in his article.

stone tools (axes and adzes, polishers and grinders, chisels,
maceheads and palettes); the beadmakers who drilled in
stone beads holes that no modern steel needle can pene-
trate and who carved pendants and used stone inlays;
the makers of shell beads from dentalium, cowrie and fossil
oyster; the flint and obsidian knappers who produced the
pressure-flaked daggers, spearheads, lanceheads, arrowheads, knives, sickle blades, scrapers and borers; the merchants of skin, leather and fur; the workers in bone who
made the awls, punches, knives, scrapers, ladles, spoons,
bows, scoops, spatulas, bodkins, belt hooks, antler toggles,
pins and cosmetic sticks; the carvers of wooden bowls and
boxes; the mirrormakers, the bowmakers; the men who
hammered native copper into sheets and worked it into
beads, pendants, rings and other trinkets; the builders; the
merchants and traders who obtained all the raw materials;
and finally the artists—the carvers of statuettes, the mod-
elers and the painters.

The cosmetics equipment alone included "palettes and
grinders" for the preparation of red ocher, blue azurite,
green malachite and perhaps galena, and "baskets or the
shells of fresh-water mussels for their containers and
delicate bone pins for their application . . [and] mirrors of highly polished obsidian to see the effect."

The oldest cloth yet discovered has been found in
Çatal Hüyük; there was nothing crude about its
manufacture. At least three different types of weaving
have been distinguished. And the skillful, richly colored
wall paintings in some of the buildings depict, among
other things, woven carpets. The men, Mellaart writes,
wore leopard skins fastened by belts with bone hooks
and eyes, and in the winter they wore cloth cloaks fastened with antler toggles. The women wore sleeveless
bodices and jerkins of leopard skin fastened with bone
pins, and string skirts weighted with little copper tubes
at the ends of the strings.

Just as these people combined manufactured cloth with
the fur clothing of huntsmen or trappers, and just as
they had added hammered copper to huntsmen's ma-

terials of bone and antler, so they had added domesticated food to wild food. The wild food included red deer, boars, leopards, and wild sheep, wild cattle and wild asses; wild nuts, fruits and berries; and eggs that Mellaart judges were from wild rather than domesticated fowl. The domesticated food included sheep, cows and goats, cultivated peas, lentils, bitter vetch, barley and wheat. The barley and wheat, although the oldest yet found, were already far removed from their wild-grass parentage. Among the varieties were naked six-row barley and hexaploid, free-threshing wheat, grains that did not enter European agriculture, it is believed, until about two thousand years later.

Like the people of the European medieval cities, the people of Çatal Hüyük obviously depended on a combination of cultivated and wild foods. But they probably ate much better than the medieval Europeans. Their skeletons, Mellaart says, show that they were well fed, healthy and tall.

Owing to fires in about 6,500 B.C., midway during tne thousand-year occupation of the site, grains were charred and preserved. This fortuitous preservation provides no record of grains five hundred years earlier but Mellaart reasons, from the evidence of grain bins, mortars and querns, that the city had cultivated grain from the time it occupied the site. It also seems to have had domesticated sheep then, but the domesticated cows and goats seem to have been acquired later. The city had dogs too, but no pigs.

The presumption must be that this civilization came directly—without a break—from the hunting life, not only because so many of the crafts were obviously derived from hunters' materials and hunters' skills, but also because of the city's art. Mellaart notes that it is "premature to speak definitively about the origins of this remarkable civilization [but] . . . the discovery of the art of Çatal Hüyük has demonstrated that the Upper

Paleolithic tradition of naturalistic painting, which died in Western Europe with the end of the ice age, not only survived but flourished in Anatolia. The implication is that at least part of the population of Çatal Hüyük was of Upper Paleolithic [the old hunting] stock."

Mellaart pays the usual obeisance to the dogma of agricultural primacy by assuming that "the new efficiency of food production" lay at the city's economic base. But having said that, he cannot swallow the idea that agriculture actually explains Çatal Hüyük's economic base. "This was not a village of farmers, however rich." He conjectures that the obviously well-organized trade may "explain the community's almost explosive development in arts and crafts," and he suggests that "the trade in obsidian was at the heart of this extensive commerce." But this too, it seems to me, is an oversimplification. Çatal Hüyük had a valuable resource and a trade in that resource, to be sure, but it had something else valuable and more wondrous. It had a creative local economy. It is this that sets the city apart from a mere trading post with access to a mine. The people of Çatal Hüyük had added one kind of work after another into their own local city economy.

Many pre-agricultural hunting settlements whose people bartered a territorial treasure may have possessed, briefly, a creative economy that flickered for a relative instant in time. But in modern and historical times, no creative local economy—which is to say, no city economy—seems to have grown in isolation from other cities. A city does not grow by trading only with a rural hinterland. A city seems always to have implied a group of cities, in trade with one another. It is thus reasonable to conjecture that, in prehistoric times too, the incipient flickers of a creative city economy could actually be sustained—as they obviously were in Çatal Hüyük—only if several little cities were simultaneously serving as expanding markets for one another.

If my reasoning is correct, it was not agriculture then, for all its importance, that was the salient invention, or occurrence if you will, of the Neolithic Age. Rather it was the fact of sustained, interdependent, creative city economies that made possible many new kinds of work, agriculture among them.

How Agriculture May Have Become a Rural Occupation

At the time the city work of growing grain and raising domesticated animals developed, there would, of course, have been no such thing as rural agriculture nor would there have been agricultural villages or settlements of any sort specializing in agriculture. In cities, agriculture would have been only a part of economies much more comprehensive, with intensively pursued commerce and industries. The rural world would have been a hunting and gathering world, sparsely dotted by small and simple hunting settlements.

Just as new rural work today develops in cities and then is transplanted, so must the first agriculture have been transplanted. The most likely reason for the transplanting would have been that animal husbandry took up too much room. Grain growing was relatively compact; it did not require enormous acreages, and in a city like imaginary New Obsidian, or even Çatal Hüyük, the people could readily tend the city fields, as people in early medieval cities of Europe did, or the early settlers of Boston. But pasturage for herds requires much land, and a limit would have been reached rather quickly to the number of animals that could conveniently attach to a Neolithic city. The solution would have been to spin off herds—transplant city herds and the work of tending them, to grazing areas more than a day's journey (for a herd) from the city. With the herds would go the herdsmen and their families; and with the herdsmen and their families would go the means to grow grain for themselves, as well as cooking equipment and other everyday necessities. Thus two kinds of rural villages, not one, would now exist at the same time in the hinterlands of cities such as Çatal Hüyük: old hunting villages, little changed, and new, radically different, agricultural villages.

An agricultural village thus would have been a specialized community, rather like a company town, to handle one fragment of a city's work. These first agricultural villages would have produced meat and wool for the city. Any other goods, including grain, they would have produced only for themselves. What they did not produce for themselves, they would get from the city in return for meat and wool. When a village ran short of seed it would get more from stewards in the city as a matter of course. When technological improvements were made in the city that were relevant to village work, the improvements would be received in the villages.

At first, villages would be located only with grazing in mind. They would be spaced far enough apart so that their herds did not impinge on one another's pasturage, but no farther apart than seemed necessary and no farther from the city than was necessary. But once these specialized and economically fragmentary settlements had been invented, a few other uses for them would become evident and would determine the locations of some. To traders, it would have seemed advantageous to locate villages as distant from the parent city as possible and along main trade routes. Villages would be like caches of food from a trader's point of view, as well as sources of many other comforts: a bit of the city along the journey. Some villages would also have been located to secure and hold fine watering places for stock, even though good pasturage was skipped over and left empty. Hunting villages would be forced to cede territory for these farm settlements and should they resist, would be fought and their people probably killed, enslaved or driven away.

If fatal misfortune dealt either by men or by nature befell a parent city, then its farming villages—if they managed to survive the disaster—would be cast loose with their incomplete fragments of a rounded economic life. These orphaned villages would of course continue to specialize—do the work they could do—but now only for their own subsistence. They would not develop further because there would be no parent city economy from which they might receive new technology. Again and again during prehistoric times, villages must have been orphaned by the destruction of cities.

When those villages lost some part of their own economic life, they would have no way to retrieve or re-formulate it. I suspect this explains the origins of nomadic herding peoples. Neolithic villagers who lost their seed grains after their parent city had been destroyed would have had no place to get more. All that would be left to them would be animal husbandry and the practice of a relatively few subsistence crafts based on materials derived for the most part from the animals. Such people would have had to become nomadic herdsmen. No doubt the city civilizations from which these nomads derived could have been traced millennia later from the languages they spoke.

While a village was still prospering and still under protection of a parent city, rural hunters of wild food who had not known city life might often have been assimilated into the village, perhaps as concubines and servants, much as they might have been consistently assimilated into cities.

But hunters and gatherers who had not been so assimilated would not have become agriculturalists even though some of their territory had been seized for pasturage and building. Sometimes they would raid villages, but the grain and animals they took would not turn them from hunting and gathering to farming. At best the raiders' use (as distinguished from merely the consumption) of their plunder would have permitted only a fragmented and barbaric type of agriculture and animal husbandry, in comparison with that of cities and their still-functioning villages.

Subtraction of Work from Rural Economies

I have been dwelling upon the fact that city economies create new kinds of work for the rural world, and by doing so also invent and reinvent new rural economies. But of course that is only part of the process by which rural economies change. Cities also subtract old work from the rural world by no longer buying former rural imports. This is what I suspect happened in the rural hinterlands of New Obsidian when wild food was no longer the chief and pressing import of the city. This same process happens all the time today. One of the old ghost towns up the Hudson River once lived on shipping natural ice to New York City—until the city began supplying artificial ice for itself. Cities never eliminate old work, either from rural economies or their own economies, by "simply" eliminating it. Always, additions of new work lie behind the eliminations of old.

Much of the work subtracted from old rural economies has been replaced by new work transplanted from cities. And this second movement is necessary to prevent cities themselves from being overwhelmed by some of their own successful economic creations. Suppose, in a Neolithic city, it had been deemed more important to retain and expand the already successful animal husbandry, right there, than to make room for newer—and hence, by definition "less basic"—kinds of work. Something had to be sacrificed: either some of the already successful, established work or else the opportunities for adding more and different work.

The reinvention of the pristine rural world, effectively

begun in Neolithic times, is still going on. Cities today are still adding new kinds of work into the remaining hunting economies: e.g., the entertainment of vacationers, performance in documentary films, the work of entertaining anthropologists. And cities are still eliminating work from rural hunting economies too. Synthetic tortoise shell, ivory and furs undermine the economic pressure to slay all the remaining tortoises, elephants and beavers.

Just as cities depend less and less upon the old hunting economy to supply them with raw materials, so do they also depend less and less upon the younger agricultural rural economy to supply them with industrial materials. Leatherlike goods without leather, cloth without cotton, flax, wool or mulberry trees, cable without hemp, perfume without factory fields of roses, drugs without acres of roots and herbs, rubber without rubber plantations, machines that need not be fed with alfalfa or oats—all these are means by which the need for industrial materials from agricultural land is diminished by city work, while the need for food from agricultural land is increased.

Meanwhile, the new work in cities—some of it—pulses out into the rural agricultural economy to construct a still younger rural, mass-production manufacturing economy, making chemicals and synthetic yarns.

Just as no real separation exists in the actual world between city-created work and rural work, so there is no real separation between "city consumption" and "rural production." Rural production is literally the creation of city consumption. That is to say, city economies invent the things that are to become city imports from the rural world, and then they reinvent the rural world so it can supply those imports. This, as far as I can see, is the only way in which rural economies develop at all, the dogma of agricultural primacy notwithstanding.

The Dogma of Agricultural Primacy

Agriculture, my friends in the anthropology department of Queens College tell me, evidently arose in three different centers: wheat and barley culture in the Middle East, rice culture in eastern Asia and Indian corn culture in America (probably in Central America). The cultivated grains came from wild grasses. The invention in America is believed to have occurred latest, and that in the Middle East the earliest, although even that is not absolutely certain because so little is known about the probable date and place of the early Asian rice culture. This is really all that is known for certain about the origins of grain culture. The rest is conjecture.

The conventional assumptions about what happened are almost wholly concerned with Middle Eastern development of grain culture, but in principle they are supposed to apply to the other two centers also. The idea is that in the Middle East little groups of hunters and wild-food gatherers, roaming about in a constant search for food, began at length to sow and to harvest patches of wild grass visited during the appropriate seasons. In time, it is supposed, this proto-agriculture produced true grains and a consequently efficient way of producing foods, and this permitted former hunters and gatherers to become peasants. After many, many thousands of years of agricultural village life, the first cities are supposed to have arisen about 3,500 B.C. in the valleys of the Tigris and Euphrates Rivers in Mesopotamia. But all this is conjecture.

How does such a theory account for the development of crossed, hybrid and mutant wheats and barleys? To be sure, it used to be supposed that purposeful plant selection would be practiced, as a matter of course, by hunting and gathering peoples, once they had reached a stage of expertise at gathering and sowing wild seeds.

But that supposition was plausible only before the botanical problems had been appreciated. Moreover, the supposition begs the question why grain culture, then, originated in so few centers instead of in hundreds of centers, or perhaps in thousands.

Some prehistorians, to get around the botanical difficulties, have suggested that crosses arose owing to abrupt changes in river levels, temporarily bringing together plants that did not normally grow together. It has also been proposed that fortuitous showers of cosmic rays created an unusual incidence of mutations among grains and thus greatly reduced the element of chance for those who might come upon them. But the trouble with relying on natural marvels is of course the question: Why did these marvels selectively transform wild grasses? Why not everything that grew?

The old idea that permanent settlements were impossible until after agriculture was invented is contradicted by so much hard evidence that many archeologists no longer subscribe to this idea, although few scholars in other fields seem, as yet, to be aware of this reassessment. The world is dotted with various kinds of Paleolithic leavings which indicate that hunters had permanent settlements. There are caves that seem to have been continuously occupied during very long periods. There are flint workings—piles of chips and discards—that mutely announce long and continuous settlement and long and continuous industry too. There are shell middens that were accrued long and continuously. There is evidence of trade goods far from their sources, hinting at home bases of some kind for the trade in amber, shells, obsidian. Moreover, unmistakably permanent pre-agricultural settlements have been located in South America, in Europe and in Asia. At least two of these, in what are now Hungary and France, go back far beyond *Homo sapiens*, to a time some 250,000 years ago or more, when men first began to use fire. Undoubtedly, pre-agricultural men migrated but, as we know from migrations in historical times, migrating people customarily leave permanent settlements and, even when the wandering covers a period of several generations, reestablish themselves in permanent settlements. A migrant need not imply a nomad.

I would suggest that permanent settlements within hunting territories were ordinary features of pre-agricultural life. They would have been as natural for men as burrows are for foxes or nests are for eagles. Almost all activities would have been carried on in the settlement and it would also have served as the base for work carried out in the field—hunting, foraging, defending the territory, and raiding adjoining territories.*

Nor is there reason to suppose that the permanent settlements of pre-agricultural people were necessarily populated only by a few families: a tiny band of hunters and their dependents. Indeed, one settlement, in what is now Syria, dating from about the same time as Çatal Hüyük but containing remains only of wild foods, contained hundreds of closely congested clay dwellings. It was continuously occupied for some five centuries and must have had a population, at any one time, of at least a thousand persons, more likely two to three thousand.

Conventionally it is assumed that pre-agricultural food was too scarce to trade because hunting populations grew to the limit of their natural food supplies and then existed on the perilous edge of starvation. Yet food-remains in some settlements indicate that hunting people did not necessarily exploit their food resources to the hilt. For instance, at some sites mammal bones are plentiful but there are no remains of the fish that must have teemed in nearby streams nor of shellfish that must have abounded at adjacent seashores. And in any case, formation and

---

*This implies that permanent settlements which grew as cities were, from the first, city-states. There would have been no such thing as a pre-agricultural city without a surrounding territory belonging to the city.

growth of cities does not depend on "surplus" food because, as we know, cities have often grown in societies
where severe hunger was endemic and terrible famines
were periodic.

In sum, the assumptions behind the dogma of agricultural primacy are at odds with much direct and indirect
evidence. The dogma relies on props of a different kind.
I have asked anthropologists how they know agriculture
came before cities. After recovering from surprise that
this verity should be questioned, they tell me the economists have settled it. I have asked economists the same
thing. They tell me archeologists and anthropologists have
settled it. It seems that everyone has been relying on
somebody else's say-so. At bottom, I think, they are all
relying on a pre-Darwinian source, Adam Smith.

Smith, whose great work, *The Wealth of Nations*, was
published in 1775, saw the same relationships between
cities and agriculture that we can observe today. He reported that the most highly developed agricultural nations of his time were precisely the nations in which
industry and commerce were most highly developed. He
saw and reported that the most thoroughly agricultural
countries had the poorest agriculture. To illustrate this
point, he contrasted the backward agriculture of agricultural Poland with the more advanced agriculture of commercial and industrial England.

Smith observed and reported something still more interesting: that it is not agriculture that leads the way for
the development of industry and commerce. He noticed
that in England the development of agriculture lagged
behind commerce and industry. The way he made this
point was to note that the superiority of English industry
and commerce over that of other nations was more
marked than the superiority of English agriculture. In
short, he reported that the really big difference in the
superior English economic development was the greater
development of industry and commerce, not the greater

development of its rural agriculture. Getting down to details, he made the important observation that the most productive, prosperous and up-to-date agriculture was to be found near cities, and the poorest agriculture was distant from them. Why, then, did Smith not make the logical inference that city industry and commerce preceeded agriculture?

To understand why, we must put ourselves in his place. His intellectual world was very different from ours, and in no way more than in its beliefs about the creation of the earth and of the life upon it. Lyell's *Principles of Geology*, which was to demonstrate that the earth is eons old, was more than fifty years in the future. At the time Smith was writing, educated men in Europe still believed that both the world and men had been created almost simultaneously, about 5,000 B.C., and that man was born into a garden. So Smith never asked how agriculture arose. Agriculture and animal husbandry were givens; they were the original ways in which men earned their bread by the sweat of their brows.

For Smith, in the 1770s, the question had to be, How did commerce and industry arise upon agriculture?—no matter what the evidence might suggest to the contrary. And so Smith had to propose a very special chain of economic causes and effects unlike any observable since, but presumably in operation at the beginning of the world. In short, he was not able to indulge his imagination while sticking to known processes; he had to invent chains of imaginary causes and effects.*

*He proposed that all clothing and housing were at first free and plentiful, but as population grew they became scarce. Why should this be, if there were more hands to make clothing and build shelter? He did not pose that question; instead he rushed on to propose that, having become scarce, they became valuable, requiring agriculturalists to become more productive so they could afford clothing and shelter. This productivity created a surplus of workers and that made commerce possible. But then why, in historical times, have

Adam Smith thus converted biblical history into economic doctrine. This seems to have been accepted as satisfactory by his contemporaries. Two generations later, it was also accepted by Karl Marx. At any rate, although Marx questioned much, and admired Darwin's work with its implications of man's long prehistory, he did not question the idea that industry and commerce had arisen upon agriculture. In this, he was quite as conservative as Adam Smith.

But now we come to a strange twist in the history of the dogma of agricultural primacy. It has continued to be accepted, though so much else in Adam Smith's, and Marx's, world has changed. What is accepted, actually, is not Smith's farrago about the beginning of economic life, but that the rise of industry, commerce and cities

---

there been economies with surpluses of workers who remained with nothing much to do? That was another question he did not pose. Instead he assumed that these first surplus workers would have found commerce and industry to keep themselves busy and would have built cities. Having done so, they would have needed food and would have increased their industrial production so that they might buy it. But why are the problems of idle and hungry city people not so simply solved as this in historical times? That was another question he did not pose.

Smith still needed to account for the fact that cities are economically more advanced than rural areas even though, as he supposed, they trail after economic advances in rural areas. He rationalized this anomaly by suggesting that industry must inherently be more capable of organization into divisions of labor than agriculture, hence capable of advancing more swiftly. But in real life, agriculture is equally available to division of labor, as it was in Smith's time when there were milkmaids and ploughboys. Indeed, when Smith, the superb economic reporter, was not troubled by being Smith, interpreter of the Book of Genesis, he used rural industry, not agriculture, as his chief illustration of how unproductive people are when they do not adhere to the principle of division of labor.

upon agriculture is explicable and unquestionable. A sentence from a history of the Rockefeller Foundation philanthropies, published in 1964, is illustrative: "When man learned to cultivate plants and to domesticate animals," it says, "society for the first time was able to plan ahead and organize itself through the division of labor." The thought is pure Adam Smith prehistory, adapted ever so slightly to acknowledge that mankind was not born with knowledge of farming.

The cartoon stereotype of the half-naked cave man, brandishing a club while he drags his woman off by the hair, is a reminder of what even the most learned people preferred to accept after they had painfully assimilated the idea that men were hunters long, long before they were farmers. It required less of a mental adjustment, evidently, to assume that the hunters must have been very primitive, and that they had no economic life more complex than that of animals. But during the past half century, archeologists have been piecing together the evidence that has made the cartoon stereotype untenable. It is clear that pre-agricultural men were much besides hunters: they were manufacturers, builders, traders and artists. They made large quantities and many varieties of weapons, clothing, bowls, buildings, necklaces, murals and sculptures. They used stone, bone, wood, leather, fur, rushes, clay, timber, adobe, obsidian, copper, mineral pigments, teeth, shells, amber and horn as industrial materials. They backed up their major crafts and arts with subsidiary goods: "producers' goods," or "input items," as economists now say—ladders, lamps and pigments, for instance, to achieve the Paleolithic cave paintings; burins to gouge out furrows in other tools; scrapers to dress hides.

At some point the question might have been asked, How did agriculture arise upon all this industry? Instead, the long economic history of man before agriculture has continued to be regarded as only a sort of prologue played out in the wilds, to be followed by the drama as already recounted by Adam Smith. A persuasive but simple fallacy continues to buttress the dogma and perhaps accounts, at least in part, for why the question has gone unasked. It was this fallacy that made me reluctant to consider that cities had come before agriculture, even after logic had forced me to face the thought. An analogy between agriculture and electricity may help explain and exorcise it. Cities today are so dependent upon electricity that their economies would collapse without it. Moreover, if modern cities had no electricity most of their people—if they could not quickly get away—would die of thirst or disease. And the most impressive and massive installations for generating electricity are in rural areas. The power they generate is sent into both cities and countryside.

If the memory of man did not run back to a time when the world had cities but no electricity, it would seem, from the facts I have just mentioned, that use of electric power must have originated in the countryside and must have been a prerequisite to city life. Here is how the sequence would be reconstructed theoretically: First, there were rural people who had no electricity, but in time developed it and eventually produced a surplus; then cities were possible.

The fallacy is to mistake the results of city economic development for preconditions to city economic development. It is so simple a fallacy and yet—like the belief in spontaneous generation—it blocks off as already answered some most interesting questions that have not been answered at all. How do cities really grow? If they create and re-create rural development, then the question to ask is, What can it be that creates and re-creates city economies?

2

How New Work Begins

Our remote ancestors did not expand their economics much by simply doing more of what they had already been doing: piling up more wild seeds and nuts, slaughtering more wild cattle and geese, making more spearheads, necklaces, burins and fires. They expanded their economies by adding new kinds of work. So do we. Innovating economies expand and develop. Economies that do not add new kinds of goods and services, but continue only to repeat old work, do not expand much nor do they, by definition, develop.

In conjecturing how animal husbandry could have begun in an imaginary prehistoric settlement, I proposed that this new work was logically added to the older work of managing wild animals before slaughter. That work. in its turn, had also been added to older work: trading **obsidian** to many people who came to New Obsidian seeking to bargain for it. And that trading service, in turn, had been added to the settlement's own way of getting obsidian: bargaining for it with the neighboring tribe whose people mined it at the volcano. And the volcano people who mined obsidian had doubtless added that work to their own still older work of preparing flints and other stones for weapons.

In short, I was presuming that each kind of new work, as it appeared in this prehistoric economy, was added logically and "naturally" to a specific bit of older work. That is how innovations are made in our own time. It is also how work has diversified and expanded during historical times.

This process is of the essence in understanding cities because cities are places where adding new work to older work proceeds vigorously. Indeed, any settlement where this happens becomes a city. Because of this process city economies are more complicated and diverse than the economies of villages, towns and farms, as well as being larger. This is why I have also argued that cities are the primary necessity for economic development and expansion, including rural development.

Obviously, cities have more different kinds of divisions of labor than villages, towns and farms do. Thus cities contain more kinds of work to which new work can be added than other settlements. But this does not tell us much because it begs the questions: How have cities acquired more divisions of labor than other settlements? And in any case, why should this process of adding new work to old occur so vigorously in some settlements, and so little or not at all in others? How does such a process start? How does it keep going? These questions and others will be pursued in later chapters, for that is what this book is about: how settlements become cities where new work is added to old and how the process is sustained in them.

But at the core of all the processes of city growth is

this root process that I described in New Obsidian—
adding animal custody to the obsidian trade, that is,
adding new kinds of work to other kinds of older work.
So before considering cities themselves we shall investigate, in this chapter, how new work is added to old.

How One Kind of Work Leads to Another

Let us begin by dissecting a few examples of innovation.
Brassiere manufacturing affords an illustration. It is work
that did not exist until the early 1920s, when it was developed in New York. At the time this happened, American women wore various undergarments called corset
covers, chemises and ferris waists. A custom seamstress,
Mrs. Ida Rosenthal, was making dresses in a small shop of
her own in New York. But she was dissatisfied with the
way the dresses she made hung on her customers. To
improve the fit, she began experimenting with improvements to underclothing and the result was the first brassiere. The customers liked the brassieres, and it became
Mrs. Rosenthal's practice to give out a custom-made
brassiere with each dress she made. Brassiere making, at
this point, was still only a side issue to the dressmaking,
a kind of accessory activity to the older work.

But the fact was that Mrs. Rosenthal had become
more interested in making brassieres than in making
dresses, and while she was turning out dresses she was
also making plans. She found a partner and together
they raised enough capital to open and staff a workroom
—a rudimentary factory—and Mrs. Rosenthal dropped
dressmaking to devote herself to manufacturing, whole-
saling and distributing brassieres. The new work now
stood as an activity in its own right.

In this process, it does not matter who carries out the
new work, as long as somebody does. It is not always the
creator of the new goods or service who presides over
its production. For example, a news item from the Soviet

Union describes an electronically operated artificial hand for amputees and persons with birth defects. It was devised, the press report said, by technicians in a laboratory serving the Soviet space program. Presumably they had been working on electronic controls for space vehicles. The report goes on to say that the Soviet government plans to put the hand into production by parceling out the various manufacturing operations to factories making radio components. This is often the way production of some new goods or service is carried out. The new work is added to older work first, and then sometimes its new divisions of labor are added to other appropriate varieties of older work.

Now let us look at a somewhat more complicated case in which one thing led to whole groups of other things. In this instance, the starting point was abrasive sand which was used by manufacturers of metal castings and other metal products in Minneapolis. The sand was produced by a small and obscure company founded in 1902, called Minnesota Mining and Manufacturing Co. This grandiose name merely represented two proprietors and a few workers who were engaged in digging, crushing, sorting and selling sand.

The first additional goods that this work led to was sandpaper. The proprietors decided to stick some of the sorted sand on paper for sale to carpenters, cabinetmakers and other woodworkers. They had not invented sandpaper as Mrs. Rosenthal invented brassieres or the Soviet technicians invented an electronic hand. Sandpaper was not new. But 3M, as this company now calls itself, was adding new work to older work nevertheless, while copying an already existing product.

The sandpaper turned out to be not much good. The trouble lay with the adhesives. Trying to solve their problem, the proprietors of 3M kept brewing new kinds of adhesives and got much interested in them, even though they did not lead to much improvement in the sandpaper. What the work with adhesives led to, instead, was some good gummed paper for use as masking tape by house painters. Making masking tape led to making other kinds of tape at 3M, and thus to a whole family of additional products, some of which were true innovations. In their order of emergence, the progeny of the masking tape were: shoe tape, electrical tape, acetate tape, pressure-sensitive adhesive tape (better known as Scotch tape), acetate fiber tape, cellophane tape, printed cellophane tape, plastic tape, filament tape, sound recording magnetic tape, nonwoven synthetic fibers.

In the meantime, the proprietors of 3M had not lost interest in other possible uses for adhesives and still another family of products branched off from that work: sandblasting stencils, automotive adhesives, industrial adhesives, marine adhesives, marine calking compounds, tile and construction adhesives, construction compounds.

The sand, from which all this had started, was not forgotten either, for in addition to abrasive sand the company proceeded to produce coated sand for polishing, then wax and varnish coatings, finely ground paint pigments, roofing granules, nonslip cleats and strips, abrasive cloth, reflective sheeting, reflective compounds, paving materials, and welding fluxes. All these were logical additions to work that began with preparing sand.

This process in which one sort of work leads to another must have happened millions of times in the whole history of human economic development. Every newspaper reports it. From only a few days' gleanings in the women's pages, one learns that a cleaner of suede clothing is now starting to bottle and sell her cleaning fluid for people who want to clean their own suede; a chest and wardrobe manufacturer is starting, for a fee, to analyze what is wrong with one's household or office storage arrangements; a playground designer is starting to make and sell equipment for playgrounds and nursery schools;

a sculptor is starting a line of costume jewelry; a designer of theater costumes is launching himself as a couturier; a couturier is starting a boutique; an importer of Italian marble is starting to manufacture marble-topped tables; a clothing store is starting classes in teen-age grooming and dieting.

Nor is the process by which one thing leads to another confined to profit-making enterprises. A hospital outpatient department is starting a home-care service; a library is starting a program of art exhibits; an art museum is starting a library. Nor is it, as we also notice from the papers, confined to useful, legal or innocuous work. Some police departments collect bribes from illegal enterprises and organize their men for collecting and rationing out the take; police sometimes add burglarizing to their work of patrolling, and other divisions of labor to dispose of the goods; sales divisions of some corporations add pimping services for important customers; some appliance repair shops start covertly selling appliances— that is, getting kickbacks from appliance retailers—and do a good business by convincing householders that serviceable equipment is beyond repair; some appliance makers add types of installment financing that amount to loan sharking and employ market analysts to tell them what the traffic will bear as well as psychologists to tell them how to make the rates sound beneficent; some government intelligence units take to stuffing ballot boxes and arranging assassinations; some beer distributors start protection rackets; some racketeers have been known to rent out their gunmen to other people who want a murder done, and to have established this added work as a regular, organized service; some city-planning departments take to scouting out and processing profitable deals for favored real-estate operators and also to organizing and running fraudulent "citizens' organizations" to help overcome public opposition.

Lest this brief catalog convey the impression that dishonest or destructive goods and services must be added into economic life along with constructive and simply innocuous ones, I would add that of course nothing precludes a society from suppressing certain kinds of new activities while permitting and encouraging others. Indeed, a society must do that or else risk nurturing activities and organizations that will devote themselves to outright destruction of useful activities and also to preventing or hampering the emergence of new and useful goods and services. The point is that new goods and services, whether criminal or benign, do not come out of thin air. New work arises upon existing work; it requires "parent" work.

How Adding New Work Multiplies Divisions of Labor

When new goods or services are added to older work, they are not added to the whole of the older work. Rather, the new work is added directly onto only a fragment of the older work. For instance, it was one specific division of labor in the whole work of dressmaking—dress fitting—that suggested to Mrs. Rosenthal the notion of adding brassieres. She added them specifically to dress-fitting work, not to that of buttonhole making, seam sewing, cutting, or any of the many other specific tasks in making dresses. Just so, the complete business of building space vehicles did not directly lead to the invention of the Soviet electronic hand, but only the work in one laboratory. Indeed, it is likely that the hand was suggested by one specific problem, in this one laboratory, which had to be solved to make a vehicular control device work. In 3M, the first addition was not made to the whole work of producing abrasive sand. The sandpaper arose from the sand sorting, not from the sand digging. And the gummed tape arose from one fragment of the sandpaper work, the business of making adhesives.

Four different kinds of enterprises—a manufacturer of

equipment for institutional kitchens, a cheese importer, a night club, and a sauce cannery—may all possibly trace back to origins in four similar restaurants. But in each case, a different fragment of the whole work of running a restaurant led to the new work. This too is one of the principles upon which I based my conjectures about how animal husbandry and grain culture may have arisen in New Obsidian. If things happened in prehistoric times as they happen now, grain culture would not have arisen, as has been conventionally supposed, upon the whole work of gathering wild plant foods, nor animal husbandry upon the whole work of hunting and capturing animals, but in each case only upon specialized fragments of the whole work.

To be sure, when new work is added to older work, it calls for more tasks in its own cause. Although the new work has arisen from a fragment of older work, that does not mean that it is itself a fragment. As soon as Mrs. Rosenthal started manufacturing brassieres, that work demanded its own divisions of labor, whole groups of them. There were all the tasks of designing the brassieres, of making, packing, selling, advertising, and distributing them, and also the tasks of financing the work, printing labels, and providing hooks, eyes, elastic and cloth. One reason Mrs. Rosenthal, her partner and their initially small staff of workers were able to manage all this was that in New York they could use many suppliers of goods and services to help them out: shippers, sewing machine suppliers, box makers, textile suppliers, bankers and so on. In sum, while many of the divisions of labor entailed in brassiere manufacturing, and especially the new kinds, were "internal," that is, within the Maidenform Brassiere Co., others were "external" and were carried on by other organizations.

But the point is that brassiere manufacturing, once it became an economic activity in its own right, multiplied into many divisions of labor; some of them had not existed before, though some had. Just so, when animal husbandry and grain culture came into the world, whether or not they came as I have reasoned, they multiplied the divisions of labor to be found in economic life.

For those who like to see a process expressed as a formula, an event such as adding brassiere manufacturing to dress fitting can be stated like this: $D + A \longrightarrow nD$. The first D stands for the division of labor of dress fitting. The A added to it is the new activity of brassiere manufacturing. The resulting nD stands for an indeterminate number of new divisions of labor.

In New Obsidian, that first D could stand for custody of imported animals awaiting slaughter; the A is the added activity of choosing and retaining breeding stock; and the nD includes all the new tasks required in domestic animal husbandry. Or the first D could stand for the work of sewing clothing from hides; the A in that case could stand for the added activity of making good hide containers to transport obsidian from the mines to New Obsidian; and the nD includes the various tasks of making the containers.

Once one gets the hang of the process, it is not only entertaining to track down the progressions of D and A that have given us modern activities like magnetic-tape manufacturing, but also to speculate about the unknown progressions in the past, as I have done. Here is a bit of speculation, offered for no reason except that I like it, concerning the possible beginnings of pottery making.

Before clay pots were made, fire sometimes had to be carried, probably from a hearth that was always under surveillance and never extinguished. It would have been carried, after baskets were made, in baskets that had been plastered inside with clay. A fire-carrying basket on which the basketry finally wore out would stand as a rough, self-fired clay pot imprinted with basket markings on its exterior, as if these were decorations. In some cases, large fire baskets may also have been made to confine fire while it was in use, much as if the clay-lined baskets were stoves.*

The next step would have been to make fire-carrying baskets, big or little, to hold different things entirely, such as small seeds or liquids. Making them would have been done by the fire tenders as a side issue to their main work. But in time some fire tenders would devote themselves entirely to this work.

The process of adding new work to old, and thus multiplying divisions of labor, can be shown also in a diagram. Here is a diagram that indicates four additions:

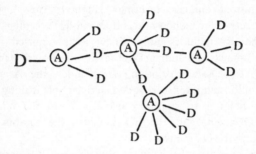

The following generalization can be stated: *Existing divisions of labor multiply into more divisions of labor by grace of intervening added activities that yield up new sums of work to be divided.* To me, the D + A   nD formula seems a handy way of expressing the process, and I shall use it again in this book.

In an economy where many new goods and services are being added, new divisions of labor multiply more rapidly than old divisions of labor become obsolete. In

*Just such fire baskets, employed to heat food in the markets, were in use in some Vietnam villages in 1959. I am indebted for this information to Mr. and Mrs. Paul Stephansen who photographed one of the baskets in stereopticon color. If the rough basket work had been knocked off, the clay would have stood as a crude, large, self-fired pot.

this way, kinds of work literally multiply, not by any economic "spontaneous generation" but rather as one thing leads explicitly to another. The greater the sheer numbers and varieties of divisions of labor already achieved in an economy, the greater the economy's inherent capacity for adding still more kinds of goods and services. Also the possibilities increase for combining the existing divisions of labor in new ways, as Mrs. Rosenthal did with the existing external divisions of labor she drew upon.

The Logic of Adding New Work to Old

In this process, as I have mentioned, the new work is logically added to old work. To be sure, the process is full of surprises and is hard to predict—possibly it is unpredictable—before it has happened. But after the fact, after the added goods or services exist, their addition usually looks wonderfully logical and "natural."

What kind of logic is this? It is analogous, I think, to a form of logic, or intuition if you prefer, that artists use. Artists often comment that although they are masters of the work they are creating, they are also alert to messages that come from the work, and act upon them. Perhaps a similar rapport is necessary in the more mundane process of adding new work to old. At any rate, messages—that is, suggestions—afforded by the parent work seem to be vital to the process.

The suggestions tend to fall into two different types: ideas suggested by the materials or skills already being used; and those that arise from particular problems in the course of the work. Sometimes the two overlap. Even when new work seems to be unrelated to skills or materials used in the parent work, we can almost always be sure that a problem of some peripheral kind in the parent work suggested the new goods or service. For example, the modern equipment-leasing business is a service that finances the production equipment that manufacturers and other producers need to carry on their work. It is a financial service that is now supplied by many banks in the United States, among others. But as an innovation, it was a service added to the parent work of food processing. A San Francisco food processor who had a small factory, but a growing business, could not get financing for the equipment he needed to expand his production. He worked out a way in which his own equipment could be financed. Like Mrs. Rosenthal, he grew more interested in this side issue than in the parent work that had given rise to it, and he founded a leasing service for manufacturers with a financing problem similar to his own.

When new work arises from parent work, that in itself does not account for the new work. Many people do not attempt new solutions to the problems that arise in their work, nor do they glimpse new possibilities in the materials or skills they use. The creator of the new work must have an insight and, combining an idea or observation with the suggestion from the work itself, make a new departure. The point is that the logic of the process is supplied by the person who is adding the new work. And this logic comes in part from antecedent work which is almost always his own but, as we shall see later, is occasionally from someone else's work that comes under his observation.

It is important to notice the kind of logic at work here so we will not be confused by supposing that other and quite different kinds of logic direct this development process. For one thing, the logic at work is *not* the logic of customers of the parent work. The new goods and services being added may be irrelevant to what customers of the older work want. For instance, 3M made its abrasive sand for customers who were metal workers. The sandpaper 3M added was not for them, but for woodworkers. The masking tape added to that was for neither metal workers nor woodworkers but for painters.

Just so, it is irrelevant to farmers who buy chemical fertilizers that the manufacturer has added the production of compounds to improve the abrasion-resistance of power shovels and the wet strength of paper overshoes.

Sometimes new goods or services do coincide with what customers of the older work want. But the added work can just as well be hostile to those interests. When Mrs. Rosenthal dropped dressmaking to devote herself to brassiere manufacturing, that act was not in harmony with her customers' interests. Ladies do not like their dressmakers to abandon them. The fact that the logic of adding new work to old is not the customers' logic may help explain why consumers' cooperatives, unlike many producers' cooperatives, have been so sterile and so inconsequential in economic history. It may also help explain some of the parodies of economic creativity we see in American automobile and soap manufacturing. The automobile makers strive to entice customers by adding superficial style changes to the product; while the soap and detergent makers claim regularly and predictably that familiar products are "New! New!" owing to ingredients so miraculous they cannot be described rationally. Perhaps such behavior results from acting almost solely upon messages that come from the sales departments.

Nor is the logic of adding new work to old the abstract logic of the economic statistician or the city zoner. These people place work into various categories such as "local services," "district retail trade," "light manufacturing," "the underwear industry," "the prosthetics industry," and so on. These are useful categories for some types of economic analysis, but insofar as they are relevant at all to understanding how old work leads to new, they interfere with our understanding.

If you will glance back at the random list of added goods and services taken from the women's pages of a newspaper, you will note that a manufactured product was being added to a service; a service was being added to manufacturing; a designer was adding manufactured products; an artist was adding artisan's products; another designer was adding manufactured products; a manufacturer and retailer was adding a different kind of retailing; an importer was adding manufacturing; a retailer was adding an educational service. The Soviet Union has a well-established prosthetics industry, but it was not from that industry that the electronic prosthesis emerged. It was not from the underwear industry that the brassiere emerged. It was neither from banking nor equipment manufacturing that general equipment leasing developed.

The point is that when new work is added to older work, the addition often cuts ruthlessly across categories of work, no matter how one may analyze the categories. Only in stagnant economies does work stay docilely within given categories. And wherever it is forced to stay within prearranged categories—whether by zoning, by economic planning, or by guilds, associations or unions—the process of adding new work to old can occur little if at all.

The conflict between the process of adding new work to old and the guilds' categories of work was a constant source of wrangling in medieval European cities. In a typical quarrel of this sort in London, the members of the Goldsmiths denounced the members of the Cutlers* thus: "In their workhouses they cover tin with silver so subtly and with such sleight that the same cannot be discerned and severed from the tin."

The trouble there was that a category of work, "goods manufactured of gold and silver," belonged to the Goldsmiths. Yet the technologically very important work of

*Who made knife handles and assembled them with parts they bought from members of two supplier guilds, the Bladers and Sheathers.

plating with precious metal was logically added to work with base metals. Incidentally, this was a case in which the added work was probably in harmony with the interests of customers of the older work. But its logic was based upon materials and skills used in making handles for knives, and probably also upon problems concerning the appearance of the finished work.

Adding Copied Work

Innovations are the most important kind of goods and services added to older work. But for every true innovator, there are many, many imitators. Innovations make up only a fraction of the many individual instances in which new goods and services are added logically to older work. Imitation is a shortcut. It seldom requires as much trial and error as innovations do.

The repairing of things is often the older work to which the newer work of making the same things is added. The Japanese used this method with great success when they began imitating Western goods during the late nineteenth century. At that time, Japan's economy was suffering severely from cheap Western imports with which her own manufacturers could not economically compete—or could not make at all. Among the imports were bicycles. They had become enormously popular in Japanese cities.

To replace these imports with locally made bicycles, the Japanese could have invited a big American or European bicycle manufacturer to establish a factory in Japan, much as the Soviet government has recently invited Renault and Fiat to establish automobile factories in the Soviet Union. In short, the work could have been transplanted into Japan from somewhere else. Or the Japanese could have built a factory that was a slavish imitation of a European or American bicycle factory. They would have had to import most or all of the factory's machinery, as well as hiring foreign production managers or having Japanese production managers trained abroad in foreign factories. In short, theirs would have been an elaborate and costly enterprise, and one more likely than not to bog down in other, unanticipated difficulties.

What the Japanese did instead was to build up their own bicycle manufacturing industry by adding new work to older divisions of labor, just as if they had been innovating. It has become a classic example of successful "economic borrowing," as imitation is called when it is encountered historically.

After bicycles had been imported into Japan, shops to repair them had sprung up in the big cities. In Tokyo, the repair work was done in great numbers of one-man and two-man shops. Imported spare parts were expensive and broken bicycles were too valuable to cannibalize for parts. Many repair shops thus found it worthwhile to make replacement parts themselves—not difficult if a man specialized in one kind of part, as many repairmen did. In this way, groups of bicycle repair shops were almost doing the work of manufacturing entire bicycles. That step was taken by bicycle assemblers who bought parts, on contract, from repairmen: the repairmen had become "light manufacturers."

Far from being costly to develop, bicycle manufacturing in Japan paid its way right through its own development stages. Moreover, most of the work of making appropriate production equipment was added to the Japanese economy too, gradually and in concert with the development of bicycle manufacturing.

The Japanese got much more than a bicycle industry. They had acquired a pattern for many of their other achievements in industrialization: a system of breaking complex manufacturing work into relatively simple fragments, in autonomous shops. The method was soon used to produce many other goods and is still much used in Japan. Parts making has become a standard foothold for adding new work. Sony, the enormous manufacturer of communications equipment, began, at the end of World War II, as a small-parts shop in Tokyo, making tubes on contract for radio assemblers, and was built up by adding to this the manufacturing of whole radios (for which some parts were bought from other suppliers) and then other types of communication and electronic goods.

Henry Ford began manufacturing automobiles almost exactly as if he had been a Japanese bicycle assembler. Before Ford started his successful firm in 1903, he had already failed twice at automobile manufacturing—once as a manager employed by others and again with a company he started himself. Both times his idea was to set up a reasonably complete, though small, automobile factory. The third time he changed his strategy. He bought from various suppliers in Detroit every single item he needed for his cars—wheels, bodies, cushions, everything. The Dodge Brothers, young mechanics who had been producing transmissions for Olds in their machine shop, expanded to make Ford's engines. They were adding work. The first Ford factory was a wooden building in a coal yard, financed by the carpenter who built it. He was adding work. The factory was cheap and it was small because all Ford did in it was to assemble parts that other people were making elsewhere.

Ford's first significant innovation of any kind—and one of the most important he was ever to make—was to promise customers that they could get a complete stock of repair parts for Ford cars. At first, he bought these parts from his subcontractors, the same people who supplied the original components. But he then began making repair parts himself, beginning with those that proved to be most in demand. Thus little by little, he added to his assembly work the manufacturing of part after part. By the time he was ready to put the first Model T into production, late in 1907, he was capable of much of its manufacture.

This sequence—first repair work on the product, then manufacturing of the product itself—is described by Hans Koningsberger in *Love and Hate in China*, in a report of a truck factory he visited in Nanking in 1965. At that time, the plant was employing about three thousand people and was producing engines for pumps and generators, as well as trucks. "[It] had its beginnings as what its founders call a 'shoulder factory': the entire equipment was carried around on the shoulders of thirty men, who ran it, and who formed a repair unit in the Communist Army. When the Army entered Nanking, these men took over an old building and set up shop, first repaiᵣ engines and then building them. In 1958, they produced their first truck."

Appropriate retailing is another common form of parent work for imitative manufacturing. At first the seller simply sells the product, then he makes and sells it. The California fruit preserving and canning industry started this way when a San Francisco retailer of imported Eastern preserved fruits added the work of preserving California fruit for local sale.

Once goods or services have been created or first imitated in a given place, still more shortcuts can often be employed by subsequent imitators. People who learn the work—or a fragment of it—in an existing organization can leave that organization and reproduce the work on their own. In Britain, this kind of event in industry or commerce is sometimes called a "breakaway." In Communist countries it is called the "cadre system." Breakaways were highly formalized in the medieval guilds. An apprentice learned the work in an existing organization, then became a journeyman employed in the same organization or others similar, and then, if all went well, he set up a shop of his own as a master and took on apprentices. In the United States, where breakaways in many types of work are common, there seems to be no name for them other than "going into business for oneself," an imprecise term that includes much besides breakaways; so I shall use the British term.

The breakaway is sometimes a straight imitation of the work done in the parent organization, or an exact imitation of a fragment of that work. But breakaways often incorporate a variation from the older work. This event is common, for instance, in magazine publishing where employees of an existing publisher break away and start a new magazine of their own. *American Heritage* magazine and *Scientific American* are both published by people who broke away from Time, Inc.; in the case of *American Heritage*, they started a new publishing company, in the case of *Scientific American*, they bought and rejuvenated an old and moribund magazine.

Many of the most economically creative breakaways have this sort of history: individuals, or a few colleagues together, leave their jobs in a large organization and independently reproduce the same fragment of work they had been doing there. Usually their customers are small organizations too. Then the breakaway adds new work to its older work. A simple example would be an art director for a large magazine who breaks away to do freelance art directing for small magazines. To this he is now able to add an organization that also designs packages. In the electronics industry breakaways of just this kind are exceedingly common. Many firms in the Los Angeles electronics industry, for instance, broke away from Hughes Aircraft, reproduced fragments of work done there, and then added to those fragments great varieties of other electronic devices and services. For reasons we shall see later in this chapter, such people would likely be unable to add their new work into economic life unless they first broke away from the parent company, reproducing the older work independently. Many fragments of already existing work become fertile only if they are first broken away from the whole work of which they have previously formed a part.

Conserving Old Work by Adding New

Old products and arts are often retained and put to new uses in economic life after new work has made them obsolete. The United States probably has more sailboats than it had in "the age of sail," although their purpose has changed. When I was a child, in the 1920s, I was urged to remember carefully the sight of a blacksmith at work shoeing a horse, for this was work expected to disappear. But in 1960, more people knew how to shoe horses than in the 1920s, although most of these were also veterinarians and had learned blacksmithing in veterinary school.

To put old goods and services to new uses, or to employ them in new combinations of work instead of jettisoning them, might well be called a "conserving" tendency in an economy. Another expression of this tendency is the "backward" application of new techniques to goods and services that would otherwise be obsolete. The phonograph is an illustration. It was temporarily eclipsed by radio and, like the blacksmith, it was supposed to disappear. It almost did in the early 1930s. But the phonograph itself was changed by incorporating some of the technology of radio; and the phonograph in turn brought changes to radio broadcasting. It was conserved to live another life.

Similarly, as Western dress for women gained favor in Japan, the disappearance of the kimono was predicted. But kimonos have been changing and, according to the *New York Times*, have been reinstated as high-fashion formal dress by the most modern young women in Japan, the students and office and professional workers. "New simplified designs, the introduction of synthetic fibers and other new materials and use of zippers and ready-tied obis" have made the kimono easier to put on, more comfortable and easier to care for, the *Times* reported, and thus popular again with the young. In short, the kimono is being conserved to live another life.

These are trivial instances, but the economic behavior they illustrate is far from trivial. It is the kind of behavior that seems to permit old crafts like handweaving, fine glassmaking or guitar making to change instead of being dropped, or being arrested and then degenerating. This kind of behavior was obviously at work in Çatal Hüyük, where people were combining the new woven clothing with sophisticated versions of the old animal-hide clothing, and trinkets of copper with trinkets of stones and shells, and radically new cultivated foods with old-fashioned wild foods, some of which would in time be cultivated too.

This tendency to conserve old goods and services is conspicuously absent in stagnated economies, although we are apt, offhand, to think of stagnation as being synonymous with "conservatism." When white sugar becomes easily available in an Appalachian settlement, sorghum pressing is abandoned. When nylon fishing nets reach a Southeast Asian village, the old net making is dropped. At its most extreme, such profoundly unconserving behavior results in the well-known havoc wrought on the cultures and economies of primitive people by contact with new goods, services and work brought in from outside.

A society's ability to conserve old skills or old goods seems to depend upon combining them with new goods or services or new purposes. But how does this happen? A very simple illustration may give a clue. Some artists of my acquaintance who were fighting a proposed expressway in New York decided, as part of the campaign, to paint a huge street banner. A banner of the weight and opacity desired, capable of withstanding the wind without being torn from its ropes, turned out to be impossible to construct until someone remembered an old-fashioned sailmaker in the second story of a loft nearby. He had never made a street banner before, but he made one now, and a good one. Here was a case in which the practitioner of the old work (to which a new purpose was, for the moment, added) was not the one who took the initiative. His work, rather, was seen—by somebody who had a problem—as appropriate work upon which to add something more. In this instance, since the sailmaker produced only this one banner, the addition of new work was ephemeral.

But much the same thing can happen on a more permanent basis. A friend of mine, Allen Block, runs a successful sandal-making business in New York. He started by designing sandals, but he did not know how to make them properly. Hence, as he was soon to learn, he did not really know how to design them either. He therefore apprenticed himself to an aged cobbler. The working quarters these two devised were almost a diagram of the act of conserving old work by adding new. From the street, one seemed to see two separate shops: at the left, with its own door and its own sign, was the cobbler's; at the right, with its own door and its own sign, was the sandal maker's. But inside, where the work was being done, the dividing partition had been removed and the two shops were one. The cobbler is dead now, but his "obsolete" skill, having been conserved, is retained in the economy to live another life.

The Infertility of Captive Divisions of Labor

I have said that the interests of old customers may or may not be served when new work is added to the old. The chances are that the new work is irrelevant to customers of the old, or even against their interests. Not all customers are consumers, in the sense that Mrs. Rosenthal's customers were consumers. Many customers for goods and services are other producers, and the goods and services supplied them go into their own work. The customers for 3M's abrasive sand were producers of metal castings. The customers of the medieval Bladers and Sheathers were the Cutlers. The goods and services supplied another producer are, of course, divisions of labor, from their buyer's point of view. There are two distinctly different ways in which relationships of this sort can be organized.

The suppliers can be independent of their customers, as 3M and the Bladers were from theirs; they can do their work autonomously, in their own organizations. But exactly the same tasks can also be organized so that the supply work is not independent. For instance, the people who made the abrasive sand at 3M could have done the same kind of work and yet could have been the abrasive-sand department of one of their large customers. People who make knife blades can work for a company that makes the rest of the knife and puts the whole thing together.

If 3M, when it was a young company, had in fact been the abrasive-sand department of a large metal-casting company, it is highly unlikely that its work would have led to additional kinds of work. In a metal-working organization, it would have been irrelevant for the abrasive-sand department to fiddle around with new products which, if they succeeded, would be of use to carpenters and house painters and of no use in working metal.

Offhand, one might suppose that large organizations with their many divisions of labor would be much more prolific at adding new work to old than would small organizations. But this is not so. In a large organization, nearly all the divisions of labor, no matter how many there are, must necessarily be sterile in this respect. The various goods and services that could be logically added to them are not logical for the customer at hand, which is to say, not logical for the organization as a whole. Worse still, the various kinds of new work that can logically be added to various divisions of labor in a large organization bear no logical relationship to one another. Picture, for example, a large manufacturer of metal dies whose abrasive-sand department has taken on the work of making sandpaper and masking tape. The personnel department has added the service of supplying part-time office workers to banks and publishers. One group of machinists has added the manufacturing of toy cars. Another group of machinists has added the manufacturing of surgical instruments. Still another group is working on a machine to improve bookbinding. The shipping department has added the manufacturing of crate linings made from foam rubber and is also making shoe innersoles from the scraps.

Quite apart from what would happen to the die business itself in this strange hive, what would happen to the various kinds of new work being added to its divisions of labor? Each would be growing at its own rate, bearing no relation to any other department's scale of production or needs. Space allocations in the organization, personnel distribution, budgeting, sales arrangements—all would become a wild, incoherent scramble. The organization would be a disorganization, a fantastic bundle of contradictions and cross purposes, related to one another only by the anachronistic bonds of a vanished community of purpose.

I have had to suggest, using a hypothetical die maker, a hypothetical bundle of new goods and services, because in real life no organization has ever grown by the unbridled addition of new work to its various divisions of labor. Even nature, as soon as an organism becomes complex, is careful to keep the reproductive cells confined to one part of the organism only.

An idea of the cross purposes and conflicts that would

arise in such an organization is conveyed in some re-
marks made in 1964 by Clark Kerr, who at the time
was president of the University of California. Dr. Kerr,
a proponent of the idea of the "multi-versity," which
would render vast ranges of services to its society, was
about to run into trouble (although he did not know it
then) with students who claimed that the multi-versity
was no longer doing a proper job of educating them because, among other things, they were being shunted aside
in favor of too many other tasks the university was doing.

Now hear a hint of the internal organizational problems that were turning up as various professors were
adding to their specialties new kinds of work for outside
customers. Dr. Kerr was discussing, in particular, the
services they added under the encouragement of Federal
research grants.

> [Other university funds] go through the usual budget-
> making procedures and their assignment is subject to re-
> view in accordance with internal policy. Federal research
> funds, however, are usually negotiated by the individual
> scholar with the particular agency and so bypass the usual
> review process. . . . These funds in turn commit some of the
> university's own funds; they influence the assignment
> of space; they determine the distribution of time between
> teaching and research; to a large extent they establish the
> areas in which the university grows the fastest. . . . The
> authority of the department chairman, the dean, the presi-
> dent is thereby reduced; so also is the role of faculty gov-
> ernment. This may have its advantages . . . [but] some
> faculty members come to use the pressure of their agency
> contacts against the university. They may try to force the
> establishment of a new administrative unit or the assign-
> ment of land for their own special building, in defiance
> of general university policy or priorities. These pressures,
> of course, should be withstood; they speak well neither
> of the professor nor of the agency. Also, some faculty
> members tend to shift their identification and loyalty from
> their university to the agency in Washington. The agency
> becomes the new alma mater. There are especially acute

problems when the agency insists on the tie-in sale (if we do this for you, then you must do that for us) or when it requires frequent and detailed progress reports. Then the university really is less than a free agent.

Dr. Kerr summed up the mess: "It all becomes a kind of 'putting out' system with the agency taking the place of the merchant-capitalist of old."

But, Dr. Kerr to the contrary, the merchant capitalists of old did not make deals with another organization's parts as if the latter were autonomous when they were not. Paul Goodman, in a letter to the *New York Review of Books* about the multi-versity problem, asked the right kind of question: "Have [the administrations] tried to shift the contracted research to non-academic institutes? No."*

The breakaway, which in essence is what Goodman was suggesting, is a means of releasing captive divisions of labor to build up, for themselves, new, autonomous organizations. It is also a means by which one man can do two different kinds of work, within two different organizations, without undermining the coherence of either.

In a small organization that is adding new work to its original work, the reproductive cells, so to speak, are almost the whole animal. The sterile divisions of labor are small in proportion to the whole. The period when an organization is most fertile at adding new work is while it is still small; its principal growth thereafter is apt to be growth in volume of the work already added.

Far from doing their proportionate share of creating new goods and services, large economic organizations are seldom able—once they have become large—to con-

---

*A very few, individually enormous, research institutes have been set up: e.g., the C.I.T. Jet Propulsion Laboratory by the California Institute of Technology and the Stanford Research Institute by Stanford University; in some ways these are more like subsidiaries of the universities, however, than autonomous organizations.

tinue adding enough new activities to keep themselves from shrinking. To compensate for this, they pick up activities that have been added into economic life outside their own organizations. Thus, American Machine & Foundry saved itself from shrinking—as markets for its old goods shrank—by picking up in rapid succession thirteen smaller companies engaged in different work: i.e., home power tools, metal furniture, special hardware of various kinds, electric relays, small motors, and a large variety of military goods. Singer Sewing Machine, having lost its once great international markets (mostly to three hundred Japanese competitors) was "expanding its electronics instrument line through the proposed acquisition of Gertsch Products," according to the *New York Times*. Ford, reported as desiring an "active operating position in new type military hardware and in the computer, semiconductor and transistor business," bought Philco. The big cigarette companies, to protect themselves against what the *Times* calls "the health threat," were embarking on new activities—bought ready-made. Philip Morris was "buying a position" in shaving supplies, packaging and chemicals; Reynolds Tobacco in fruit juice, shoeshine equipment and metal foil. 3M, so prolific at adding new activities to work with those grains of sand, has, now that it is large, taken to buying activities; one of its recent purchases has been Thermo-fax.

Whenever a large organization sickens or its profits fall off, the first tonic prescribed is the purchase of already created work. Thus Newton N. Minow, called in some years ago to aid the enfeebled Curtis Publishing Co., announced, "I will try to help Curtis find the right mergers and acquisitions."

When organizations that are already large decide to embark on a program of adding new goods and services, they seldom start by adding onto the divisions of labor they already have. They buy up others, to provide parent work for the new purposes they have in mind. Thus, in the early 1920s, when the management of du Pont, an already huge gunpowder trust, had determined to build a diversified chemical industry, the firm acquired, in *Fortune*'s words, "a host of smaller companies to give it a position in paints and finishes, dyes and pigments, acids and heavy chemicals, cellulose plastics and coated textiles, and, through rights purchased [from French firms], in rayon and Cellophane."

We are accustomed to the fact that old giants like General Motors are formed of great numbers of once independent firms which were valuable to the combine precisely because they had already added successful activities to their parent work. It is the same with new giants. Litton Industries, for example, a small microwave-tube manufacturing company in the early 1950s, founded as a breakaway from Hughes Aircraft, had become by 1963 the hundredth largest industrial corporation in the United States. It had purchased thirty-nine other companies. When the proprietors of Litton resolved to "dominate the low-priced arithmetic field," they set about doing so by buying a calculating machine company; a company that had an automated system for control of retail inventory and that manufactured tags, tickets and labels; a company that made adhesives for the backs of labels; another making office furniture; another making trading stamps; and a paper mill. Explaining how his enterprise had gotten into "everything from computers to shipbuilding," Litton's president told a *Time* magazine reporter, "We have never acquired companies as such. We have bought time, a market, a product line, a plant, research time, a sales force. It would take us years to duplicate all this from scratch."

When large organizations actively try to add new goods or services to those they already produce, they create, like special reproductive organs, special divisions of labor for that purpose called research and development departments. These are substitutes, or surrogates, for the great body of sterile divisions of labor. But by definition, the parent work on which R & D can build, in comparison with the organization's total work, is exceedingly limited. And even within these limitations, the new work that the researchers find it logical to develop frequently turns out to be irrelevant or hostile to the interests of the organization as a whole. Hence we have the paradox of useful inventions neglected by the very organizations that have "taken the trouble" to develop them. The infertility of large organizations is not a new phenomenon. Consider the infertility of the American railroads which, in their heyday, were the largest of the country's corporations. Equally, the great Renaissance trading organizations, the largest companies of their time, were anything but fertile at adding further new goods and services into economic life.*

If large organizations were fertile in proportion to

*Robert Lekachman has drawn to my attention the interesting case of International Business Machines. The initial growth of I.B.M. was typical: while it was still small, it bought the rights to an invention, the electric typewriter, which had been turned down by the large typewriter manufacturers, and the company grew with growth in volume of its new work. But after the company had already grown very large, it added the 360 Computer, and this was not simply the addition of another machine to its line of products. I.B.M. had to change radically to offer analysis, programming and training services to its computer customers and to establish computer centers where, in effect, it rented time, equipment and personnel to clients. In short, it had to become a service organization too; the company was radically reconstituted by its management. Having grown large, it behaved like a small company again. The point is, if an organization behaves as if it were small, by adding new work in rather radically different categories from the old—and not by purchasing going concerns, but by internal change—it must also behave like a small organization in another respect: it must undertake radical organizational changes, become so flexible as to remake itself, in effect. Even then, of course, most of its divisions of labor must still remain infertile.

their divisions of labor and to their extraordinary ability to get development capital, then backward countries that harbor large and powerful economic enterprises (as backward and poor countries typically do) could depend upon these to generate the great numbers of necessary new goods and services that are missing. But that is not how economies develop.

All this does not mean that large organizations are not useful in economic life; they often are. It only means that the new goods and services for the future are not going to be built, in any great numbers, upon them and their divisions of labor. Some kinds of production cannot well be carried out except by large organizations with many internal divisions of labor. Such organizations are, by definition, relatively self-sufficient and use few external divisions of labor. They are often transplanted to the rural world where they establish company towns. Otherwise they convert existing cities into company towns. Development of almost everything else halts in a city that becomes dominated by one or a few huge organizations, although this is not, of course, the only reason cities stagnate and economies stop developing.

Large and successful organizations are awesome. It is easy to believe that almost anything is within their power and that they hold the future development of an economy in their hands. Perhaps this is why it is commonly believed, even by many economists, that an economy's expansion depends upon expansion of already existing activities and upon further development of work undertaken by already large and successful organizations.

But such organizations and their work do not forecast the future. Rather, they themselves are results of economic creativity in the past. Because of the necessary sterility of most of their divisions of labor, it is not in their power to develop more than a minute fraction of a developing economy's future new goods and services. Indeed, where large organizations are relied upon for economic expan-

sion and development—that is, where small organizations find little opportunity to multiply, to find financing,
and to add new work to old—the economy inevitably
stagnates. When the stagnation becomes serious, there are
no longer things for large organizations to buy up to keep
themselves from shrinking.

In short, it is not the success of large economic organizations that makes possible vigorous adding of new
work to older work. Rather, when this process operates
vigorously, it depends upon large numbers and great
diversity of economic organizations, some of which, of
course, grow large in their heydays.

Adding and Dividing Work

Ancient people seem to have understood perfectly well
that economic life is a matter of adding new goods and
services. But instead of seeing the logic and order by
which this happens, they saw magic. Important activities
had been given to men or taught to men in remote times
by gods; they had been stolen from gods; they had been
brought along, like a trousseau, by demigod progenitors
of people.

Herodotus, who was much too sophisticated and curious to be satisfied by old tales of that sort, was forever
noticing where things seemed to have come from. After
a trip among the Libyans he reflected: "It is evident, I
think, that the Greeks took the 'aegis' with which they
adorn statues of Athene from the dress of the Libyan
women; for except that the latter is of leather and has
fringes of leather thongs instead of snakes, there is no
other point of difference. Moreover, the word 'aegis'
itself shows [the derivation]; for Libyan women wear
goatskins with the hair stripped off, dyed red and fringed
at the edges, and it was from these skins that we took our
word 'aegis.' . . . Another thing the Greeks learnt from
Libya was to harness four horses to a chariot." The

Gyzantes, another people, are well supplied with honey, "much of it made by bees, but even more by some process which the people have discovered." The Barcaeans learned how to detect the military mines dug by Persian sappers during a siege: "A metal-worker very ingeniously discovered the saps in the following way: he went all round the inner circuit of the town wall with a bronze shield, with which he kept tapping the ground, and getting a dull, dead sound in every place except over the saps, where the bronze of the shield echoed and rang. In these places the Barcaeans dug countermines and killed the Persian sappers." Indeed, nothing seems to have delighted Herodotus more than evidence that people think up new goods and services for themselves.

The Romans understood, evidently, one part of the process $D + A \longrightarrow nD$. They knew that new economic activities rise upon older activities. They had a legal principle, *solo cedit superficies*, which probably dated from the early days of the Republic and which meant that the ownership of an added activity follows the ownership of the basis upon which it is added. Martial complained that the jurists interpreted the principle to the detriment of writers and the benefit of publishers who grew rich by dispatching "to the confines of Britain and frosts of the Getae" verses which "the centurion hummed in his distant garrison," while they paid no royalties. The argument accepted by the jurists was that the verses were merely an addition to the base (or parent) work of publishing. Although Roman society exemplified division of labor, as virtually all men and a great many animals do, the Romans do not seem to have identified it as a principle of the organization of work. Thus, they seem not to have identified the *bases* upon which new activities are added. Perhaps if they had, the writers could have made a better legal case. In short, the Romans seem to have understood the "$+A$" part of the formula, but not what went before and after it.

On the other hand, Adam Smith, who identified the principle of the division of labor and explained its advantages, seems not to have recognized that new work arises upon older divisions of labor. Smith's analysis is dramatized in the chief and most frequently cited example he used to illustrate the principle of the division of labor—the work in a pin-making factory. Pin making was an eighteenth-century example of English mass production, and Smith described it thus:

> One man draws out the wire, another straights it, a third cuts it, a fourth points it, a fifth grinds it at the top for receiving the head; to make the head requires two or three distinct operations; to put it on, is a peculiar business; to whiten the pins is another; it is even a trade by itself to put them into the paper; and the important business of making a pin is, in this manner, divided into about eighteen distinct operations, which, in some manufactories, are all performed by distinct hands, though in others the same man will sometimes perform two or three of them.

Ten men, Smith said, could in this way turn out twelve pounds of pins in a day, or about 4,800 pins apiece. "But if they had all wrought separately and independently and without any of them having been educated to this peculiar business, they certainly could not each of them have made twenty, perhaps not one pin in a day."

So far so good. But then Smith assumes that this same principle also accounts for the existence of pin making itself. He called pin making simply a larger division of labor. But was it? If so, of what larger work had it been a division?

Pins of the kind Smith was describing were first manufactured in England in conjunction with the craft of making wire carding combs. The Carders and Pinners were companion guilds for this reason. The wire bristles for carding combs were sometimes prepared in the same shops where the frames were made and the whole cards, as they were called, assembled. But sometimes the bristles were prepared in independent shops by brakemen (a name that may have been derived from braking, the old word for separating fibers) who bought iron ingots from smiths, drew them into wire, made the wire into bristles and sold the bristles to cardmakers. In either case, the first four tasks of bristle making were essentially the same work as Smith described in the first four pin-making tasks: "One man draws out the wire, another straights it, a third cuts it, a fourth points it. . . ."

Bristle makers, engaged in making a tool for the textile industry, were almost making pins. But when some of them actually did so (probably early in the fourteenth century), they were not further dividing the labor of making carding combs. Nor were they further dividing the labor of making bristles. They were not dividing at all. They were adding a new complexity, pin making, to an older simplicity, bristle making. From this addition came the rest of the divisions of labor in pin making that Smith describes: "A fifth grinds it at the top for receiving the head; to make the head requires two or three distinct operations; to put it on, is a peculiar business; to whiten the pins is another; it is even a trade by itself to put them into the paper. . . ."

The fact that Smith's mistake was subtle and casual has only rendered it the more obfuscating and durable. Smith gave to division of labor unwarranted credit for advances in economic life, a mistake still much with us. *Division of labor, in itself, creates nothing.* It is only a way of organizing work that has already been created. Even the first four labors of pin making did not exist until making metal carding combs was added to economic life. Division of labor is a device for achieving operating efficiency, nothing more. Of itself, it has no power to promote further economic development. And because it does not, division of labor is even extraordinarily limited at improving operating efficiency in any given work. All further increases in efficiency, once existing work has been suitably divided into tasks, depend upon the addition of new activities. The machine that made pin making automatic, and rendered all the tasks described by Smith obsolete at a stroke (though adding different ones) was a device that a New York machinist created and put into production in a pin factory of his own about fifty years after Smith's description. He had been a designer of machines for industrialists. To this work he added, on his own behalf, his new kind of pin-manufacturing work, cutting across categories of work when he did so. Smith had supposed that improvements to pin making would come, possibly pin-making machines, but he also supposed that this change would be extracted somehow out of the existing work of making pins—not built upon some other work entirely.

Dividing existing work into tasks is by no means confined to advancing economies. It is also practiced in the most stagnant economies, where men and women spend their entire working lives at very specialized tasks: tapping rubber trees, or herding goats, or loading bananas, or twisting fibers, or dancing in temples, or mining salt, or crushing ore, or carrying baskets of dirt for public works, or cultivating corn and beans. A stagnant economy may lack almost everything, but not division of labor.

When finer and finer divisions develop unhindered, they do not advance the efficient organization of work, as we all have reason to know from experience with bureaucracies. A New York City school principal has commented, "One must petition and patiently wait for the replacement of a pot or pan in the students' lunchroom instead of just having the school dietician go out and get it." But no doubt this sensible fellow, while waiting for pots and pans, had been teaching the young that division of labor, owing to its efficiency, is the secret of man's extraordinary economic life.

It is ironic that division of labor gets no credit for its genuinely bountiful effect. It prepares the way, it provides the special footholds, for adding new goods and services into economic life. Ants, no matter how efficiently they divide their tasks, do nothing so terrifying and wonderful. Seen as a source of new work, division of labor becomes something infinitely more useful than Adam Smith suggested when he limited its function to the efficient rationalization of work.

3

The Valuable Inefficiencies
and Impracticalities of Cities

People who think we would be better off without cities,
especially without big, unmanageable, disorderly cities,
never tire of explaining that cities grown too big are, in
any case, inefficient and impractical. Certainly, as we all
know, the most routine and ordinary activities—getting
people to work, moving goods around, keeping trees
alive, making space for school playgrounds, disposing of
garbage—absorb ridiculous amounts of energy, time and
money in cities, as compared to towns and villages. And
it does seem as if big cities are not necessarily efficient
for producing goods and services. Factories move to the
outskirts and the suburbs, and to small and distant
towns, often for reasons of efficiency.

All this is true. Cities are indeed inefficient and impractical compared with towns; and among cities themselves, the largest and most rapidly growing at any given

time are apt to be the least efficient. But I propose to argue that these grave and real deficiencies are necessary to economic development and thus are exactly what make cities uniquely valuable to economic life. By this, I do not mean that cities are economically valuable in spite of their inefficiency and impracticality but rather because they are inefficient and impractical. Now that we understand how new work arises upon older work, we are in a position to understand this paradox.

Efficient Manchester, Inefficient Birmingham

Let us begin by examining city inefficiency from the point of view of two English manufacturing cities, Manchester and Birmingham. Back in 1844, a character in one of Disraeli's novels said, "Certainly Manchester is the most wonderful city of modern times. It is the philosopher alone who can conceive the grandeur of Manchester and the immensity of its future." The remark, says the city historian, Asa Briggs, in *Victorian Cities*, was representative of "most contemporary social comment." Manchester, of course, also occupies a very special place in economic history because Marx and Engels were so greatly interested in it. Marx based much of his analysis of capitalism and its class struggles upon Manchester. He, like Disraeli, saw it as a prophetic city, although ominous in its prophecy rather than grand.

What impressed Disraeli, Marx and their contemporaries, and what made Manchester seem to them—for better or worse—the most advanced of all cities of the time was the stunning efficiency of its immense textile mills. The mills were Manchester. By the 1840s their work dominated the city completely. Here, it seemed, was the meaning of the industrial revolution, arrived at its logical conclusions. Here was the coming thing. Here was the kind of city that made all other cities old-fashioned—vestiges of an industrially undeveloped past.

Even those observers and commentators, and there were many of them, who were appalled by the sordid living conditions and terrible death rates of Manchester, and those who saw, as Marx and Engels did, how immense and ominous was the social and economic gulf between the few mill owners and their poor and hopeless masses of workers, even they believed that the terrible efficiency of Manchester was a portent of the cities of the future—if not all cities, at least capitalist cities.

Birmingham was just the kind of city that seemed to have been outmoded by Manchester. "It was always a peculiarity of Birmingham," wrote a London journalist of the 1850s whom Briggs quotes, "that small household trades existed which gave the inmates independence and often led—if the trade continued good—to competence or fortune." Briggs adds that these endeavors often led to failure too.

Birmingham had a few relatively large industries, although nothing remotely approaching the scale of Manchester's, and even these accounted for only a small part of Birmingham's total output of work and total employment. Most of Birmingham's manufacturing was carried out in small organizations employing no more than a dozen workmen; many had even fewer. A lot of these little organizations did bits and pieces of work for other little organizations. They were not rationally and efficiently consolidated. There was a lot of waste motion, overlapping work, duplication that could certainly have been eliminated through consolidations. Furthermore, able workmen were forever breaking away from their employers in Birmingham and setting up for themselves, compounding the fragmentation of work there.

It was also a little hard to say just what Birmingham was living on because it had no obvious specialty of the kind that made Manchester's economy so easy to understand and so impressive. To try to describe Birmingham's economy then (or now) is not easy. It was a muddle of oddments. In the old days, saddle and harness making seems to have been the chief industry, but all sorts of other hardware and tool manufacturing had been added to the manufacture of hardware for saddles and harnesses. In the seventeenth and eighteenth centuries, the city had enjoyed a large trade in shoe buckles, but the shoelace put an end to that. A rising button industry had more than compensated for the loss. Some of the button makers used glass decoratively and this had afforded opportunity to makers of bits and pieces of colored glass who, working from this foothold, had managed to build up a considerable local glass industry. In the nineteenth century, Birmingham was also making, among other things, guns, jewelry, cheap trinkets and papier-mâché trays. The work of making cheap metal toys led to making cheap steel penpoints. The work of making guns afforded opportunities for making rifling machines and other machine tools.

All this, of course, was just the sort of old-fashioned muddling that people in England of the 1840s and 1850s were accustomed to see going on in cities. It was not modern. It was not an expression of the new age. It afforded no particular new portents, either terrible or grand. At the time of all the intellectual excitement about Manchester, nobody was nominating Birmingham as the city of the future. But as it turned out Manchester was not the city of the future and Birmingham was.

Manchester's efficient specialization portended stagnation and a profoundly obsolescent city. For "the immensity of its future" proved to consist of immense losses of its markets as other people in other places learned how to spin and weave cotton efficiently too. Manchester developed nothing sufficient to compensate for these lost markets. Today it has become the very symbol of a city in long and unremitting decline. Its idleness and underemployment and the hardships of its people would be much greater than they are, were it not for the migration of young people, decade after decade and generation after generation, to London, Birmingham and overseas cities in search of more opportunity. The economy of Birmingham did not become obsolete, like Manchester's. Its fragmented and inefficient little industries kept adding new work, and splitting off new organizations, some of which have become very large but are still outweighed in total employment and production by the many small ones.

Today, only two cities in all of Britain remain economically vigorous and prosperous. One is London. The second is Birmingham. The others have stagnated one by one, much as Manchester did, like so many lights going out. British town planners, ironically, have regarded London and Birmingham as problems, because they are places in which much new work is added to old and thus cities that persist in growing. The British New Towns policy was specifically devised to discourage the growth of London and Birmingham and "drain it off." Birmingham's economy has remained alive and has kept up to date. Manchester's has not. Was Manchester, then, really efficient? It was indeed efficient and Birmingham was not. Manchester had acquired the efficiency of a company town. Birmingham had retained something different: a high rate of development work.

Efficiency as it is commonly defined—and I do not propose to change its definition, which is clear and useful—is the ratio of work accomplished to energy supplied. We can speak of high or low rates of efficiency because, in any given instance, we have two relevant factors to measure: input of energy, and quantity and quality (value) of work accomplished. We can compare the measurements in one instance with measurements in other instances. Manchester turned out a great deal of cloth relative to the energy supplied by its workers and by those who served the needs of the workers in the city.

But these particular measurements are not relevant when development work is wanted. A candy manufacturer, reminiscing to a *New Yorker* reporter about the first candy bar he developed as a shipping clerk in a candy factory, recalls, "I showed it to my boss and he was very happy. 'How many of these can you make in a minute?' he asked me. 'In a *minute*?' I said. 'It took me four months to make this one!'" Suppose it had taken him eight months? Or two months? That measurement has nothing to do with the operating efficiency envisioned by his boss.

Efficiency of operation, in any given case, is a sequel to earlier development work. Development work is a messy, time- and energy-consuming business of trial, error and failure. The only certainties in it are trial and error. Success is not a certainty. And even when the result is successful, it is often a surprise, not what was actually being sought.

A low rate of efficiency in production work means that the person or organization doing the work is going about it ineptly. But the exorbitant amounts of energy and time and the high rates of failure in the process of developing new work do not mean the development work is being done ineptly. The inefficiency is built into the aim itself; it is inescapable. There is no systematic way to evade it. The president of du Pont, a company that has tried to systematize its development work to the highest degree possible, has told a *Fortune* reporter that only about one out of twenty of those research projects that the company decides to develop further after initial exploratory work turns out to be useful to the company. The fact that an organization engages in large-scale production, which is what makes a large organization large, and that it produces very efficiently too, does not mean that the efficiency spills over into development work.

Indeed, development work is inherently so chancy that by the law of averages, chances of success are greatly improved if there is much duplication of effort. The U.S.

Air Force's analytical organization, the Rand Corporation, having been assigned to study how waste could be eliminated in the processes of military development work, came to the conclusion that although duplication of effort was theoretically wasteful, it was not wasteful empirically. For one thing, the report said, different people brought different preconceptions to development work and there was no way of telling in advance which might prove fruitful or where it might lead. Eminence or reputation or even past success was not a reliable indicator. The report cited, as an illustration, the fact that in 1937 when the jet airplane engine had already been developed in Britain (largely in Birmingham, as it happens), a committee of distinguished aeronautical experts in the United States, to whom this event was not yet known, having studied the possibilities of jet propulsion, came to the conclusion that it was not practicable. It was their recommendation that attempts to develop jet propulsion be dropped. The Rand researchers said that they had found definite waste, and a lot of it, in the development work of the military establishments; it was the great waste of administrative man-hours and energy devoted to trying to eliminate duplicated effort. Just so, when Pasteur, that wise old man, begged for enlarged support of the biological sciences, he begged for *multiplication* of laboratories.

The shorthand formula that I used in the preceding chapter to summarize the process by which work multiplies when a new activity is added to an older division of labor, $D + A \longrightarrow nD$, looks rather neat and tidy. The tidiness is deceptive. It leaves out the trial and error, which is always there in real life. How many brassieres did Mrs. Rosenthal experiment with before she got the one she manufactured? The formula needs a TE in it, for trial and error: $D + nTE + A \longrightarrow nD$. Even so, the formula holds true only when there is a successful end result that is put into production, yielding its new divisions of labor. When an attempt to add new work to old is tried, experimented with, and does not work out, we get only D + nTE.

What was going on in Birmingham at a great rate, as opposed to Manchester, was much trial and error, sometimes leading to successful new activities and sometimes not. In effect, the city contained a great collection of mundane development laboratories. This fact was not obvious because the "laboratories" were also doing production work. Viewing the city's economy as a whole, one can think of it as a great, confused economic laboratory, supporting itself by its own production. Of course, taken as a whole, it was also inefficient.

Manchester's staggering productivity and efficiency were not so unprecedented as the observers of the 1840s thought. The machines were new, but history records a multitude of cities that poured their economic energy into repetitions of the same work with immense efficiency and which put no energy, or almost none, into development of new goods and services. Coventry had done this, also with textiles, in medieval times. Medieval Europe had an odd word, *dinanderie*, for brass vessels. Dinant, in the Lowlands, one of the most important and prosperous of medieval cities, had made such a success with its brass kettles and pots that, like Manchester, it had specialized merely in repeating its success. Dinant was extraordinarily productive—for a while.

At least as long ago as 2,500 B.C. there were cities of "terrible efficiency," according to the archeologist Stuart Piggott in *Prehistoric India*. He was referring to Mohenjo-daro and Harappā, the twin capital cities of an ancient empire of the Indus. Mohenjo-daro and Harappā were marvelously developed, to a point. But at some time before 2,500 B.C. development work had halted. They added no new goods and services from that time on, it seems, nor did they make any improvements in their old products. They simply repeated themselves. Their production must have been stupendous. The same standardized bricks were used in truly staggering quantities, not only in the cities themselves but throughout the scores of towns in the empire. The same wonderfully accurate stone weights, in multiples and fractions of sixteen, were turned out endlessly. And the voracious wood-fired kilns belonging to the two cities mass-produced so many identical pottery cups that Piggott speculates that it may have been the custom to drink from a cup and then break it. One suspects they had more cups than they knew what to do with.

But while other people were developing the spoked wheel and the light chariots made possible by spoked wheels, Harappā and Mohenjo-daro kept turning out only clumsy, solid wheels and cumbersome, heavy wagons. While other people were learning to strengthen bronze weapons and tools with a thickened central rib, and to make the heads of these with hollow hafts so handles could be fitted into them, Harappā and Mohenjo-daro kept turning out only one-piece, flat, easily broken implements. At length the Indus River at Mohenjo-daro became a lake of mud.* The mud flows engulfed the city and undermined many buildings. The people seem to have been incapable of any response that involved changed ways of doing things, or new ideas. After every mud flood they rebuilt exactly as before, with their interminable bricks, and the quality of the work deteriorated steadily until it was no longer done at all. The mud floods cannot be described as the "cause" of Mohenjo-daro's decay because a similar decline was evident in the other city of Harappā and throughout the empire, alongside a similar, endless repetitiveness of old work. The response to the mud floods was merely one dramatic symptom of the all-pervading stagnation.

* Just why is uncertain. I suspect that the immense destruction of forests, unremitting over a period of more than five centuries, to feed the mass-production brick and pottery kilns caused erosion and silting.

The Conflict Between Efficiency and Development

If we were to measure the economic development rate of a city, we could not do so just by measuring its output in a year or any group of years. We would have to measure, rather, the additions of new work to its older output, over a period of time, and the ratio of the new work to the older work. Then, to speak of a low or a high development rate, we could compare the rates of addition of new goods and services during different periods and the rates of addition among different cities.

Suppose, for example, that the monetary value of all the work done in Birmingham had been added up for a given year—say, 1840. Then ten years later, in 1850, statisticians might make the same assessment, but keep separate the value of goods and services of kinds that had not yet been produced in Birmingham in 1840. The ratio of these new goods and services to the value of all goods and services in the Birmingham of 1840 would yield a percentage figure, a development rate for the decade.

In 1860, the value of goods and services of kinds that had not been produced in the city in 1850 could be added up and then figured as a ratio to all the goods and services produced in 1850. The result would be a development rate figure for the decade 1850–60, as well as for the decade 1840–50. And so on, decade by decade. Had such figures been worked out for Birmingham and for Manchester, it would have been clear that Birmingham had a consistently high rate of development work and Manchester a consistently low rate. It would have been clear which was likely to be the city of the future.

No such measurements were made then, of course; nor are such measurements made now. But even so, gross observation tells us something about cities' development rates. Hong Kong must have a fantastically high rate.

Tokyo obviously does; indeed, most Japanese cities do, unlike, say, most British or most American cities nowadays. Soviet planners complain that much new work is established in Moscow while little arises in the small and medium-sized Soviet cities that have high rates of underemployment. Harappā and Mohenjo-daro must have had high development rates at a relatively early period in their histories, then rates of virtually zero for the last five or six centuries of their decaying existence. Detroit had a high development rate through most of its history and a very high rate indeed at the time the automobile industry was being developed there. But since 1920, Detroit has had an exceedingly low rate. It has become much like Manchester. In Boston, after more than half a century of low development rates, science-based industries were developed rapidly and in profusion beginning in the late 1940s. This new work would surely have been reflected in a much improved rate for Boston between 1940–50 and 1950–60, but that does not necessarily mean more than a temporary spurt. A high rate may, or may not, still be maintained there, but I suspect it is not; if it were, rather rapid development of other kinds of new goods and services would, by now, be showing up in Boston's economy.

Beginning in about 1800, New York enjoyed tremendously high rates of development for twelve or thirteen decades. That they have continued is unlikely, for many recent signs inform us to the contrary: absolute declines in the sheer numbers of enterprises in New York; persistent growth in the numbers of idle and underemployed poor; remarkable growth of unproductive make-work in the city bureaucracies, make-work which, more and more, is depended on to take up the slack of insufficient useful work for the city's high school and college graduates; piling up of undone work and unsolved practical problems; lack of new kinds of manufacturing work to compensate for the losses of old; a seemingly compulsive repetition of existing ways of doing things even though it is evident that what are being compulsively repeated are mistakes; lack of local development capital for new goods and services, accompanied by a surfeit of capital for projects that destroy existing enterprises and jobs, and quantities of capital for export. All these are classic signs that a great city is dying economically and their clear evidence in New York announces that the city's once vigorous development rates have been declining badly for some decades and that the decline is probably accelerating.

Any given city's performance at developing new work can change radically. Even Manchester's did; for a brief period, at the time it was developing its textile industry, Manchester's development rate was obviously high. A city's ability to maintain high development rates is what staves off stagnation, and allows the city to continue to prosper. The fact that a high development rate must be maintained is obviously little understood, nor does it seem understood that efficiency fails to make a city prosper. The commissioners of the housing agencies of New York City sincerely believe that they have been benefiting the economy of the city by reducing the numbers and varieties of New York's enterprises in the cause of efficiency for those retained. It is the boast of one of these commissioners, one that he often repeats with pride in public, that in the new Lower East Side, rebuilt under the city's auspices, each new store the plans have permitted takes the place, on the average, of forty older stores that have been wiped out. By such means, he reports, the city is being made efficient. Of course the Lower East Side, once fabulously productive in developing work, is now almost an economic desert. But the commissioner is quite right: it does have more efficient stores.

Is it not possible for the economy of a city to be highly efficient, and for the city also to excel at the development of new goods and services? No, it seems not. The conditions that promote development and the conditions that promote efficient production and distribution of already existing goods and services are not only different, in most ways they are diametrically opposed. Let us consider a few of them.

Breakaways of workers—especially very able workers—from existing organizations promote the development of new work as well as the creation of new organizations. But breakaways are not good for the parent company; they undermine its efficiency. To the company or companies in control, one of the advantages of a company town is that breakaways are not feasible there. And in any settlement where breakaways are inhibited, by whatever means, the development rate must drop, although the efficiency of already well-established work is apt to climb. Rochester, New York, used to be a city in which immense numbers of breakaways occurred. It was rather like Birmingham in this way. Moreover, so many Rochester breakaways were creative and successful, particularly in the development of a great variety of fine scientific and advanced technological equipment, that during a period in the late nineteenth and early twentieth centuries it would have appeared that Rochester was destined to become one of the country's most economically creative and important cities. But George Eastman, of Eastman Kodak, put an end to that. One reason he was able to establish his new company was that Rochester businesses were already doing highly advanced work in precision manufacturing and in the making of optical and other scientific products.* Once Eastman had developed Kodak into a strong company (a rapid progress, in part owing to Eastman's own development work and in part due to his purchases of other camera and film companies),

---

*The optical work had begun in the mid-nineteenth century, notably with the work of Bausch & Lomb which began as a little firm making spectacle frames to which the proprietors added the making of lenses.

Eastman fought breakaways from his company with every means at his command; and he was successful. He entangled in long and bitter law suits the men who had the temerity to try to leave him and form their own enterprises. And as Eastman Kodak, an efficient organization, came to dominate the economic, the political and even the cultural life of Rochester, breakaways from the city's other industries also dwindled.

In the more than half a century since Eastman made Rochester into an efficient company town, only one other enterprise there, Xerox, has created notable new work. Xerox started as a small photo-supply company, named Haloid, that had formed before Eastman dominated the city. Possibly because it was so small and obscure, it managed to exist "in the shadow of Eastman," as the city's historian, Blake McKelvey, has put it. Then, shortly after World War II, Haloid added the new work of making photo-copying paper and machines for using it. The Xerox process had not been invented by Haloid,* but Haloid bought rights to it—as so often happens in such cases—after the innovation had been turned down by many large companies. Xerox's success, great as it has been, has not transformed Rochester back into a vigorous, developing city. It would take many organizations and people adding new work to old, and much diversity of development, to accomplish that.

Now consider for a moment the question of suppliers of bits and pieces of work to other producers. Many relatively small suppliers, much of whose work duplicates and overlaps, are indispensable to a high rate of development. But they are not efficient, neither in respect to their own work nor the operations of the producers who buy from

---

* It was invented by a worker in the patent department of an electrical equipment manufacturer in New York to solve a problem that had arisen in his own work: the expense and inconvenience of obtaining copies of drawings and other documents used in patent research.

them. For example, during the years when the automobile industry was developing in Detroit, those who tried manufacturing cars were very numerous; nobody knows exactly how many there were, but there were more than five hundred, possibly more than seven hundred. And the suppliers of bits and pieces of work to these producers were even more numerous. Indeed, some of those suppliers became automobile manufacturers themselves; Buick, for instance, began with sheet-metal work, Dodge with supplying engines. But a multiplicity of small, duplicating, overlapping suppliers was not an efficient arrangement for the three huge manufacturers who came to dominate the Detroit industry. Supplying parts to them became, beginning in the 1920s, a "simple" business. According to a report on the industry made by *Fortune* in 1946, it was "at times brutally so. . . . Prices are low, profit margins narrow and volume requirements high. Together these mean mass production with consequent heavy investment in plant and machine tools. Second, the list of customers is extremely small. Loss of a single account can frequently be catastrophic. . . . Finally, the market for original equipment parts is precisely the market for automobiles, no more and no less." This is not a portrait of supply industries that can engage in development work, but it is a portrait of highly efficient suppliers.

Consider also the conflict between development and efficiency as it applies to the work of investing development capital and supplying working capital. The most efficient way to invest capital (whether by government, by semipublic, or by private lenders and investors—it does not matter) is through a relatively few large investments and loans, not through many small ones. If small loans are made, it is most efficient to consolidate them, in effect, by making them only for purposes that have already become standardized and routinized. To put capital into the purchasing of enterprises that produce goods and services already developed is more efficient than to put it into development of new enterprises and new work. Also, it is efficient to invest development capital in a sure thing—if in new work, then in new work for which customers are guaranteed in advance. It is efficient, for example, for banks to lend to enterprises, even small ones with experimental products, if the borrowers have contracts for military development work from governments. The companies' development expenses will be covered in this way, and the companies enjoy the possibility of large production contracts later.

But for a city to develop new work at a high rate means that its enterprises must have access to much inefficiently dispensed capital: many, many small loans and investments, a high proportion of them out of the routine; still other, relatively large, loans for swift expansion of goods or services that seem to be working out experimentally but which must go into larger-scale production to become practicable—although it is not a certainty they will be. And both kinds of investments must be available from a variety of sources because preconceptions infuse the businesses of investing and lending money as surely as they do other endeavors. Not everyone sees the same investment opportunities in the same ways. Not everyone glimpses an opportunity.

Consider too the physical arrangements that promote the greatest profusion of duplicate and diverse enterprises serving the population of a city, and lead therefore to the greatest opportunities for plentiful divisions of labor upon which new work can potentially arise.*

*For reasons I have analyzed at length in *The Death and Life of Great American Cities*, enterprises serving city consumers flourish most prolifically where the following four conditions are simultaneously met: 1) different primary uses, such as residences and working places, must be mingled together, insuring the presence of people using the streets on different schedules but drawing on consumer goods and services in common; 2) small and short blocks; 3) buildings of differing ages, types, sizes and conditions of upkeep, intimately mingled; and 4) high concentrations of people.

It is most efficient for large construction firms to produce monotonous multiples of identical buildings; it is most efficient for architects to design multiples of identical buildings. Superblocks are more efficient than smaller blocks because there are fewer crossings and traffic can flow more efficiently; when there are fewer streets, utilities can be distributed more efficiently and of course the maintenance of streets costs less.

Indeed, numerous small enterprises, just by existing, are in conflict with the economic efficiency of a city's large and well-established enterprises. The student newspaper of Columbia University, back in February, 1964—more than four years before the great eruption of student protest concerning the university's expansion and building policies (among other things)—was complaining editorially as follows:

> In the original quadrangle of the campus . . . the University constituted a dead center of academic buildings, separated from the neighborhood and lacking its total life. But this center was small. . . . As Columbia has expanded, the central area has grown. The policy has been to build new structures as close to the old ones as possible. The justification has been the convenience of adjacent classrooms and offices [i.e., efficiency of university administration]. But with expansion . . . stores and services have begun to disappear. . . . The disappearance of variety saps the life of the community. The lack of stores and services adds another problem. As buildings are demolished, many of the comforts of student life—a good restaurant or a convenient laundry, for example—become available only with difficulty.

Just by being present and in the way, other enterprises thus conflict with the efficiency of the university—not, to be sure, the university as a body of students and faculty, but the university as an administrative enterprise. But here is the point: the administrators determine what is efficient for the university and what is not.

Just by being present, many small enterprises conflict in still another way with the efficiency of large enterprises.

One of the great advantages of a company town, for the company, is that there are few alternative ways for people to earn their livings. But this does not promote economic growth. Consider, also, the conflict as it affects individuals who might add new work to old. From the viewpoint of efficiency, a man or woman trained to specific work, and good at it, is best kept at that kind of work as long as needed. But from the point of view of economic development, a man or woman trained to specific work is most valuable if he adds something new to that work, if he changes what he does. Of course he may fail.

Thus, one of the social preconditions for economic development is not so much the opportunity for a person to change his work (and his class) from that of his father, as is often supposed, but rather the possibility of changing radically his own work and his own place in society during his own working life. This is not the same as being given the opportunity to train for work that has already been established by others and to engage in it, even though the change is a step upward. China, during its long stagnation, exemplified the institution of the public talent hunt. Poor peasant boys of exceptional talent could compete for prestigious places in the bureaucracy, the occupations at the top of the economic heap in China, and could become members of the upper class in consequence. This was useless as far as economic development was concerned, for the talented boys were simply moving from one kind of well-established work to another kind of well-established work.

To be sure, all the conditions that promote efficiency within city economies are not in conflict with conditions that promote development of the economy. A large city is a large market for many things. As we shall see in the following chapter, even a small city is a relatively large market for a few specific and special supplies. The concentrated market is, in itself, an efficient thing. And its chief characteristic, that it is concentrated, makes it possible for small, fragmentary, exceedingly special, weak or much-duplicated enterprises to operate with considerable inefficiency and yet often get away with it. But apart from this, as far as I can see, the conditions in a city that promote efficiency of operation are in conflict with the conditions that promote development work.

The Impracticality of Big Cities

Size, in cities, is relative. What seems big for one period of history is small for another. A city that is large for its time is always an impractical settlement because size greatly intensifies whatever serious practical problems exist in an economy at a given time. Today, in large American cities, air pollution and overdependence on automobiles are two obvious examples of chronic, unsolved problems, most acute in the largest cities. Yet consider the great cities of the last century without electricity, with their high infant-death rates and their tremendous numbers of young orphans, with their immense numbers of dray animals, their stinking stables, their flies, streets running with horse urine and manure, their terrible and unrelievable summer heat. They would seem to us impractical and they were.

Consider how impractical the cities of the fourth or fifth millennia b.c. must have become when their populations outgrew the water supplied by local streams and springs. No wonder the earliest engineering projects were water works. Behind the assumption that agriculture must have preceded cities stands the assumption that cities were impractical before agriculture. No doubt they were. Shortages of wild food in poor years must have been terrible for unusually large concentrations of people in hunting societies. Consider, also, the impracticality of the little cities of tenth- and eleventh-century Europe. Their unusually large populations—for that time—depended for most of their plant food upon fields close by the walls and gardens inside the walls, and it was impractical to abandon such fields and gardens, or to let them lie unused for years, as could be done with exhausted fields in the scantily populated countrysides and manor settlements. Consider how impractical the Renaissance cities were: they experienced a population explosion of draft animals at a time when Europe was not yet cultivating suitable fodder crops.

To store food so it does not spoil is always a problem. Again and again old solutions have become inadequate as growing cities have had to find ways to store large amounts of food in limited spaces and yet move it in and out of storage rapidly. Fires are a danger anywhere; in cities they can be immense disasters. The same is true of floods or contaminated water. And how impractical it was, in cities, to supply thousands of rooms individually with fuel and light, the more so because the city's work—unlike so much country work—could not slacken merely because it was cold or the day was dark. Until deadly epidemics could be controlled, all cities were impractical.

Moderate-sized cities—what are now deemed to be "cities of practical size"—are practical only because problems were solved in the past in cities that had grown to "impractical" size. To limit the sizes of great cities as is often advocated, because of the acute problems arising from size, is profoundly reactionary. Cities magnify an economy's practical problems, but they can also solve them by means of new technology.

Once a serious practical problem has appeared in an economy, it can only be eliminated by adding new goods and services into economic life. From this solution to city problems comes true economic growth and abundance. No city by itself develops all the various goods and services required to overcome its complex practical problems, at least not in historic times and probably not in prehistoric times either. Cities copy each others' solutions, often very swiftly. They also import each others' solutions, by importing relevant goods to solve the problems.

Practical problems that persist and accumulate in cities are symptoms of arrested development. The point is seldom admitted. It has become conventional, for instance, to blame congested and excessive automobile traffic, air pollution, water pollution and noise upon "rapid technological progress." But the automobiles, the fumes, the sewage and the noise are not new, and the persistently unsolved problems they afford only demonstrate lack of progress. Many evils conventionally blamed upon progress are, rather, evils of stagnation.

Consider, for example, the problem of mechanical noise. Noise has become so pervasive in large American cities that the phrase "noise pollution" has been coined to suggest its positive harmfulness. When mechanical noise first became a problem, an evasion of the problem was arrived at: zoning noisy industries into special areas. The practice did not combat the noise, only shunted it aside. In the meantime, mechanical devices increased while methods for diminishing the problem went undeveloped. The solution, of course, is new goods and services. Francis Bello, *Fortune*'s specialist on technology, has listed some of them: equipment that sets up opposite, canceling patterns of sound; mounts that eliminate vibrations; new acoustical materials and treatments. He wrote, back in 1955, that these devices for countering noise at its sources had been feasible for some time, but had gone undeveloped. They remain undeveloped. Excessive noise is not a problem of progress, but evidence of stagnation. The same can be said of the problem of overdependence on automobiles. The problem and all its far-reaching consequences grow worse, but not because of progress.

Solutions to most of the practical problems of cities begin humbly. When humble people, doing lowly work, are not also solving problems, nobody is apt to solve humble problems. It is instructive to examine the curious difference in ancient Rome between the water supply to the city and the water supply within the city. The aqueduct system was begun early and was improved and elaborated by Roman engineers through the centuries as the city grew larger and more complex. Fountains and hydrants brought plentiful water from distant sources to most quarters of the city. But otherwise, Rome's plumbing was almost as primitive as that of a village. Not that the Romans were incapable of plumbing work: the large public baths had water piped in, and systems for circulating and heating it; the rich had intricate and clever water clocks, and beautiful waterworks in the gardens of their villas. But apart from rather minimal supplies to the first floors of some residences of the wealthy, Rome's utilitarian water needs were amazingly neglected. Martial complained, for example, that his town house lacked water although it was near an aqueduct. Water for dwellings, shops and almost all public buildings was brought in by hand labor. The *aquarii*, slave water carriers, were the lowest and most hapless of workers in a city whose work was increasingly done, as time passed, by slaves. Juvenal called the water carriers the scum of the slave population. The slaves themselves were not free to develop their work by building plumbing systems nor could they even experiment with such possibilities.

The drainage situation was similar. The sewers of Rome were begun by 500 B.C. and they too became marvels of engineering. But, according to Jérôme Carcopino in *Daily Life in Ancient Rome*, although a few houses in Pompeii were sensibly connected to the drainage system (including connection of upstairs latrines), "the drainage system of the Roman house is merely a myth begotten of the complacent imagination of modern times." Slaves carried out waste water and sewage. When some people in an economy are forestalled from solving practical problems, but others doing other work are not, the solutions to practical problems become strangely lopsided and problems accumulate.

Cities as Mines

Let us now look a little way into the future. If we observe the acute practical problems of cities in highly advanced economies today, we may be able to glimpse some of the forms economic growth could take in the highly advanced economies of the future—wherever such economies may prove to be. Waste disposal will do as an example, for in many different forms—air pollutants, water pollutants, garbage, trash, junk—wastes have created highly acute problems for large cities. They cause lesser problems, which are nevertheless chronic and unsolved, outside of cities.

Although the cities of the United States are making little or no progress in coping with wastes, hints and clues to solutions do appear. What they portend, I think, is not waste "disposal," but waste recycling. Odd little news items about wastes crop up. The *New York Times* describes an apparatus produced by a Japanese manufacturer that bales assorted trash and garbage, compacts it under hydraulic pressure, and encases the resulting dense, solid block in asphalt, cement, vinyl or iron sheeting, depending on what is wanted. Bacteria are killed in the process. The blocks can be made in almost any shape desired, for use in building. Those sheathed in metal can be welded together. According to the company's American representative, who was interviewed by the *Times*, the process—apart from the usefulness of its product—is fifty to seventy-five percent cheaper than incineration. The largest machine the company produces can handle three thousand tons of waste in twenty-four hours; the smallest, 150 tons in twenty-four hours. The same company produces an older apparatus for pressing stripped automobile bodies into solid, small blocks for economical handling as scrap—manufacturing to which the company logically added its new device.

A manufacturer in Washington, D.C., advertises a device to be installed in buildings in place of a garbage incinerator. It reduces the bulk of garbage and trash by about seventy-five percent for purposes of collecting it easily and economically. The containers filled with compacted garbage are supposed to be removed by a trash-collecting contractor, and empties left in their place. This of course is not, in itself, a method of recycling waste, but it hints at the sort of auxiliary systems that will be needed for getting some wastes from their places of production to points of processing.

Here and there, garbage is being processed into compost. The *Times*, which seems to employ someone deeply interested in garbage, has described a little factory in Brooklyn, New York (run by the proprietor and a part-time helper) that converts restaurant garbage into lightweight, pulverized, dehydrated garden compost. The income from the sale of the compost is clear profit; the proprietor of the plant pays his costs by means of the silver he retrieves from the garbage and sells back to the restaurants. St. Petersburg, Florida, has a considerably more elaborate plant that handles unsorted garbage and trash. First the material goes through a magnetic separator to remove metal, which is sold as scrap; then the rest of the material is ground up, soaked, digested (by bacteria), dried and screened to yield a compost that is inert—it has no nutritive value left—but is useful for soil conditioning, a job that chemical fertilizers cannot do. It is a small plant, handling only a hundred tons of refuse a day. Its products do not pay for its operation, but that is one of the most interesting things about it. The difference between its income from sales and its costs is paid by the municipality in the form of a fee of $3 per ton for disposing of the garbage and trash, an arrangement that the municipality finds economical. One glimpses how waste recycling can be made economically feasible even while it is still in a primitive and experimental state.

The conventional approach to the problems of air pollution is to ban, or attempt to ban, fuels that contain high volumes of pollutants like sulfur dioxide. I suspect this is a futile effort. Of course it can reduce pollution from given smokestacks, but as the number of smokestacks increases, the pollution increases accordingly, even though higher-grade fuels are used. One is dealing with a problem by simply attempting to "subtract" it, an approach that seldom works. A much more promising idea was described in a technical article in *Public Service Magazine* of September, 1964, by a vice-president of the Pennsylvania Electric Co. of Johnstown, Pennsylvania. He reports that a test was run in one of that company's coal-burning plants, beginning in 1961, to capture sulfur dioxide in the stacks and convert it to sulfuric acid, which of course is one of the most basic and heavily used chemicals in modern economies. In the test, ninety percent of the sulfur dioxide was captured from ordinary, low-grade bituminous coal containing about a three-percent sulfur content. In a twenty-four-hour day, this amounted to about 1,050 tons of sulfuric acid at a seventy percent concentration, which at the time of the test had a delivered market price of $8 to $10 a ton. The cost of capturing and converting it was $7 a ton. In effect, the process amounts to a new way of mining sulfur for sulfuric acid. The same approach, in principle, has been used rather widely to capture particulate air pollutants such as fly ash and soot, both of which are recycled. Fly ash is used to make cinder block. But there remains, I should think, enormous opportunity for capturing and recycling various gases which are not only dangerous in the air but also potentially valuable.

Of course a few waste-recycling industries are already very profitable. The machinery scavengers of Chicago have built up an economically valuable, world-wide trade about which I shall say more in Chapter Six. Chicago has also been a center for the remanufacturing of scrapped automobile parts. This too has interested the *New York Times*, which reports: "Formerly remanufactured parts were put together in tiny garages on a hit-or-miss basis and the quality was suspect." That was the development stage of the work; now it is well established and has arrived at respectability. The report goes on: "Now there are at least 1,000 remanufacturers of all sizes and the whole business has evolved into a large, efficient, mass-production operation. To the delivery docks of the companies come weekly thousands of used parts that are then disassembled, cleaned, reconditioned with new components, tested and shipped out to retail outlets. . . . Ninety-seven percent of all starters replaced today are rebuilt starters; 81 percent of replacement generators are rebuilt; 78 percent of clutches; 77 percent of carburetors; 66 percent of brake components, and 62 percent of water pumps." To indicate the savings to consumers, the report notes that a rebuilt four-barreled carburetor costs approximately $35 compared with $55 for a new one.

One of the oldest forms of waste recycling is the reprocessing of waste paper. One producer of book paper advertises that its papers are more resistant to deterioration from humidity and temperature changes than paper made from new pulp, and accompanies these advertisements with striking photographs of New York City, which it calls its "concrete forests." This fancy, that the city is another kind of paper-yielding forest, is rather apt; but the metaphor of the waste-yielding mine may be more comprehensive. For in the highly developed economies of the future, it is probable that cities will become huge, rich and diverse mines of raw materials. These mines will differ from any now to be found because they will become richer the more and the longer they are exploited. The law of diminishing returns applies to other mining operations: the richest veins, having been worked out, are gone forever. But in cities, the same materials will be retrieved over and over again. New veins, formerly overlooked, will be continually opened. And just as our present wastes contain ingredients formerly lacking, so will the wastes of the advanced economies of the future yield up ingredients we do not now have. The largest, most prosperous cities will be the richest, the most easily worked, and the most inexhaustible mines. Cities that take the lead in reclaiming their own wastes will have high rates of related development work; that is, many local firms will manufacture the necessary gathering and processing equipment and will export it to other cities and to towns.

How will the mines be organized? First, it is useful to distinguish between two great classes of wastes: those that are carried by water, and all others. Leaving aside the water-borne for the moment, consider the fact that all other wastes must be collected from their points of production by people. This is true even of the wastes that now go into the air. It is impossible to "control" air pollution.* That is to say, it is practical only to trap pollutants before they get into the air—to prevent air pollution. Such captured wastes, like the sulfuric acid at the electric plant, have to be collected by somebody, just as any other non-water-carried wastes must be, and sent on from their point of collection to processors or reusers. The sulfuric acid produced at the electric plant illustrates what I think is the main difficulty in waste recycling but also the great opportunity to organize the new industries. The production of the sulfuric acid at the electric plant is not sufficiently large to interest the electric company itself in going into the business of stockpiling acid, finding various customers, and shipping it. Yet the acid is worth collecting; indeed, in this case, a chemical company contracted to pick it up at the electric plant and pay for it. In large

*An Air Pollution Control Board—the popular nomenclature in American cities—is, on the face of it, a preposterous body.

cities, the multitude of other fuel users who now float off sulfur dioxide into the air—hospital heating plants, factories, apartment houses—produce even less of it, taken individually, than an electric plant does, although in sum their production is enormous. They are not about to add thousands upon thousands of little chemical distributing businesses into the economy, out of their own chemical wastes. In the same way, somebody who has old machinery to get rid of seldom finds it worth his while to hunt up a reuser of that particular apparatus. The job is better done by somebody who mines old machinery from many different factories. Even he may not be the one who finds the ultimate reuser; he may be a middleman collector who sorts what he collects and resells it to specialists who know the markets for various categories of second-hand machinery.

When waste recycling is at a primitive stage, as it is at present, the collector of second-hand machinery, the collector of waste paper, the collector of restaurant garbage all engage in feasible occupations, but not of the sort necessary if waste recycling is to develop much. Picture so simple an establishment as a single household and its wastes. Imagine that one serviceman calls who is interested only in old metal, another who is interested in waste paper, another in garbage, another in discarded wood furniture, another in used-up plastics, another who wants old books (but only if their bindings have gilt letters; another serviceman is interested in the others), and so on. A family would be driven crazy by this traffic, let alone by the necessity of separating and storing for various intervals the various wastes. An economy in which wastes have become an acute problem is precisely an economy in which this sort of thrift is a nuisance to the producers of wastes and not worth their while.

But diversity of wastes can in fact be advantageous, if properly handled. The more highly developed waste recycling becomes, the more valuable is this very diversity of materials. The aim must be to get all the wastes possible into the system—not only those that are already valuable at a given stage of development, but also those that are only beginning to become useful and those that are not yet useful but may become so.

A type of work that does not now exist is thus necessary: services that collect all wastes, not for shunting into incinerators or gulches, but for distributing to various primary specialists from whom the materials will go to converters or reusers. The comprehensive collecting services, as they develop into big businesses, will use many technical devices. They will install and service equipment for collecting sulfuric acid, soot, fly ash and other wastes in fuel stacks, including gases that, at present, cannot yet be trapped. They will supply and handle containers for containerized wastes and will install fixed equipment such as chutes, probably by employing subcontractors. Who will develop the comprehensive collecting services? My guess is that the work, when it does appear, will be added to janitorial contracting services— a kind of work itself that as yet hardly exists except for the benefit of relatively few institutional and other large clients, and is not notable for yielding development work. But in economies where people doing lowly work are not hampered from adding new work to old, we may expect that just such lowly occupations as janitorial work will be the footholds from which complex, prosperous, and economically important new industries develop.

Comprehensive collectors of wastes may at first derive their incomes like the St. Petersburg trash and garbage processing plant which gets a $3 fee per ton for handling wastes and derives the rest of its income from sale of its products. Just so, comprehensive waste collectors may at first be paid fees—either directly by those whose wastes they collect, or indirectly by them through taxes, or by a combination of both. This will cover the services of handling wastes not yet convertible or valuable for reuse. But they will also derive income from the wastes they do pass on. As proportions of unused wastes become smaller and the income derived from sales becomes larger, comprehensive collectors will compete for the privilege of doing the collecting work free, just as some collectors of profitable special wastes now do. Eventually they will compete for collection rights by offering fees for waste concessions, again just as some collectors of special wastes now do. In large cities, the comprehensive collectors will handle and distribute annually many, many millions of tons of materials and will supply immense numbers and varieties of converter industries and recyclers of special wastes.

Water-borne wastes present quite different problems and possibilities. Although water does the initial collecting work, water is difficult to mine. Current methods of treating sewage and obtaining its products—purified water and residues—are very expensive, cumbersome and slow, and they require large spaces considering the yield. Sewage-treatment plants are consequently few compared with the need for them. Waters polluted by industrial wastes are similarly expensive to mine. The paper industry of the Soviet Union is now polluting the waters of Lake Baikal in Siberia, an action that Soviet conservationists warn will be disastrous to the fresh-water life in the lake, life that is unique for having evolved, during long ages past, in isolation from life in other bodies of water. The justification for this vandalism, like the justification for the destruction (which has already been accomplished) of almost all life in Lake Erie by sewage and industrial wastes, is that treatment to remove the pollutants—or to divert them into other bodies of water, at best an evasion—is too expensive.

Thus the first priority in dealing with water-borne wastes, in view of the difficulty of mining them, is to keep them out of the water to begin with, if at all possible—to collect them in some other way. This is indeed possible with some water-borne wastes: those that are in the water only and solely because the water is a means of carrying them away from the point of production. Human excretions are in this category; to carry these wastes away by flowing water is extraordinarily primitive. It is amazing that we continue to use such old-fashioned makeshifts. Excrement in sewage complicates the handling of all city waste waters, including even the runoff from rainstorms, and exacerbates all the problems of public health connected with water pollution.

Economies that develop in the future will, I think, turn to the use of chemical toilets.* The residues in the toilets will be collected like any other non-water-borne wastes. In effect they will be ash—"burned" to small amounts of dehydrated and sterilized phosphates and nitrates—collected about once a year from any given household toilet, more often from public facilities. Other kinds of wastes that will be kept out of water are analogous: they are in the water only because it is now the economical medium for carrying them, in lieu, often, of comprehensive waste-collecting services. Garbage from food-packing plants is an example.

So-called heat pollution, resulting when hot water is dumped into streams and lakes, leads to highly complex deterioration of water because of the destruction of cleansing biological cycles. This damage will cease in economies that continue to develop, because the hot water will be piped and recycled to yield its heat and so save fuel. Still other industrial wastes in water will diminish, or at

*These, of course, already exist but have not been developed except for use in situations where water is very scarce or where connecting it to toilets is impractical. Chemical toilets for standard use will probably not be developed or manufactured by existing manufacturers of bathroom fittings. It was not the makers of iceboxes who developed electric refrigerators, nor makers of coal stoves who developed the electric stove business; no more should we expect makers of flush toilets to develop practical chemical toilets of the future.

worst increase less rapidly than they now do, because of their own recycling. For instance, reuse of paper somewhat reduces the effluents from papermaking, which are most severe in the pulping operations. Aluminum reducing causes much water pollution, but recycling waste aluminum causes less. And still other processes that currently pollute waters will decline owing to obsolescence. Vehicles using electricity will indirectly reduce water pollution from oil refining, for example. The remaining industrial pollutants will be chiefly those integral to manufacturing. Water, in enormous bulk, is a necessary ingredient of many processes: not only papermaking, oil refining and aluminum reducing, but also dyeing, textile manufacturing, sugar refining, and brewing, to name a few common examples. We may expect that some types of manufacturing which do not yet exist will also use water as an ingredient and thus will add to the industrial wastes that unavoidably enter water. But here an analogy with the problems of disease may be to the point. Medical workers who do not have to care for patients suffering from smallpox, cholera, bubonic plague, typhoid, scarlet fever, diphtheria, tuberculosis, infantile paralysis, measles, scurvy, malaria, advanced syphilis, hookworm, yellow fever, and so on, and researchers who do not need to investigate these diseases, have more time to care for victims of unconquered afflictions and to investigate the mysteries of their diseases. Just so, economies in which the many relatively easy problems of waste recycling have been solved will be in good position to deal with harder problems.

Certainly one of the hardest problems will be to find ways of mining—or, to look at it the other way around, purifying—great volumes of unavoidably polluted fresh water swiftly, cheaply and at the site of the pollution. It is my conjecture that these techniques will be built upon an entirely different kind of water treatment for a wholly different purpose: the mining of ocean waters swiftly and cheaply for minerals. And that work, I think, will be built upon still different work: the techniques for extracting fresh water cheaply and swiftly from ocean water—something that is now almost possible.

In the past, when acute city practical problems have been solved, the solutions have not been an economic burden upon their societies. On the contrary, solutions have increased true economic abundance, true wealth. Of course more workers have been needed to do the previously undone work, but the costs of doing undone work have not been at all analogous to adding unproductive bureaucracies, nor the cost of maintaining idle people on welfare. Just so, we may expect that the solving of pollution and other problems arising from wastes, while requiring many workers, will not be an economic burden upon the developing economies where such problems are, in fact, solved. On the contrary, all the wealth extracted from recycled wastes, plus pure air and pure water, will represent increases in true abundance. Indeed, much of the new work, we may expect, will wholly or partly support itself even during its difficult trial, error and development stages.

Population and Resources

A developing economy needs increasing numbers of workers, which of course means a growing population. And a developing economy also increases the natural resources it can draw upon for its population, rather than diminishing its store of resources. When people added grain culture and animal husbandry, they were expanding, not diminishing, the natural resources they were capable of using. Modern men have done the same by adding chemical fertilizers and oil drills and thousands of other goods and services; and future developing economies will surely tap immense new resources in the sea, among others. To be sure, developing economies are all too ruthless to nature, but their depredations do not compare in destructiveness to those of stagnating and stagnant economies where people exploit too narrow a range of resources too heavily and monotonously for too long, and also fail to add into their economies the new goods and services that can help repair their depredations.

The effects of economic stagnation upon nature are veiled when populations are so scanty and so primitive in their technologies that anything they do has relatively little effect upon the rest of the natural world. But once a society has developed its economy appreciably, and thus has increased its population appreciably too, any serious stagnation becomes appallingly destructive to the environment. Common sequels in the past have been deforestation, complete destruction of wild life, loss of soil fertility and lowering of water tables. In the United States, lack of progress in dealing with wastes, and overdependence on automobiles—both evidence of arrested development—are becoming very destructive of water, air and land.

Wild animals are strictly limited in their numbers by natural resources, including other animals on which they feed. But this is because any given species of animal, except man, uses directly only a few resources and uses them indefinitely. Once we stopped living like the other animals, on what nature provided us ready-made, we began riding a tiger we dare not dismount, but we also began opening up new resources—unlimited resources except as they may be limited by economic stagnation.

Analogies of human population growth to animal population growth, based on the relation of population to current resources, are thus specious. The idea that, under sensible economic planning, population growth must be limited because natural resources are limited is profoundly reactionary. Indeed, that is not planning for economic development at all. It is planning for stagnation. So little does this seem to be understood, that it is becoming conventional (especially among the very well-off) to assume that poor and unproductive people cause their own poverty by multiplying—that is, by their very numbers. But if it is true that poverty is indeed caused by overpopulation, then it follows that poor people ought to prosper wherever populations decline appreciably. Things do not work out that way in the real world. Entire sections of Sicily and Spain have become almost depopulated by emigration. Yet the people remaining do not prosper; they remain poor. In the United States, the poorest counties experience prolonged out-migration and absolute population drops, but the economic situation of the people who remain is not improved as a result. It often grows steadily worse. McDowell County, West Virginia, once had a population of 97,000 persons living primarily—and poorly—upon the coal mines. By 1965, the population had fallen to 60,000 persons but they were worse off, according to a report in the *New York Times*, than they had ever been before and were kept going by charity. In Fauquier County, Virginia, which has, according to the *Times*, twelve millionaires and three thousand indigent black families, a free maternity clinic has been established which, upon request, sterilizes poverty-stricken women. At the time of the *Times'* report, in 1962, the operation had been performed upon sixty-three women. This service may improve the economic condition of the twelve millionaires by reducing the cost of welfare. But anyone who thinks it is going to bring prosperity to the indigent black families is naïve indeed. Ireland, before the potato famine, had almost nine million persons. They were very poor. From starvation, disease and emigration, they were swiftly reduced to less than three million. The fewer poor people were still poor. Their marriage and birth rates became the lowest in the world but this did not make Ireland well off. One wonders how much a population is supposed to be reduced before prosperity ensues.

Furthermore, if people cause their own poverty by their own numbers, it follows that if a given population is reasonably scanty to begin with, it will not be poor. Yet countries that have always been thinly populated, and have rich resources besides, are quite as liable to poverty as heavily populated countries. Thinly settled Colombia, for instance, has topsoil rich and deep beyond the dreams of Iowa, and high-grade iron ore beyond the dreams of Japan, yet Colombia festers in poverty and economic chaos worse, if anything, than densely populated India. If densely populated Japan and Western Europe were poor and if thinly populated Colombia, the Congo and Brazil were prosperous, then a rather nice case might be made for the idea that overpopulation causes poverty.

Birth control has much to recommend it. It is a great force for the social and economic liberation of women, and no doubt will prove even more so in societies of the future that make use of women's potentially splendid abilities to add new work to old. Birth control is also perhaps a major human right, although certainly not so vital as the right to have children. But birth control as a prescription for overcoming economic stagnation and poverty is nonsense. Worse, it is quackery. It carries the promise that something constructive is being done about poverty when, in fact, nothing constructive may be happening at all. The economies of people are not like the economies of deer, who wax fat if their numbers are thinned.

Earlier in this century, it was conventionally supposed by American philanthropists that poverty is caused by disease. Healthy people, it was reasoned, would be more productive, have more initiative, be more capable of helping themselves, than people in ill health. Poverty was analyzed as a vicious circle in which poverty leads to disease and disease reinforces poverty. Measures to combat disease turned out to be quite successful at combating disease, irrelevant for combating poverty. They helped lead to the situation that is now being diagnosed as a different vicious circle—poverty-overpopulation-poverty. To seek "causes" of poverty in this way is to enter an intellectual dead end because poverty has no causes. Only prosperity has causes. Analogically, heat is a result of active processes; it has causes. But cold is not the result of any processes; it is only the absence of heat. Just so, the great cold of poverty and economic stagnation is merely the absence of economic development. It can be overcome only if the relevant economic processes are in motion. These processes are all rooted, if I am correct, in the development work that goes on in impractical cities where one kind of work leads inefficiently to another. Let us now get down to examining the movements that go on within the economies of cities—the little movements at the hubs that turn the great wheels of economic life.

4

How Cities Start Growing

We now know a few general things about the economy of cities: that cities are settlements where much new work is added to older work and that this new work multiplies and diversifies a city's divisions of labor; that cities develop because of this process, not because of events outside of themselves; that cities invent and reinvent rural economic life; that developing new work is different from merely repeating and expanding efficiently the production of already existing goods and services, and thus requires different, conflicting conditions from those required for efficient production; that growing cities generate acute practical problems which are solved only by new goods and services that increase economic abundance; and that. the past development of a city is no guarantee of future development because the city can stop vigorously adding new work into the economy and thus can stagnate.

Young Detroit is as good a place as any to observe the beginning of a city economy. When Detroit began its growth in the 1820s and 1830s, its chief export was flour. The city-to-be was a cluster of grist mills, frame houses, cabins, dirt streets, taverns, docks, small workshops and a fort, carved into the wilderness north of Lake Erie on the Detroit River. For the people in the settlement, for the garrison at the fort and for the nearby farmers, the workshops produced some everyday necessities: candles, shoes, hats, a little cloth, whiskey, soap, saddles and harnesses, wagons. Almost every little settlement of the time supplied such goods for itself and its nearby hinterland.

But the workshops of young Detroit that are important to our story were not these; rather, we are concerned with shops that served the flour trade itself. Near the flour mills were shacks where mill machinery was repaired and new parts and machinery were made to equip the growing numbers of mills. Along the waterfront were small shipyards where passenger ships and ships for the flour trade were built to cross the Lakes. By the 1840s, some of the Detroit yards had found customers for their ships in other Lake ports and even along the coast. Soon the Detroit yards were building ocean-going cargo vessels. These were not sailboats, but steamships. Detroit shipyards were among the first in the world to build steamships. Just how the work of making the marine engines began is obscure, but it is believed to have been added, by machinists, to the older work which they had been doing for the mills. What is certain is that as the export work of the shipyards grew, the yards supported a growing collection of engine manufacturers and parts makers, as well as suppliers of other fittings and materials for the ships. By the 1860s, marine engines themselves were a major Detroit export. Some even found their way to Europe.

While the engine business was growing, it was supporting a growing collection of its own suppliers: shops that made parts and tools, others that supplied metal. The most important were the refineries and smelters that supplied copper alloys, made from local ores, to shops where brass valves and the other bits of engine brightwork were manufactured. The refineries too began to find customers outside of Detroit, and soon they became so successful that between about 1860 and 1880 copper was Detroit's largest export.

In about 1880, the local ores ran out. The refineries thereupon closed down in Detroit and their proprietors built new plants in the mountain states near new mines, and out there they established company towns. Detroit, which was thereafter a copper importer, had thus generated one of its own imports, just as I have imagined that New Obsidian did when herds of sheep were spun off from the city to new villages in the rural world. The loss of the copper business was not an economic disaster to Detroit because the sequence I have been describing was only one of many that were developing simultaneously. By 1880, Detroit had produced so many exports—paints, varnishes, steam generators, pumps, lubricating systems, tools, store fixtures, stoves, medicines, furniture, leather for upholstery, sporting goods—that they soon more than compensated for the loss of the refineries.

This was the prosperous and diversifying economy from which the automobile industry emerged two decades later to produce the last of the important Detroit exports and, as it turned out, to bring the city's economic development to a dead end. The Chinese ideogram for "crisis" is composed of the symbols for "danger" and "opportunity"; just so, a very successful growth industry poses a crisis for a city. Everything—all other development work, all other processes of city growth, the fertile and creative inefficiency of the growth industry's suppliers, the opportunities of able workers to break away, the inefficient but creative use of capital—can be sacrificed to the exigencies of the growth industry, which thus turns the city into a company town. This is what eventually happened in Detroit with the automobile industry. Perhaps it might have happened earlier with the copper industry, had that not been transplanted rather soon after its first swift growth, leaving Detroit free to develop further new goods and services.

The Reciprocating System

But we are concerned now with what happened when Detroit was first building up its economy. The flour it originally exported was served by the shipyards, which soon began to export their own products. Meanwhile the shipyards were served by the engine makers who soon began to export their own products too and the process repeated itself once again in the case of refined copper. At any given moment during these events, Detroit contained industries producing exports, and industries supplying the exporters. To indicate such a distinction, economists sometimes speak of "primary" and "secondary" city work, for the fact that some industries arise to serve others has long been recognized.* The conception that I am now about

*These customary terms have a slightly different meaning from exporting industries and local suppliers because "primary" industry refers only to major export work (especially that based on use of a natural resource), and "secondary" industry is often so designated although it produces exports. In short, customary usage blurs a distinction between work that is exported and work that is sold to other local producers, which is precisely the distinction with which we are here concerned.

Readers who are familiar with the work of Professor Wassily Leontief and his students at Harvard will recognize a kinship between the distinction I am making and input-output analysis, but also an important difference. In input-output analyses, marine engines are always input items; but they can be either export items in a city economy or local producers' goods, or both.

to introduce is that a city's exports and some of the goods and services produced locally to serve the export work act together to create an economic reciprocating system.

We find reciprocating systems all about us, in nature as well as in man-made contrivances. An animal eats, hence has strength to find food; hence it can eat, hence has strength to find more food. Within the animal's body are hundreds of other reciprocating systems: the heart pumps blood through the lungs and the blood is oxygenated; the blood supplies oxygen to the heart muscles and they are enabled to continue working; the heart pumps blood through the lungs and the blood is oxygenated; the blood supplies more oxygen to the heart muscles. Outside the animal countless reciprocating systems are also at work. The branch of knowledge called ecology is the analysis of reciprocating systems that maintain whole cycles of life in the sea and on land. It may be that all self-sustaining systems are reciprocating. But in a reciprocating system, if any one part of the process halts, the whole system fails.

The system with which we are now concerned is simple, being built wholly of exported goods and services and the local industries that supply things to the exporting industries. But unless some among those local industries take to exporting products of their own, the system halts. And if new local industries do not arise as older ones take to exporting their work, the system likewise halts.

This simple reciprocating system functions in cities not only when they are first forming and growing, but as long as their economies grow and diversify, no matter how complex the cities themselves become. We see it at work, for instance, in Birmingham, England, when that city first began to grow in the sixteenth and seventeenth centuries. It is believed that Birmingham's first exporters of any significance were makers of saddles and harnesses. Some of the local suppliers to Birmingham's exporters were lorimers, people who made saddle and harness hardware. Birmingham's lorimers were evidently soon not only exporting saddle and harness hardware themselves, but other types of hardware as well. Two centuries later, in a more complex Birmingham, the same process was still at work. The local glassmakers who supplied bits of decorative glass to exporters of buttons became exporters of glass themselves. And today we continue to see this process at work in a very complex Birmingham. Makers of transistors for Birmingham's electronics exports also export transistors. The point is that although this system comes into play at the beginning of a city's growth—indeed, causes its growth as a city to begin—the process does not disappear when other and more complex city growth systems come into play later.

When I was imagining how New Obsidian grew, I conjectured that such a system was at work. An example I made up was the local production there of hide bags for carrying obsidian exports down from the mines to the settlement. These bags, I suggested, also became exports. In the real city of Çatal Hüyük, it is likely that drills, polishers, hard clay stamps, and possibly even looms, became exports after they were first created to supply producers within the city, among them producers of exports. Although this reciprocating system was at work in Detroit when the copper companies formed and grew there, the copper companies did not repeat the process when they established company towns in the mountain states. The transplanted refineries were already big and relatively self-sufficient. They were able to supply most of their own needs within their own organizations. In their company towns, no independent supply organizations could arise and then begin to export goods of their own. The company towns thus created no additional economic reasons for their existence, as do even little cities that grow only briefly.*

*In Scranton, Pennsylvania, for example, which stagnated when it became a successful coal-mining city, the first export

A young, small city necessarily has a meager economy. Most of what it produces, especially for its own small population, is ordinary and routine. The consumer goods and services that it produces locally for its own people and its immediate rural hinterland certainly cannot compare with those of the larger and older cities with which it trades. Young New York shipped beaver fur for hats to London, but it did not export hats to London consumers. Novosibirsk, the Soviet science city, does not export much, if anything, to Moscow from its relatively small local consumer economy.* On the contrary, Novosibirsk is undoubtedly a heavy importer of goods from Moscow's large consumer economy.

What, then, does a young and still relatively small city have that is out of the ordinary? It has two things only. If it is a city at all, it has its own export work which, by definition, is not duplicated in all other settlements of similar and larger size; if it were, nobody would send for it. But to have an export is not enough; inert towns have exports—for instance, the company towns established by the Detroit copper refiners. A young city also has its enterprises which supply components to its exported work. These goods and services that supply the export economy of the little city are not duplicated everywhere for the reason that the export work they are serving is itself not du-

---

of the settlement was not coal, but iron and iron forgings. Among the local suppliers to producers of forgings were miners of anthracite coal, which the forges used for fuel. The mining companies, having started as local suppliers, began exporting the coal that was soon to become the city's chief export.

*Indeed, according to a letter published in *Trud*, Moscow's trade-union newspaper, and quoted in the *New York Times* in May, 1965, working women in Novosibirsk (signers of the letter included a physician, an official of one of the city's cafeteria administrations and four factory workers) were outraged at the meagerness and the slow growth of that young city's consumer services and goods.

plicated everywhere—the ships that served the Detroit export trade in flour, the buckles supplied to exporters of saddles in Birmingham. That is why, and only why, these goods and services too may well be potential exports and the supply-export reciprocating system of city growth can begin to operate.

One of the great debates in the history of embryology was between proponents of "preformation" and "epigenesis." The first group erroneously believed that the development of an embryo was a process of enlarging what was already there. The proponents of epigenesis believed that development of the embryo was a process of gradual diversification and differentiation of tissue from an initially undifferentiated entity. It was they who were on the right track. A city is not an animal, but I think there is an apt analogy here. People who think of cities simply as towns that have kept growing larger are believers in a "preformation" theory of city growth, an enlargement of what is essentially already there. I am arguing, rather, an "epigenesis" theory of cities: the idea that a city grows by a process of gradual diversification and differentiation of its economy, starting from little or nothing more than its initial export work and the suppliers to that work. If I am correct, cities radically differ in their growth processes from inert towns and from villages *even when they are still as small as towns or villages.*

Depot Cities

Detroit and Birmingham began as "manufacturing cities." That is to say, their first export work was something manufactured or processed in the settlement. To be sure, these cities were also engaged in trade, but the trade at first was based upon these exported manufactures and the goods and services for which they were exchanged. But some cities begin mainly as trading centers or depots, convenient sites where merchants establish themselves and

deal in goods that are not necessarily produced or processed in the settlement itself or destined for buyers in the
settlement. Many port cities have begun as depots; so have
many inland cities on river fords or important trade-route
junctions.

It is often supposed that a city's early exports, and
especially its origins as either a manufacturing city or a
depot city, mark its character thenceforth. But this is not
so. Venice, for centuries the very queen of trading cities,
did not begin as a depot but as a salt-processing settlement. Its traders in salt must have added to this work the
business of general trade. London became a depot early,
almost certainly by the tenth century, but its position as a
center of general trade may well have been built upon food
processing, as Detroit's was. At any rate, an important
export of London when it was young and small was salt
fish, which was processed there. Paris' position as a depot
may have been built upon—or reinforced by—its vineyards and its wine making.

Pittsburgh did not begin as a manufacturing city but as
a depot. Osaka, which is now nicknamed the Chicago of
Japan, meaning that it is a great manufacturing center,
only last century bore the nickname, City of Merchants.
Chicago itself, although it processed and shipped timber
and flour, was also a depot city from the first. It was
called the Great Northwestern Exchange early in its
history. Dinant, the medieval city that literally went to pot
by overspecializing in the manufacturing of brass vessels,
may have begun as a depot city. Mohenjo-daro and
Harappā, the once-great cities of the Indus that stagnated
so drastically before 2,500 B.C., were great trading cities
in their time. Piggott, enumerating the goods and materials brought from afar and found in their ruins, lists asphalt,
alabaster and (probably) soapstone from Baluchistan; gold,
lead, tin, turquoise, lapis lazuli and (probably) silver from
Persia; hematite (iron oxide used for dyeing cotton cloth)
from islands of the Persian Gulf; shells, agates, carnelians

and onyx from the far southern coast of India; dried and salted fish from the western coast; copper, lead and semi-precious stones from Rajputana; deodar wood from Kashmir and the Himalayas; and jadeite from either Tibet or Burma. But Mohenjo-daro and Harappā, or one of them, may well have started with manufacturing; at any rate, red dyed cotton cloth seems to have been a major export at the time when their trade was far flung and their imports were gathered from many places. If a city starts as a producing center, merchants there soon add general depot services. If it begins as a depot, suppliers to the work of trade itself soon add manufacturing; for trade requires many goods (e.g., ships, wagons or other carriers, containers, processing work, tools for the processing) for its own operations.

The great medieval fairs of the twelfth century were, of course, immense centers of trade where great numbers of merchants gathered. But the fairs did not become manufacturing centers and they did not become cities either. They proved to be ephemeral. Today they are deader than Troy; even their names—Thourout, Messines, Bar-sur-Aube, Lagny—are hardly remembered. Yet such medieval cities as London, Paris and Hamburg, which started several centuries earlier than the fairs as smaller trading centers and perhaps as centers of seasonal trade at that, early became centers of general craft manufacturing too. How, is a puzzle that I have not found explained except by abstractions such as "growth of industry and trade." But using the principle of reciprocating growth, based on exports and the industries that help supply the export work, I think we can figure out what happened.

In *Medieval Cities*, Henri Pirenne, the great Belgian economic historian, describes the traders of the tenth century who dealt in the meager raw materials of Northern and Western Europe—hides, wool, tin, salt fish, furs—and the precious goods of the East filtering through Venice. The traders, according to Pirenne, lived a "roving and hazardous existence." They emerged, he conjectures, from "the crowd of vagabonds drifting about all through society, living from day to day by alms from the monasteries, hiring themselves out at harvest-time, enlisting in the armies in time of war and holding back from neither rapine nor pillage when occasion presented. It is among this crowd of foot-loose adventurers that the first adepts of trade must, without any doubt, be looked for."

In the squalid little crossroads camps and ports where these vagabond traders rested, heard the news, bartered, and made up their caravans or flotillas for the next venture, there must also have been many others of the same kind who did not become traders. These would have been runaways, misfits and ordinary hungry people who preferred to take their chances where things seemed to be happening instead of perishing passively on land that refused to support them. No doubt these permanent hangers-on in the camps and ports would have liked to become traders too. But most of them lacked the luck or the capacity, or else had the misfortune (under the circumstances) to be women. But there was work of other kinds besides trading to be picked up in these settlements. One could stable and pasture the pack animals and riding horses of overland traders; supply, clean and repair the ships of voyagers; even build ships for merchants or for raiders or for defense against raiders; obtain and butcher game for arriving parties of travelers, or cook for the transients; guard and repack cargo; make barrels and chests; load animals, wagons or ships; provide beds; serve as concubines; or act as all-purpose servants and casual laborers.

There was valet work to be picked up: cleaning and laundering tunics, cloaks and hose, and cleaning and repairing other travel-worn gear—shoes, leather girdles, saddles and saddle bags. When personal gear of this kind was worn out, the logical places for the vagabond traders to buy new equipment and clothing were the ports and crossroads camps. And the logical people to provide the replacements were the casual servants who had started by doing valet work but now were ready to begin making things on their own.

At first the cloth and the leather goods they provided were no better or worse than the everyday clothing that the traders wore to begin with, which had been made in peasants' and yeomen's households or by impressed peasant labor for manor households. That is to say, the quality of the work would have been poor, for after the fall of Rome weaving and other crafts throughout Europe had degenerated.* The wool which valets used to make tunics, cloaks and hose-wrapping for the traders probably came out of the traders' own bales. And from the traders' bales of hides came the raw materials for the traders' shoes, girdles and saddles, for which finished articles the traders paid in extra materials or perhaps in coin. In this way the valets began to accumulate working capital.

During the course of the tenth or eleventh centuries, the vagabond traders of Europe were to become better dressed than the peasantry and fitted with better saddles than even the feudal gentry had, for the most part; for the weavers and leather workers who emerged from the class of servants in these trading settlements were beginning to specialize in craft work, just as their neighbors were specializing in butchering, or running cookshops, or keeping inns and stables, or making wagons, or coopering or maintaining brothels. Some of the cloth and leather

---

*For instance, apart from Venice, almost the only settlements in tenth-century Europe where cloth of good quality was made were a few Friesian villages in Flanders. Their scant output was the cloth of kings. Charlemagne sent a gift of Friesian cloths to Harun-al-Rashid, the Caliph of Baghdad. Like the rare and expensive silks and beautiful rugs of the East that found their way in minute quantities through Venice, Friesian cloths in the tenth century would have been goods for traders to sell to the rich and mighty.

work became valuable enough to put into trade. It was in this way, I suspect, that certain medieval settlements became more than merely trading centers. They were on their way to becoming craft manufacturing centers also.

It is important, however, to understand that either of two things could have happened next, with momentously different results. If the traders, some of whom were now becoming respectable merchants, had added the craftsmen's work to their existing lines of merchandise, then the craftsmen in the ports and camps would have remained no more than local suppliers of goods to merchants, the only difference being that they would now have been supplying the merchants with goods to be traded, as well as with goods for their personal use. This was evidently the case in Scotland, where craftsmen in the Scottish burghs did supply their wares to already existing merchants. Throughout medieval times, the Scottish burghs enforced a separation between the work of craftsmen and the work of trading, according to Unwin in his *Studies in Economic History*. Unwin blames this arrangement—accurately, I think—for stultifying the medieval industrial development of Scotland and rendering the burghs weak and economically backward compared to the developing little cities of England and the Continent. The reason such an arrangement is apt to be stultifying is that general merchants do not seek out the best markets for each specific kind of goods in which they deal, while people who specialize in specific goods are apt to specialize in their search for markets too. Such an arrangement also hampers craftsmen from adding new work to old work if the new work does not interest merchants of the older goods and services.

One is reminded of India, where Hindu craftsmen belonged to one group of castes, while mercantile work was reserved to men in another—standing next higher—and no one crossed the line from one to the other. To this day, Hindu craftsmen traditionally belong to the same great caste grouping as servants, which also suggests that perhaps craft work, as a formal occupation, arose in India upon older, servants' work as I have conjectured it did in the early medieval European cities.

An alternative to the arrangements in Scotland and India was for craftsmen to become merchants of their own craft work. For reasons I shall explain in a moment, it appears that this is what must have happened in the early days of such medieval cities as Paris, London and Hamburg. By specializing in the sales of their own craft goods, merchant-craftsmen could expand their markets and thus the production in their cities. This increased production for export would have supported growing groups of local, subsidiary craftsmen in the cities, who supplied goods, services, equipment and parts to the export craft work. The structures of the medieval guilds suggest that this is the way things did, in fact, happen. From the time they are first documented, in the twelfth century, the guilds were of three different types: merchant guilds, strictly local guilds, and craft guilds.

The richest, most prestigious, and probably the oldest were merchant guilds whose work corresponded to that of the old traders. The structure of these guilds was simple. Although they contained apprentices and other workers, all their master members were engaged in long-distance buying and selling. No matter if they were called Fishmongers or Vintners, in their trade they were as eclectic as the merchants of the Grocers, whose very name (meaning people who dealt in gross lots) proclaimed the general nature of their trade work. That is, they sold what they came by. But by the twelfth century, many had settled down with warehouses, counting houses and agents in this city and that.

At the other extreme were the humble guilds and parish organizations of tradesmen who did no long-distance trading. The bakers, butchers, coopers and wagoners were typically in this group. They bought their supplies from the merchants of the first category and sold their goods locally. Their master members were shopkeepers who kept workshops.*

The third type were the craft guilds, such as the Weavers and Saddlers. From the first, craft guilds had a structure different from the others. Some of the masters were merchants, selling their wares outside the city and, at least sometimes, buying materials outside the city too. Yet these men were also "of the craft." Other masters in these guilds were shopkeepers, who traded only within the city, often selling their wares to merchant-craftsmen.

There is no doubt about why the craft guilds had this structure; well-documented events from the early thirteenth century on show us. Typically, before a craft was institutionalized as a guild, it had this history: it began as local work supplying producers' goods and services to members of other craft guilds or merchant guilds in the city, as the Dyers, for instance, served Weavers, or as the early-thirteenth-century makers of brass vessels in London, the Potters, sold to merchants; but then some of the people doing this craft work in the local economy of their cities became exporters of their goods and services on their own account. That is, for example, some dyers took to importing cloth woven elsewhere, dyeing it, and exporting it; some potters took to exporting pots themselves and some also added to their pot making other work for export, such as bell casting (although they still called themselves potters). If one reviews the electronics enter-

---

*Local retail shops in our sense, selling goods not made on the premises, were still unknown. According to Duby and Mandrou, in their *History of French Civilization*, retail shops first appeared in Paris in the thirteenth century. The earliest sold manuscripts—hitherto made only in monasteries—copied by poor students in their garrets; art objects being resold by their owners; and objects made by fine artisans unable to maintain workshops of their own.

prises that formed twenty years ago as local industries in
Los Angeles or Tokyo, supplying goods and services to
other producers in those cities, one finds that some of them
remain local industries while others are exporting their
work. Were they organized as guilds at this point, they
would have the same structure as craft guilds for the
reason that some local work had become export work.

The interesting thing is that the medieval craft guilds
had this structure from the very first, which means that
events that shaped this structure must have occurred early
in the medieval cities—indeed, must have been involved
in forming them as cities. The Weavers of London, for instance, were already institutionalized before London itself
had a city charter. Taken together, the three types of
guilds give us a picture of the economy of a city that is
not only valid for medieval times but for our own times
as well: local goods and services that remain local; exports, starting with the initial exports; and local goods and
services that become exports.

The Export-Multiplier Effect

When the exports of a settlement increase, the local economy of the city grows too. This local growth results from
what economists call "the multiplier effect." The phrase
usually refers to jobs; that is, each additional job created
by a city's export work adds other jobs in the city's local
economy, to supply and serve the growing numbers of
workers and their families. And there may also be more
work to be done, as we have seen, supplying goods and
services to producers of the growing export work itself.
This growth in the local economy is possible because the
growing export work earns more imports for the city.
Some of these increased imports go directly back into the
growing export work. Other imports go into the local
economy where they are incorporated into goods and serv-

ices consumed by the city's growing population; others are destined for the local industries that supply components to the export work.

Settlements vary enormously in the proportions of their earned imports that go into the local economy and the proportions that bypass it by going directly back into export work. The mayor of a Maine resort town, whose chief export work is entertaining tourists, has remarked that nearly every dollar spent by the tourists goes right out again to buy the food, pillowcases, gasoline and other things those same tourists consume. The larger a city's own collection of various local industries that supply goods and services to producers of export work, the larger will be the total multiplier effect from increases in export work.

But to get a large multiplier effect, local work done for exporting organizations must be done in local establishments independent of the exporting organizations themselves. Manchester's cotton mills or Pittsburgh's steel mills are integrated. As exporting organizations they do not support many independent local enterprises supplying the mills with materials, machines, parts, repair work, and so on. The new jobs created by the mills for their growing export work—in the days when the number of jobs was still growing in those mills—resulted in relatively little more industrial growth in Manchester and Pittsburgh than that enjoyed by the expanding mills themselves. Of course, even in these cases, there was a multiplier effect because of the growth of local goods and services supplying consumer goods to the growing numbers of export workers and their families. But even the local job growth from this source has probably been rather low in Manchester and Pittsburgh because those cities have contained relatively few autonomous producers within their local economies, hence relatively few who could add to their older work the work of manufacturing goods for local consumers—and few too who could supply bits and pieces to other producers who might undertake such manufacturing. Such cities import a high proportion of finished consumer products rather than materials to make consumer products locally. The multiplier effect from growth in a city's export work is thus not a fixed ratio for all settlements alike. Nor is it a fixed figure over time within a specific city.

Since another kind of multiplier effect also operates during city growth, as I shall explain in the next chapter, it seems to me useful to call what is generally referred to as the multiplier effect, meaning a city's growth of local work owing to growth of its export work, by a name a little more precise than is now conventionally thought necessary: the *export-multiplier* effect. Thus we may distinguish it from the other type of multiplier effect, when we come to it in the next chapter.

The important point is that a high export-multiplier effect creates "more room" in the framework that we call the economy of a city. The local economy can add new work, including the experimenting and trial and error that go into the development of much of the new work. The local economy has room for the multiplying divisions of labor that result from carrying the process $D + nTE + A \longrightarrow nD$ to successful conclusion. As I mentioned earlier, a developing economy in which new goods and services are being added to economic life is an expanding economy. Indeed, it must be an expanding economy because the very process of adding new work to old multiplies divisions of labor. But for expansion to be possible at all, there must be settlements where more room, quite literally, is being made for new divisions of labor. And this room cannot be made after they appear, for then, by definition, there will have been no room to permit them to have made an appearance. The necessary room, rather, must be created by events set in motion before the new work and its multiplied divisions of labor appear. The generation of new exports provides this room for local expansion of work, owing to the export-multiplier effect. That effect is thus of the essence in the reciprocating system of city growth I have been describing in this chapter.

It is conventionally assumed that increased local jobs in the economy of cities are mere passive sequels to the growth of the export work. But, in the reciprocating system which I have described, they cannot be such. Some of the new local work must also be a precursor of new exports. Only a rather small part of a city's total local industry that supplies goods and services to the city's current exporting organizations need be, at any given moment, in process of producing export work in its own right, for the reciprocating system to be kept functioning. But, of course, the larger the stream of new exports, the faster the reciprocating system can operate, and the more room it can produce in the city's local economy for still further economic trial, error, development, and multiplying divisions of labor. A diagram showing the generation of new exports from a city's local industries serving already existing export work, together with the multiplier effect, is to be found in Section I of the Appendix, for those who wish to see these movements in graphic form.

Specious "Causes" of City Growth

The mouth of the Connecticut River, the largest river of New England, is so fine a site for a depot city that had a major city grown there, we may be sure it would have been accounted for in the geography textbooks by its location at the river mouth. But in reality, this site has brought forth only the little settlements of Lyme and Old Saybrook. At the time Washington was designated to be the capital of the young United States, Americans seem almost universally to have believed that because it was to be the capital, it was destined to become a great commercial and industrial city too, a London, Paris or Rome.

But cities simply cannot be "explained" by their locations or other given resources. Their existence as cities and the sources of their growth lie within themselves, in the processes and growth systems that go on within them. Cities are not ordained; they are wholly existential. To say that a city grew "because" it was located at a good site for trading is, in view of what we can see in the real world, absurd. Few resources in this world are more common than good sites for trading but most of the settlements that form at these good sites do not become cities. Among the best natural harbors in Britain, for example, are those belonging to the settlements of Ipswich, Yarmouth, King's Lynn, Sunderland, South Shields, Lossiemouth, Shoreham, Stornoway and Greenock.

Many and many a name on the map of the United States tells of a fine trading location and high hopes: Centropolis, Central City, Center Junction, Centerton, Centralia, Center Port, Centerport, Centreport. . . . Mark Twain, in *Life on the Mississippi*, tells how the people of Hannibal expected their settlement to grow automatically into a city when the railroad came through, and then were baffled when most of the trains went right by, as the riverboats had done before them. Many cities engaging in enormous trade occupy notably inferior trading sites. Tokyo and Los Angeles are examples. A senator from Maine—a state with many fine harbors but no very consequential cities—once told the people of Los Angeles, "You have made a big mistake in the location of your city." He was annoyed because Los Angeles, in the 1920s, was lobbying for Federal funds to build itself a port. "You should have put it at some point where a harbor already exists," he scolded, "instead of calling on the U.S. government to give you something which nature has refused!"

Even for a settlement to have become an important depot does not insure its subsequent growth as a city. Sag Harbor at the eastern end of Long Island (a magnificent depot site), and Portsmouth, North Carolina (where now not even the mailboat stops), commanding Pamlico Sound with its extensive waterways penetrating the interior, were sufficiently important soon after the American Revolution to be sites of customs stations. Plymouth, at the time of Queen Elizabeth I, was a more important port—although not a more important commercial and industrial city—than London. Many depots established by colonial powers in Latin America and Africa have not grown further as cities. But colonial depots are not always inert; Hong Kong has become one of the world's great industrial and commercial cities.

We are all taught in school that New York grew so rapidly after 1825 "because" of the Erie Canal. Did it really? Then why not Jersey City? Jersey City had as good an access to the Erie Canal and the Atlantic Ocean as Manhattan did. It also had the added advantage of being on the mainland. Alexander Hamilton, observing the start of Manhattan's rapid development and growth (beginning soon after the close of the American Revolution), and shrewdly noting that Jersey City had an even more advantageous location, buoyantly predicted that Jersey City would become "the metropolis of the world." In the quarter century before the canal opened, New York—which had been relatively stagnant throughout the colonial period—was developing new goods and services so rapidly that by 1824 it had already outdistanced Philadelphia, formerly the chief manufacturing city of the country, in the number of its factories and the varieties of its manufactured goods, although not yet in their total value. Development and growth processes were going on in New York that cannot be accounted for, retroactively, by the canal. To be sure, New York's high rate of development work put the canal to heavy use after it was built. But lesser cities found no such potent magic in the canals they built in emulation of New York.

The great capitals of modern Europe did not become

great cities because they were the capitals. Cause and effect ran the other way. Paris was at first no more the seat of the French kings than were the sites of half a dozen other royal residences. Indeed, until the twelfth century, Orléans, another center of trade, was more imposing than Paris as a seat of king and court and as a cultural and educational center too. Paris became the genuine capital only after it had already become the largest (and economically the most diversified) commercial and industrial city of the kingdom. Berlin was not even the capital of its province—Brandenburg was—until after it had become the largest, and economically the most diversified, commercial and industrial city in Prussian territory. London was neither de facto nor formally the capital of England— Winchester was the secular capital and Canterbury the ecclesiastical capital—until the eleventh century when, London having already become the largest (and economically the most diversified) commercial and industrial center of the kingdom, it became de facto capital and then, gradually, the formal capital. In the ancient city-states and empires, the cities were capitals because they were large and strong enough to export their city governments, first to the hinterlands beyond the home territory and then frequently farther, and were handsomely paid for their rule. Thus Rome's government first governed only Rome, but ultimately government became Rome's chief export work—in principle, much like other local goods and services becoming exports.

A settlement to which the work of government is given as its chief or initial export work may become a great city. Constantinople did. But it is more common for small settlements that are selected arbitrarily as capitals to develop no other appreciable economic reasons for being. Washington, Ottawa, The Hague, New Delhi and Canberra are examples; probably Brasilia will prove to be another. Many provincial or state capitals are thoroughly inert towns or stagnated little cities. A capital with government work as its initial or chief export work has much in common, economically, with a company town.

In the case of some cities, no given advantage can be found to "explain" their existence in a specious way. All that Birmingham seems to have had, to begin with, was a good supply of drinking water—no novelty in Renaissance England. Alcaeus made the point in 600 B.C. when he wrote of the cities of Greece, "Not houses finely roofed nor the stones of walls well built nor canals nor dockyards make the city, but men able to use their opportunity."

5

Explosive City Growth

This chapter concerns itself only incidentally with how cities generate new exports. We shall concentrate instead on what cities do with some of the imports they earn by generating those exports.

At the end of the last century, as we noted, Tokyo was importing large numbers of bicycles. When these bicycles broke down or wore out, repairmen in Tokyo began making new parts for them. Soon these same repairmen began to specialize in making this part or that. And eventually manufacturers contracted to buy large numbers of parts from repairmen and put the parts together. By this means they manufactured whole, new bicycles in Tokyo, and Tokyo's imports of bicycles were replaced by locally manufactured goods.*

*Economists customarily call such an event "import substitution," but I shall call it "import replacement," because

As cities grow, they replace the imports which they earn from neighboring cities, as well as from outside their nations. For reasons we shall come to, the process of replacing imports is apt to cause cities to grow explosively. Episodes of explosive growth can recur again and again during the life of a city as new and different imports are earned, then replaced. But before going into that, let us examine a little more closely just what happens when a city replaces an import with new local work, as Tokyo did with its bicycles.

First of all, before the process could occur at all, two sorts of events had to have taken place. Tokyo had already become a good market for imported bicycles; and this meant it was becoming a place where it was worthwhile for somebody to make them. Also, before the bicycles were actually manufactured there, workmen in the city were learning how to manufacture them, even though their work at first had a different purpose. The production of bicycles could be logically added to work that was already being done in Tokyo.

When Tokyo was still importing bicycles, they had to be paid for by exports from the city—in this case, since the bicycles came from abroad, exports to foreign countries. But even if the bicycles had been imported from Osaka or some other city in Japan, they would have been paid for by Tokyo's exports to other parts of Japan. But once Tokyo itself began to manufacture bicycles, they no longer needed to be paid for by exports from the city. To be sure, most of the materials that went into the bicycles still had to be imported and paid for, but the cost was not nearly as much as that of whole, imported bicycles.

---

the verb form, "to substitute for imports" is awkward, while "to replace imports" does not have this disadvantage. Also, I am going to draw some conclusions about the effects of import replacement that have not been drawn in conventional treatments of the subject, so perhaps it is as well, in any case, to use a new phrase.

This difference in cost permitted Tokyo to import other things instead. The change meant, of course, that the places that had been manufacturing bicycles and shipping them to Japan lost some of their export business. But this is not at all the same as saying that Tokyo was importing less than it imported before. Tokyo, rather, shifted its imports to things other than bicycles. The foreign bicycle companies' losses were other people's export gains as Tokyo became an expanding market for other goods and services instead.

Let us go back, just for a moment, to our imagined pre-agricultural city, New Obsidian. When New Obsidian was able to replace its former imports of wild animals and wild seeds with its new city-produced domestic animals and cultivated grains, it was thus able to import other things in place of the wild food it had originally bought: pigments, copper, furs, bundles of rushes, antlers, timber, hides and thongs, shells and so on. Some of these it could import in larger quantities than before, now that it did not want wild food from its customers for obsidian; others it perhaps imported for the first time. Some of these new imports went to clothe or decorate the increased numbers of workers in New Obsidian, now that the city had added the new industry of raising food. But others were "extra." From the point of view of New Obsidian, it was just as if the city's imports had increased greatly—although in fact they had only shifted in composition. But New Obsidian had everything it had had before, plus those new imports. For all practical purposes, the city's imports had "grown," just as surely as if the city had earned all those additional imported things by increasing its exports greatly. It had earned them, instead, by quite a different process: by replacing a former import. The apparent growth of a city's imports—because of a shift in their composition—is the key to the import-replacing process of city growth and its momentous consequences.

My conjecture about what happened in New Obsidian

when it replaced its imports of wild food derives from what actually happens in our own cities when imports are replaced by local work and the composition of imports consequently shifts In the case of Tokyo, some of the "extra" imports were undoubtedly food and other consumer goods that came from outside the city to supply the increased numbers of workers and their families, for of course when Tokyo began to produce bicycles for itself the city needed more workers than formerly. So let us add to the materials imported into the city, for the bicycle manufacturing itself, the necessary new imports for the increased population generated by the new industry. Whatever difference remained between the total cost of these imports and the cost of whole, imported bicycles could be spent on still other imports which Tokyo had not previously earned.

As far as the rest of the world was concerned, its total economic activity had neither diminished nor increased because Tokyo was making its own bicycles. But the economy of Tokyo itself had expanded, and thus the total of all economic activity in the world had expanded. So we can see that the process of replacing imports is a good deal more important than just moving production of bicycles from this place to that. The process of replacing imports is not equivalent to moving work out of a city—like spinning off an animal herd from New Obsidian or a copper refinery from Detroit. Nor is it equivalent to moving production from one city to another, if imports in the receiving city are not thereby being replaced. I plan to argue, later in this chapter, that this process of replacing present imports, and buying others instead, is probably the chief means by which economic life expands, and by which national economies increase their total volumes of goods and services.

In the meantime, let us pursue one more question concerning those bicycles: the economic feasibility of producing them in Tokyo instead of importing them. When the bicycles were manufactured in Tokyo, the retail price of a bicycle there went down. The home-produced bicycles were cheaper than imported ones. By definition, then, it was economically feasible to produce bicycles in Tokyo. If the Tokyo products had cost customers more than imported bicycles, their local production would not have been feasible (although the government might have made it artificially so by means of an import tax or tariff on the foreign makes).

But what does "economically feasible" really mean? Does it mean only that the bicycles could be produced in Tokyo; and that there was a sufficiently large and solvent market there to make their production worthwhile; and that some savings could be made in the transportation costs which the customers for the imports had to bear? No, it means something more. It means that the local costs of producing bicycles were not prohibitive. When those local costs were paid, there was still enough margin in the sale price of the bicycles to cover the rubber, the steel and whatever else the industry had to import from outside Tokyo. Or, putting it the other way around, it meant that the cost of the goods and services that had to be imported into the city was not so high that it left too little margin in the sale price to cover local costs of the work.

Bicycle manufacturing in Tokyo might not have been economically feasible if the manufacturers had been so foolish as to attempt to copy slavishly the production methods being used, say, in the great factories of the American bicycle trust in Hartford at the time. Those methods would have required the Tokyo manufacturers to build large new factories that would involve great expense before anything could be earned from them. The manufacturers would have had to import many expensive machines too, and would have had to pay for expensive imported management services in the factory or else for sending managers abroad for training. But by tailoring their production methods to Tokyo's existing capacities—a creative thing to do—and by using many already existing local producers who needed only to expand work they were already capable of doing or to adapt it somewhat, the manufacturers made the new work economically feasible.

We see the same principle at work when highly developed economies replace handmade imports with work produced by machine. Such new local work—whether grinding and mixing spices, or printing cloth or tooling leather—might not be economically feasible if it all had to be done by hand. Sometimes the replaced import in such a case is not as good as the handwork that is being imitated; sometimes it is. But again, production methods are not being slavishly copied. The local imitations are tailored to local technical capabilities.

The Mighty Economic Force Exerted by This Process

We are considering a process of immense, even awesome, economic force. Perhaps an idea of its mighty force can be conveyed by considering, first, two untypical instances in which the replacement of imports has rescued cities from what otherwise would have been dire temporary or permanent economic distress.

Ordinarily, when a city is rapidly producing for its own market many things that formerly had been imported, and thus rapidly shifting the composition of what it continues to import, its export work remains at much the same volume as before or else it expands. In such cases, the city's increased growth from the work of producing former imports is pure increment, an absolute expansion of its economy. But sometimes, owing to unusual circumstances, a city's export work may drastically decline at the very time other work in the city is growing through local production of former imports. In such a case, the replacement work is unequivocally responsible for the city's continued growth.

In Los Angeles this unusual situation occurred at the end of World War II when new local production of goods and services compensated for enormous losses of export work and was responsible for more growth besides. During the war itself, there had been immense increases in Los Angeles exports. And in spite of wartime shortages, imports into Los Angeles had soared too—imports incorporated into the war goods the city was producing, and imports also to help clothe, shelter and feed the workers and their families. But even before the war's end, the export work began to decline and it declined still more during the next four or five years. I shall mention only the principal losses.

Aircraft manufacturing, the city's largest industry, laid off about three-quarters of its workers by the end of 1945 and operated at about that reduced level, sometimes lower, for the rest of the decade.* Shipbuilding, the second largest wartime industry in Los Angeles, almost closed down. The Hollywood motion picture industry was in the beginning of its decline. Petroleum, once the city's largest export and still an important one until 1946, was thereafter lost to the city's export economy because people in Los Angeles itself took to consuming so much gasoline that the city ran a "deficit" and became a petroleum importer. Some of the city's oldest depot services were lost, those concerned with nationwide distribution of the citrus fruits, walnuts and avocados grown in the city's hinterland. This loss was incurred when the groves were up-

*The same kind of decline did not occur in most large industries in the country; e.g., Chicago's steel industry (begun about the turn of the century to replace imports from Pittsburgh), the automobile industry, the chemical industries, garment industries, construction industries, all converted rather quickly from war work.

rooted to build suburbs and highways and—still farther out—to make way for truck farms to feed growing Los Angeles. I have been able to find no figures for the total number of export jobs lost in Los Angeles between 1944 and 1950. But some idea is conveyed by the fact that aircraft jobs alone declined from 210,000 in 1944 to 60,000 at the end of 1945 and shipbuilding from 90,000 to 18,000. Later both declined still more, though more slowly. Besides the export jobs themselves, other work was lost: that of supplying parts, tools or services to the export industries, and all sorts of goods and services to the export workers and their families. All this export-multiplier work was lost along with the export work.

In 1949 the Los Angeles export economy was probably at its nadir—perhaps lower than at any time since the Great Depression. At the war's end, many people had, in fact, predicted severe economic distress and depression for Los Angeles. They would have been right if the city had had nothing to grow on but its export work and the multiplier effect of that work. But as it turned out, work and jobs in Los Angeles did not decline; they grew. In 1949 Los Angeles had more jobs than it had ever had before. The city's economy had expanded while its exports had been contracting! What was happening, of course, was that Los Angeles was replacing imports at a great rate.

Much of this new local production work was being done by new local companies or by older ones that were adding new work, and most enterprises, in both categories, were small when they began replacing imports. The new enterprises started in corners of old loft buildings, in Quonset huts and in backyard garages. But they multiplied swiftly, mostly by the breakaway method. And many grew rapidly. They poured forth furnaces, sliding doors, mechanical saws, shoes, bathing suits, underwear, china, furniture, cameras, hand tools, hospital equipment, scientific instruments, engineering services and hundreds of other things.

One-eighth of all the new businesses started in the United States during the latter half of the 1940s were started in Los Angeles. Not all were replacing former imports, nor did all of them succeed. There was much trial and error. But many were replacing imports, and many did succeed.

Some of the companies started at this time were to become highly successful exporters—for example a company making sliding glass doors for local house builders. It was started in 1948 by a young engineer who had broken away from his job in the materials laboratory of Douglas Aircraft, had attempted to manufacture a furnace that had swiftly become obsolete, and had then started the door business in a Quonset hut with a young architect as partner and $22,000 in capital. The company succeeded locally and then became an exporter. In 1955, when it moved into a new plant costing $450,000, it had already become the largest supplier of sliding glass doors in the United States, exporting far and wide. Scores of important new exports and hundreds of lesser ones were to come out of new local work started in Los Angeles at this time.

While new companies were starting, still other imports in Los Angeles were being replaced in a different way. Many former exporters to the city were opening branch plants there to produce their goods and services close to what had already become a large market for their work. Among others, the automobile companies of Detroit opened new branch factories in Los Angeles and enlarged old ones. Their big suppliers opened Los Angeles branch plants to manufacture components for the cars. From the viewpoint of Detroit, the automobile industry was decentralizing and Detroit was losing export work it would otherwise have had. But from the viewpoint of Los Angeles, imported work was now being produced locally and other imports could be bought. Exports for the Los Angeles economy emerged from the branch plants too. The city was soon to become an exporter of "Detroit" automobiles throughout the territory west of the Rocky Mountains.

But since these and other branch plants were producing standard products being produced in other places too, their products did not become nationwide exports.

Though Los Angeles' imports, like its exports, were much reduced from former levels in the years following the war, and were lower than they would be later, the city was still able to import enough to obtain the materials for its new, locally produced goods and services. And so many goods and services formerly imported were now being produced in the city instead, that the imports the city could "not afford" were not missed. The city had those goods and services anyhow. So great was the city's shift of imports from finished goods to materials for work now done locally, that the city could actually afford "extra" imports, not imported before—such as the petroleum. Los Angeles could also import more of some things it had previously imported and had not replaced by new city work, such as additional farm produce that came, in part, from the new truck farms beyond the city. Thus, far from seeming to have declined (although they had), the city's imports seemed to have grown, just as if they had been earned by a growing export economy.

From the point of view of the world outside, Los Angeles was buying as large a quantity of imports as it could have bought in any case. But without the replacement and shift of imports there would have been many idle people in the city, at a much lower standard of living. The replacement work had not only expanded the total of economic activity in Los Angeles, but in the United States and in the world as a whole.

Similarly, in Shakespeare's time, a mighty episode of import replacing in London more than compensated for the immense losses incurred at that time in London's export work.* London in the late sixteenth and early seventeenth

---

*The reasons for these losses were different from the reasons for Los Angeles' losses, but they were probably comparable in severity. England's foreign trade was badly depressed

centuries must have been replacing many of its domestic imports but, as always, replacements of foreign imports were more obvious because the foreign imports (and in many cases the people doing the new local work) were so obviously exotic. So many foreign workers from the Continent set themselves up so rapidly in business in London that, ac-

---

at the time, which meant declines in London's formerly large foreign exports (and imports). In addition, the city's domestic exports, to other English cities and rural districts, dependent upon markets in those cities, must have been declining badly too because virtually all the old cities of England at this time, with the exception of London, were afflicted by a gratuitous—indeed, self-imposed—economic stagnation.

While it is apart from the present point, the nature of this stagnation is interesting. What had been happening in the provincial cities was the reversal of the former freedom of English craftsmen to become exporters in their own right, and hence the suppression of new exporting organizations and new export work. In Newcastle, for example, a craftsman was no longer allowed to import or export a cargo for himself; the trade of the city was given, by its own government, as a monopoly to a powerful merchant company whose members had obviously come to dominate the power structure of Newcastle. To make sure that craftsmen could not evade this prohibition, or rival merchants live on business from them, the regulation also forbade skippers or merchants to act as agents for craftsmen trying to export their own work.

Many of the old cities of England never recovered from the stagnation they brought upon themselves at this time; thenceforth they were more or less inert towns. It was almost certainly economic repression of this sort—sometimes enforced by trading companies, sometimes by old and well-established guilds—that the saddlers of Birmingham, then obscurely beginning its growth, were evading. Such cities as Birmingham and Sheffield, just formed and beginning to grow at this time, retained the old economic freedoms lost for the time being in many other settlements of England dominated by powerful but decadent and stagnant guilds and trading companies.

cording to Unwin, the new industrial suburbs, rapidly building up at the time from Clerkenwell to Whitechapel, took on a strong foreign flavor. Shakespeare himself, according to A.L. Rowse, lodged for a time in the household of a Huguenot maker of French headdresses who had moved his work to London. The new shops of Blackfriars contained much locally made luxury goods that Englishmen had formerly had to seek out abroad. A case could be made that the economic success of the golden age of Elizabethan England—and the initial capital for the foreign voyages of its great captains—depended on the fortunate circumstance that London was engaged in replacing imports at the time. How poor, and how economically stagnant and weak, England would have been without this movement!

As I have said, cases like these, in which exports are declining while imports are being replaced, are exceptional. Usually a city's exports are not declining while local goods are replacing imports. When export work is growing at the same time, a city's economy grows from the combination of these forces. But in these cases, also, the mighty economic force exerted by the replacement of imports can be discerned because growth is much too abrupt and rapid to be accounted for by growing exports alone. For example, Chicago, during its first episode of import replacing, multiplied itself almost by seven in a single decade, growing from a population of 12,000 to 80,000 between 1845 and 1855. And this was not a growth of an idle city population, but of people with jobs and opportunities; it was growth of Chicago's economy. Chicago at this time was a depot. It handled and processed goods, mainly flour and timber, shipped to Eastern markets through the Great Lakes and on the new railroads, and it served as a distribution point for products from the East shipped to the Midwest. Its depot work was growing and so were new exports which it had already generated (some machinery manufacturing, shipbuilding, a little regional banking), and which had grown out of its original work. But Chicago's exports were not growing at such a rate that they and their multiplier effect could account for the city's fantastic growth of jobs.

What was also happening was an extraordinarily swift development of the city's own production for its own market. Chicago at this time was replacing many of its imports almost as rapidly as they were earned and found a market in the city. This is evident from the fact that at the beginning of the decade Chicago, like any other little Midwestern depot settlement, was importing most kinds of city-made goods and was supplying for itself only the kinds of things that every town supplied. But by the end of that decade it was producing a very large range of the common city-made goods of the time and some of the luxuries too—clocks, watches, medicines, many kinds of furniture, stoves, kitchen utensils, many kinds of tools, most building components.

Chicago was still not thought of, in 1855, as a manufacturing city although it obviously was one; it had not become much of an exporter of manufactured goods thus far except to its immediate hinterland. Yet it was manufacturing a great deal, chiefly for its own population and its own producers. Furthermore, its manufactures were so diverse that no particular product seems to have been of special importance in itself; that is apt to be the case when a city is replacing many different imports rapidly with local work.

The great cities of the world have had many repeated episodes of replacing imports and of explosive growth. Nobody knows when London had its first. It certainly had one in the thirteenth century (among other imports that London replaced at that time were the brass vessels it had previously been importing from Dinant, the city that overspecialized in its brass work and so had no other exports to make up for its losses when it lost that). But that was probably not London's first episode of import replacing and explosive growth. Paris, incidentally, was replacing its imports from Dinant at about the same time as London. In the twelfth century, Paris had been no larger than half a dozen other French commercial and industrial centers, notable perhaps only for being less specialized in any way than the others. But in the thirteenth century Paris grew so rapidly that it became five or six times as large as any other French city, and this growth cannot be accounted for by any equivalent growth in exports. It was marked, however, just as we would expect, by an amazing growth in Paris' own local economy; that is, in the comprehensiveness of what Paris provided for its own people and its own enterprises.

Ancient Rome's first explosive growth—at least its first momentous episode—occurred at the beginning of the fourth century B.C. The city fathers tried to stop the great growth of the city at that time with programs of emigration and by discouraging immigration. But the mighty economic force exerted by the growth of Rome's local economy was not halted. I say growth of Rome's "local economy" because, as far as is known, this expansion cannot be accounted for by growth of Rome's exports at the time. The surge has long puzzled historians for that reason and also because it cannot be explained by conquest. Rome's first conquests—of Latium and then swiftly of the Italian peninsula—followed this episode. As Rome did, the ancient city-states typically rose like rockets to sudden size and power after earlier stages of gradual, relatively slow and obscure growth.

Wherever cities grow at all, they experience growth explosions of astonishing power. Villages and towns do not grow this way; but then they do not become cities, either. Even small cities that have grown only briefly, and then have stagnated decisively, have had at least one period of extraordinarily abrupt and rapid economic growth tucked into their histories. Often we can tell just when it happened by observing the architectural period of most of the little city's buildings; so much was built in a single swift interval.

Although cities do not import less when they replace imports than they otherwise would, they do import less from some places as they shift to new purchases from others. What happens to cities that lose exports when their customer cities begin producing the same things for themselves? Stagnant cities lose out.* They fail to develop new exports that compensate for the losses. Creative cities do develop new exports that take the place of the old. Indeed, replacements of old imports and shifts to new ones by other cities afford to creative cities great new opportunities. Their own new and unprecedented exports can find new and growing markets.

The Import-Replacing Multiplier Effect

The city where I grew up, Scranton, Pennsylvania, experienced its first and only episode of rapid import replacing and explosive growth from about 1905 to 1920. Scranton's growth, at that time, was due to a combination of two causes. Its exports were growing.† It was also producing locally many humdrum former imports: beer

---

*As they also do when they lose export work that has become obsolete, and export industries that are transplanted into the countryside.

† Especially coal, textiles and a correspondence school that educated people by mail. The textile plants, for the most part, were transplanted industries, located in Scranton because the wives and daughters of the coal miners provided a pool of very cheap labor. The correspondence school had begun locally; its early students were chiefly miners who had had to leave school to work at a young age but were studying at home to qualify themselves as foremen, supervisors and mining engineers. To such courses of study the school added hundreds of others, and in time enrolled students from many countries of the world.

(legally until Prohibition, illegally afterwards), stationery, tombstones, stock brokerage services, mattresses, potato chips (called Saratoga chips because that was where they had first come from) and so on. But other goods and services, apart from locally produced former imports, were rapidly added into Scranton's local economy at that time too. Among them, I am glad to say—because they meant much to me as a child—were a zoo, a museum of natural history and a central public reference library. Several hospitals were added, several stuffy but imposing clubs, several department stores, such city departments as fire fighting and public health services, and a trolley-car system. With the exception of the trolley cars, which were among the first in the United States (and which were later painted fuchsia or silver or sky blue and had flowered chintz seat covers), these goods and services were already familiar in many other cities. But however familiar elsewhere, they were new to Scranton. They had not even been imported. Small cities, during explosive growth, almost always "round themselves out" with various goods and services already familiar in other cities but not previously available locally. The rounding out is apt to include a broadened range of financial, legal, warehousing and printing services too.

The economy grows in still another way: when imports are replaced, a city is almost sure to produce—for its own market—more of those things than it had previously imported. This happens because the very act of replacing former imports creates more jobs. Once Scranton began to produce tombstones, there were more jobs in Scranton for tombstone workers, and thus, eventually, more customers for tombstones. Once Chicago began making lamps for itself, there were more people to use lamps there. After San Francisco began producing jam and jelly instead of importing preserves from Boston, San Francisco contained more people to eat jam and jelly. Such increases in the local market will amount to little if a city is replacing

only one or two of its imports. But when it is replacing
many kinds in rapid succession or simultaneously, the new
markets in the city for each item amount to a considerable
increase over the previous markets. Just as export growth
creates a multiplier effect, so do replacements of imports.
But there is a vital difference between the two effects.

In the case of an export-multiplier effect, some of the
new imports earned by the export growth go directly back
into the export work, the way ore imported into Pittsburgh goes directly into exported steel, or a high proportion of the textiles imported into New York go into exported clothing. The other imports earned by exports go
into a city's local economy; but even so, many of them go
indirectly into the export work that earns them. In the
case of an import-replacing multiplier effect, however,
none of the different (seemingly additional) imports go
either directly or indirectly into exports from the city. All
are added to the growing local economy. The greater volume of the locally produced jelly, lamps or tombstones—
relative to the imports they replaced—is one result. The
rounding out of the local economy is another. And because the employed population is growing, there are of
course increases in production of things the city was already producing for itself anyway, before the import replacing; say, houses, ice cream, grade-school education.

In sum, the multiplier effect from import replacing is
far more potent than the multiplier effect from growth of
exports, because all shifted imports go to swell the local
economy. An equivalent amount of imports earned by
export growth do not. After a city has experienced an
episode of import replacing and import shifting, its local
economy is thus much larger than it was before the
episode: not only larger absolutely but also *larger in proportion to its exports and imports.*

Accurate statistics do not exist today on ratios between
the export economies and local economies of cities, especially large cities. Many attempts have been made to

compile such statistics but they contain a great deal of guesswork for the reason that the statistics are collected according to categories of activities (e.g., services, transportation, manufacturing, construction, entertainment, "other"), not according to actual destinations of the goods and services. The statistics usually also contain a major flaw: a poor job, if any, is done separating local producers' goods and services from exported goods and services. The division usually made is that between misleadingly named "non-basic" activities, meaning goods and services for the local population, and equally misleadingly named "basic" activities. The latter usually means exports and producers' goods and services supplied to exporters; but in practice there is immense confusion between these latter and producers' goods and services supplied to producers of local consumer goods. Nevertheless, rough and even ill-conceived as available statistics are, they indicate that, as a rule, the larger a city the larger is its local economy in proportion to its exports and imports.*

Import replacing and its potent multiplier explain why large cities have local economies proportionately so large. For those who wish to see the import-replacing process shown graphically, along with the resulting proportionate changes among the parts of a city's economy, a series of diagrams appears in Section II of the Appendix.

The question arises as to why all cities do not replace their imports from time to time. Why do some, like Scranton, do so significantly only once while others, like London,

---

*For instance, one study of "basic" and "non-basic" work shows the following numbers of "non-basic" jobs for every ten in these cities' "basic" economies: New York, 21; Detroit, 12; Cincinnati, 17; Albuquerque, 10; Madison, 8; Oshkosh, 6. The cities are listed in declining order of population. If local producers' goods and services supplied to export work were carefully separated from the exports themselves, the differences would be much greater and more startling.

do so again and again? The answer is that if a city stops generating new exports after an episode of import replacing, it will not earn many more imports to replace. It will not have the grist, so to speak, for another episode. Anything that halts the export-generating processes of a city ultimately kills the import-replacing process too.

When cities that have already had import-replacing episodes in their past, and thus already have large and comprehensive local economies, go on to replace imports rapidly yet again, they garner an economic margin in their local economies for adding extraordinary, even unprecedented, goods and services. It was just such cities, already big but growing rapidly, that first made important use of electricity, telephones, indoor plumbing, and so on. It was just such cities that took the lead in overcoming epidemics. It will probably be in just such cities that current acute practical problems are first overcome—and in which new ones will come to light. Large margins for new local goods and services are necessary to solve the big problems that become acute in such cities at times when the same problems are still only chronic in other places.

There is also room for extraordinary growth of learning and the arts in the large local economies of big cities. Scholars and artists are not out hoeing corn for the same reason that people administering antitetanus shots are not out hoeing corn either. Shakespeare's theater found room in a city economy that had grown room for it. This does not explain Shakespeare's genius, but it does explain why there was scope for that genius in the local economy of London rather than in Newcastle or, for that matter, in the local economy of Stratford-on-Avon.

The proportionately large local economies of large cities also explain why there is room in them for old crafts and old institutions even though so many new things are added. When the motion pictures come to an inert town or a stagnant little city, the opera house closes or converts to motion pictures; there is not room in the economy for both. When television comes, the motion picture theater may close. But cities that replace many imports from time to time have room for jumbles of old and new things. At the very time when the greatest numbers of new things are being added, the local economy is also expanding most rapidly.

Although there are extraordinary opportunities to add unprecedented new goods and services into the local economies of already large and rapidly growing cities, the opportunities of course are not necessarily put to use wisely or productively. They can be frittered away and often have been. Perhaps the biblical Tower of Babel is as good a symbol as any: once upon a time a city achieved an immense opportunity for extraordinary work in its local economy, but misused it only on sterile vainglory. Nevertheless, the wastes of great economic opportunities in cities do not negate the fact that such opportunities for new and creative goods and services do arise. And at some times, in some places, people have used the opportunities well: to bring useful and wonderfully creative achievements into the world.

The Explosions

Let us go back to examining a young city that has just begun its growth. It is generating new exports from its meager local economy, as described in Chapter Four. It grows steadily but gradually, along with the steady but gradual growth of its exports. No matter how gradual this growth, if the city continues to generate new exports, sooner or later it must build up a rather large and diverse quantity of imports. At some point, inevitably, the time arrives when production of a few of those imports is economically feasible within the little city.

If people there are already doing work to which the

new work can be added, if they can find space in the right places for producing some of the former imports locally, if they can get capital, and if they are not either overtly or covertly prohibited from replacing imports (as people in colonial economies often are, for example), some of the imports will soon be replaced by local work. And now the city grows from this new work, at the same time shifting its imports and adding more local work from the import-replacing multiplier effect. Therefore the city has become a place where production of a few more of its various imports is economically feasible. Again replacements are made. Again some of the city's imports shift, and the city grows. Therefore the city has become a place where local production is now feasible that would have been out of the question when the process started. Torrents of various imports are rapidly replaced. The growth of the city has become so swift by this time that some of the very imports to which the city shifted earlier in this episode are themselves being replaced later in the episode. This is a process, in short, that inherently builds on itself and accelerates. An import-replacing episode, once it is vigorously under way, is so mighty an economic force that it does not seem to halt until it has reached its own conclusion.

But inevitably, the time comes when so many imports have been replaced that the current imports of the city have shifted overwhelmingly to: a) rurally produced goods; b) goods and services for which the city still affords a market too small to be worth producing locally for; and c) goods and services the city still lacks the technical capacity to produce. Suppose, during this process, the city's exports have been growing. Then imports have not only been shifting their composition; they have been increasing too—certainly in quantity and probably in variety. In this case, either the candidates among the imports for local production have become more numerous than they otherwise would have been; or else the moment has been hastened when the production of some of them becomes economically feasible. Thus the swift growth of a city's exports can prolong an episode of import replacing and explosive growth. Or the export growth can shorten the intervals between bursts so one burst follows quickly upon another.

During the great growth explosions of New York City in the last century and the first quarter of this century, the city's exports were also growing rapidly. The great explosions of growth in Tokyo since the war and of such cities as Hong Kong, Moscow and Milan have surely been intensified and prolonged because exports from those cities have been rapidly growing too. After an episode of explosive growth has died down, a city has in its local economy much new potential export work, as will be explained in the next chapter.

If the city does indeed continue to generate new exports, it will not only compensate for its own inevitable losses of exports—which must occur in any case—but it will also build up new funds of replaceable imports. Then, in time, the city will experience another episode of import replacing, import shifting, and exceedingly rapid growth.

So what we have here, if this summary is correct, is another reciprocating system of growth, though more complex than the one described in the preceding chapter. Its workings can be stated this way: a city builds up its imports and thus becomes capable of replacing many of them. By doing so it becomes capable of generating more exports. It thus builds up imports and becomes capable of replacing many of them. By doing so it becomes capable of generating more exports. It thus builds up imports . . . and so on.

Few sights are more flabbergasting than the sheer quantity and diversity of work and working places concentrated in a great city. How do such immense concentrations of work come to be? The answer, I think, is in the working of this remarkable reciprocating system.

Import Replacing and Economic Growth Rates

One consequence of replacing imports, a consequence which I mentioned at the beginning of this chapter, is the expansion of the sum total of all economic activity. I would now like to suggest that this process may be, in fact, the chief cause of economic expansion. There are several reasons for thinking so.

A national economy's rate of expansion—conventionally expressed as a percentage growth rate from year to year—is a sum of economic growth in all parts of the economy, less any contractions of economic activity during the same period. It is a net rate. Some places in the nation, such as stagnant regions or declining cities, may show no growth at all; in any case, their expansion is less than average. They have dragged the rate down. Other places—cities with the most rapidly growing economies—have a much higher rate of economic growth than the average. They have raised the net rate. Of course the same cities are not continually and steadily doing most to raise the net growth rate—only those growing explosively at the time. Not all the cities of a rapidly expanding economy are simultaneously replacing imports rapidly. The economy is a little like a corn popper in which not all the kernels are popping simultaneously; but all the time corn is popping.

A circumstance still more persuasive than comparative growth rates within a nation suggests that the process of import replacing may be the chief cause of economic expansion. Consider the fact that when cities rapidly replace imports, three direct results follow:

1. The sum total of economic activity expands rapidly.
2. Markets for rural goods increase rapidly because of shifts in the composition of city imports.
3. Jobs in cities grow very rapidly.

These in turn are the three major characteristics of an economy with a high growth rate—and they are rather strange characteristics. For example, if there were no real world against which to test theories, one might plausibly suppose that numbers of agricultural workers would increase in an economy where solvent markets for agricultural goods are increasing very rapidly. But just the opposite happens in the real world. Great surges of agricultural expansion coincide with great surges in city jobs —not great surges in rural jobs.* Rural jobs, in fact, decline proportionately, and even absolutely, at precisely the times of great surges in a nation's agricultural production; of course, as we have seen, the workers who do remain in agriculture become more productive.

Now, because it has long been observed that the three changes I have listed occur simultaneously in an economy, if they occur at all, many attempts have been made to explain how they cause one another. One such recent attempt, put forward because past explanations are clearly unsatisfactory, is the study, *Why Growth Rates Differ*, published in 1967 by the Brookings Institution of Washington, D.C. The study notes accurately that the rapid economic expansion of the European Common Market in the 1950s was accompanied by large movements of workers from agriculture into industry. It also points out that the relatively slow growth rate of the economy in the United States during the same period was accompanied by only small movements of workers into industry from agriculture. (Many workers in the United States at this time moved from agriculture into idleness and makework, a point the study evades.) The study then goes on to pro-

*This, of course, is not at all the same as saying that great surges of agricultural expansion necessarily coincide with great surges in city *populations*. The populations of cities with stagnant economies can grow mightily as people move from poverty-stricken countrysides to idleness in cities, a situation that can occur in highly developed—but stagnating —economies as surely as in underdeveloped, stagnant economies. It is occurring widely, for example, in the United States now.

pose this connection: an economy's growth rate is largely determined by how many workers it has in agricultural jobs of low productivity, hence how many workers it has available for other work. But then what of India? Or Mississippi, or Egypt, or Portugal, or Peru?

The fallacy lies in the assumption that events happening together somehow cause one another. Yet events can all be different effects of a common cause. I am proposing that this trio of events is caused by rapid local production of former imports in cities. If this is so, it follows that the development and prosperity of underdeveloped, have-not countries, including the development and prosperity of their agriculture, must depend upon replacements of their city imports. This means replacements of many present imports from currently more highly developed economies, as well as replacements of imports that cities in such countries must generate, as exports, to one another.

If Japan had depended upon increasing her exports of silk, or other raw material, instead of rapidly producing in her own cities many of the imports the silk bought, Japan would today be a most backward and poverty-stricken country. The shifts of imports in Japan's cities have been so heavily to goods that cannot be produced in the cities that these imports also include much that cannot be produced anywhere else in Japan. That is why Japan can be a modern industrial nation, although it has hardly any iron and must import most of its fuels too. Japan does not waste its fund of imports on things its cities have been able to replace, nor does it go without those things.

The Parentage of Embryonic Cities

When I was discussing, in Chapter Four, how cities begin growing, I left hanging the question of how an embryonic city first creates its original export work. Also unanswered was the question of how an embryonic city happens to have an expanding market for its early export work. These questions are crucial. An embryonic city must have an expanding market for its initial exports; otherwise, its local economy cannot expand either, and so cannot generate new export work.

By definition, the earliest cities had only the rural world and each other as customers for their initial exports. At first they must have exchanged with each other only the natural resources from their own territories. As their exports to one another grew, so must their local economies have grown—very gradually, very slowly—and so must their imports from the surrounding rural peoples have grown gradually and slowly. Then the embryonic earliest cities must have exchanged some of the craft goods made within their own communities. The craft goods could eventually have been replaced in the importing cities, that is, the little pre-agricultural cities could have engaged in mutual economic borrowing. There must have been many such instances when craft imports were replaced. Then, once the wild-food imports from the rural world were replaced and cities grew explosively (for the time), the formation of new cities would no longer be quite so chancy as before, nor their initial growth so slow. For from this time on, new embryonic cities could find ready-made expanding markets for their initial export work in older, explosively growing cities, just as in our own times and in historical times, older cities have provided the expanding markets for the initial exports of embryonic cities. Let us trace some of these relationships backward in time to see how the economies of new cities are born of the markets in older ones.

London has afforded an expanding market for the early export work of many younger cities—from Hong Kong to New York. The London market has also sometimes helped revive stagnant cities. Copenhagen, for example, was a poor and stagnant city in the early nineteenth century, and Denmark was then one of the world's poorest countries.

Starvation and disease had kept the country's population almost static for seven centuries. Occasionally, during the long poverty, there were fleeting periods of better times, when now and again the Lubeck or the Amsterdam market bought Danish grain, horses and bullocks. But these gains were temporary; no new work to speak of, no new streams of Danish exports, were built upon this trade. (Small wonder, for the trade was usually handled by rural landlords who had set up tight trading monopolies in the ports and, for anyone but these merchant-landlords, economic opportunity was nonexistent.) In the eighteenth century, Denmark had even lost most of this rudimentary trade owing to the growth of cheaper and more plentiful Dutch and English agricultural produce, and her people were on the thin edge of starvation.

Denmark could produce food, plenty of it, but it was not doing so because it lacked the city growth processes we have been discussing. There was no mechanism at work by which the economy could expand. Then, in the second quarter of the nineteenth century, London's explosive growth and its great shifts of imports afforded a new chance. Once again, Danish produce was in demand and this time the goods were chiefly processed in Copenhagen and shipped through Copenhagen, and in Copenhagen the new opportunity for city growth was at last well used. From its supply work to the trade and the processing, the city generated new exports—and indeed is still doing so today. In a short time, Copenhagen began to produce locally some of the imports it was earning, shifted its own imports, and provided an expanding market, itself, for rural Denmark and for many other places.

In the United States, the westward economic expansion has been conventionally depicted as a rural movement. In fact, the westward expansion included the establishment of scores of settlements that grew rapidly into cities. Those cities, when their growth began, did not find the expanding markets for their initial exports in the wilderness or in the cabins of poor pioneers and homesteaders. They found their markets—their economic reasons for being—in older cities of the Eastern seaboard and abroad. The rural West, in its turn, found its markets in these Western cities.

Sometimes the older cities of the East and of Europe provided expanding markets at one remove for embryonic frontier cities. This, for instance, was how Detroit found an expanding market for its initial export of flour. The flour was shipped mainly to the West Indies. But the reason the market for North American flour in the West Indies had grown, and was still growing, was that the market for such products of the West Indies as limes (for the British Navy), rum and turpentine had grown, and was still growing, in England. This particular three-cornered trade, as it was called, with the West Indies at one of its corners, gave many an American city its start, beginning with colonial Philadelphia. But behind such trade lay import shifts and expanding markets in English cities, especially London.

The earlier effects of London's great import shifts in Shakespeare's time preceded even the Pilgrims to New England. Samaset, the Indian chief who amazed the Pilgrims by addressing them in broken English, had already put in a summer's work with an English fleet fishing off Cape Cod, most probably for the London market. Samaset coveted steel hatchets for his people. Apparently these had been refused him and his men by the English fishermen. The Indians were hopeful that the new little settlement at Plymouth would become a source of hatchets for them, and so it did. After the first hard years, Plymouth paid off its debts for the Atlantic passage and for supplies bought on credit, and the settlement went on to prosper owing to London's expanding market for Plymouth's exports of beaver pelts (bought mostly from the Indians) and clapboards. A lot of clapboards manufactured in Plymouth and in embryonic Boston must have helped feed the Great Fire of London.

But of course London itself was once an embryonic city and, far from providing an expanding market for others, could not have begun its growth as a city without an expanding market for its own initial exports. During the shrouded years between the fall of Rome and the emergence late in the tenth century of the embryonic medieval cities, London was probably a very rudimentary trading settlement. Bede described it in the eighth century as the "mart of many nations resorting to it by sea and land." Probably its trade was seasonal, like that of Dragor in Denmark at this time and the rude Baltic ports where furs and minerals seem to have been exchanged, but only at certain times of the year, set by custom. The line between bartering and raiding must often have been unclear to the people who fared among these settlements, and it must have been a line frequently crossed. London's chief goods for barter were probably salt fish. Trade among such settlements in the eighth and ninth centuries must have been rather like the earliest trade among the earliest cities: small, increasing as yet infinitesimally if at all, and consisting of exchange in almost nothing except a few territorial natural resources, sometimes processed but usually not.

How slow the growth of Europe's trading settlements (including London) might have been if, like the earliest cities, they had continued to have only each other and the rural world as markets is a question that cannot be answered—as is the question whether these rudimentary trading posts would, indeed, ever have grown into cities at all. Dragor, for instance, did not. But fortunately for the economic life of Europe, these eighth- and ninth-century trading settlements did not, as it turned out, have to recapitulate the chancy first growth of the earliest cities with no older cities to serve as expanding markets. For in the tenth and eleventh centuries Venice had become an explosively growing city with an expanding market for raw materials from the west and north of Europe. It was this market that made possible the relatively swift economic growth of Europe that followed. Venice required materials such as leather (especially cordovan, processed and handled in the settlement of Cordoba in Spain); tin, some of which probably moved through London; the Friesian cloths of Flanders; wool, moving not only into and through London, but into and through many another trade depot; perhaps wine as well as wool from Paris and its vicinity; furs from Germany and Muscovy; and amber, that ancient Baltic resource. Some of this trade was three-cornered: London, for example, supplied fish to expanding little inland Continental cities; Cordoba supplied some of its leather to the now expanding little market in London.* But behind all this lay the import-shifting, explosively expanding market of Venice. It was this trade, stretching through the ports and inland depots of north Italy, up into the Continent westward and north, curving east again through the North Sea and the Baltic, which was pursued by those tenth-century vagabond traders, described by Pirenne as being drawn from the riffraff of Europe.

But of course Venice at one time, far from providing an expanding market for embryonic cities and, through them, for the rural world too, had itself been an embryonic city. Where did it find its own initial expanding markets? The poor, fish-eating, marsh-dwelling, perhaps fugitive Veneti of the fifth and sixth centuries gathered salt. Almost surely the first significant and expanding market they found for this salt—and probably, soon, for timber too—was in Constantinople. Venetian merchants took to trading with the old cities of Islam and long continued to do so, although this trade with the infidels was regarded as a scandal by the rest of European Christendom.

* Which is why the early leather workers of the city were called "cordwainers." Later the term came to mean the makers of fine shoes, but at first it included all craftsmen using fine, soft leather.

Constantinople, where Venice found an expanding market, was not always so. Once it too had required expanding markets in older cities. Its customer cities—not only for the government services that had been transplanted from Rome to Constantinople (which was previously the old, small city of Byzantium), but also for its commercial services—were other cities of the Roman Empire. Rome had provided the initial expanding market for some of these. Others were older than Rome, but even some of these had had stagnated economies revived by import shifting in Rome, much as Copenhagen was revived by import shifting in London. Rome was a mighty market for imports, the mightiest in the history of the world until recent times. "Into her three ports of Ostia, Portus and the emporium beneath the Aventine," wrote Carcopino in *Daily Life in Ancient Rome*, "poured the tiles and bricks, the wines and fruits of Italy; the corn of Egypt and Africa; the oil of Spain; the venison, the timbers and the wool of Gaul; the cured meats of Baetica; the dates of the oases; the marbles of Tuscany, of Greece, and of Numidia; the porphyries of the Arabian Desert; the lead, silver and copper of the Iberian Peninsula; the ivory of the Syrtes and the Mauretanias, the gold of Dalmatia and of Dacia; the tin of the Cassiterides, now the Scilly Isles, and the amber of the Baltic; the papyri of the valley of the Nile; the glass of Phoenicia and of Syria; the stuffs of the Orient; the incense of Arabia; the spices, the corals, and the gems of India; the silks of the Far East."

What immense, and repeated, episodes of import replacing and import shifting in Rome must have lain behind that flow. We get a faint hint of their magnitude from the establishments of the foreign shipfitters on the Piazzale delle Corporazioni of Ostia, who had evidently transplanted work to the market, rather like people who established branch plants in Los Angeles. As Carcopino lists them, there were fitters of Alexandria; fitters of Narbonne and Arles in Gaul; of Cagliari and Porto-Torres in Sardinia;

Carthage; Hippo-Diarrhytus, the modern Bizerta; Curbis, now Courba; Missua, now Sidi Daud; Gummi, now Bordj Cedria; Musluvium, now Sidi Rekane; and Sabratha, the ivory port of the desert.

Not only Rome, but many another city of the Roman Empire replaced imports and, just as happens in cities of our own time, many of the replaced imports became exports for the cities that had replaced them. The Russian classicist and historian, Michael Rostovtzeff, tells, in *Rome*, of the earthenware vessels of eastern design that spread over the Roman world. At first they were imported into Italy from Greece and Asia Minor. But before the second century B.C. these imports had been replaced in Italy and had already become specialties of, and exports from, Italian cities, particularly those of north Italy. "In the first century A.D. southern Gaul begins to compete," Rostovtzeff continues, and "in the second half of the century the manufacture moves farther north, and reaches the Rhine in the second century. These vessels now conquer not only the northern and northeastern markets but Italy as well; and simultaneously Asia Minor is producing the same article after the same patterns for the southern and southeastern markets. In the second century A.D. all the provinces, both East and West, are turning out in immense numbers the earthenware lamps which had once been almost a monopoly of the workshops in north Italy. . . . Indeed local imitations of the products from great centers of industry crop up everywhere."

Just as happens in our own times, cities that did not generate new exports lost out economically as a consequence of import replacing in customer cities, although during the centuries of the most vigorous import replacing in the Roman world, the total economy was rapidly expanding, just as we would expect. But during this movement, Greek manufactures, once widely exported, "disappeared almost entirely from the world's markets." The cities of Greece were generating no new exports; they had stagnated.

In the second century A.D., when the wealth of the empire seemed to be at its height, an ominous stagnation was actually setting in almost everywhere, and development rates in the cities of the western empire must have been in process of declining to almost nothing. "Nothing now," notes Rostovtzeff of the later empire, "except articles of luxury accessible to few, finds a distant market." What this means, of course, is that new work was no longer being added to old, new exports were no longer being generated in the cities. And of course there were then no more new imports of any significance for customer cities to replace. The little movements at the hubs had ceased, and the great wheels of economic life were grinding to a halt.*

---

*Not only did creation of new goods and services cease, but improvements were no longer being made to old products. Of the later empire, for example, Rostovtzeff notes, "The quality [of manufactured products] grows inferior; there is less both of mechanical skill and beauty. Technique becomes monotonous and somewhat old fashioned. . . . It is important also to note this: ruins and tombs have yielded up objects of Roman production by the hundred thousand, and these warrant the assertion that practically no new discovery was made in technique: on the contrary, many earlier discoveries fell into disuse."

Nor did new settlements established in distant provinces at the height of the empire's power and extent become self-generating cities, as so many earlier Roman provincial centers had been for at least a time. They remained, rather, centers of administration only, government company towns. When Roman administration was withdrawn from Britain, for example, the Roman settlements there almost immediately collapsed. They had developed no other significant economic reasons for being.

Unwin, commenting on the fact that cities were no longer centers of economic opportunity (as they once had been) in the western empire, notes that their inhabitants had become so oppressed by the official taskmasters that they "had to be prohibited from fleeing into the country." And of course he was speaking of "free" inhabitants, not slaves.

But let us go back to Rome before its abysmal stagnation and economic decay. Once Rome itself had been an embryonic city which needed expanding markets for its own initial exports. When Rome was still only an inconsequential little settlement occupied by herdsmen (who were possibly also raiders) on a hill protected by ravines—the hill that was to become the Palatine—looking across at another hill occupied by the Sabines, the Etruscans had a dozen flourishing cities in Etruria to the north. The three most ancient of these cities were on the Tyrrhenian coast; the younger were inland. Presumably those cities traded with each other. Certainly they traded with older cities of Phoenicia, Cyprus and Assyria, and with Urartu, a once-rich city-state in the area of Mount Ararat in Asia Minor. These Etruscan cities were Rome's first customers, her first markets of any consequence. How did they come to provide expanding markets for Rome? I suspect it began with import replacing by the Etruscans, for they did replace imports. They had once, for example, imported metal work from Urartu, and possibly from other cities also. But subsequently, the Etruscans had become great metal workers on their own behalf. After mining pockets of ore near their cities, they proceeded to undertake large iron-mining operations on the nearby island of Elba. When the Etruscans shifted imports, their cities must have become expanding markets for materials they had previously bought either in much lesser amounts or not at all. And it is then that Rome would have found its initial export opportunities. But what specific goods or services could Rome have supplied? My guess is leather—cattle hides. Embryonic Rome was well qualified to process and dispatch cattle hides. The very word for money in Latin, *pecunia*, comes from the word for cattle, *pecus*.

What I am saying is that every city has a direct economic ancestry, a literal economic parentage, in a still older city or cities. New cities do not arise by spontaneous generation. The spark of city economic life is passed on from older cities to younger. It lives on today in cities whose ancestors have long since gone to dust. New York, far from having sprung from the Erie Canal (a mere artifact of New York), is more likely the great-great-great-great-grandcity of Urartu, say, by a descent that traces back through London, Venice, Constantinople, Rome, and Vetulonia or Tarquinii, oldest of the Etruscan cities. These links of life may extend—perilously tenuous at times but unbroken—backward through the cities of Crete, Phoenicia, Egypt, the Indus, Babylonia, Sumeria, Mesopotamia, back to Çatal Hüyük itself and beyond, to the unknown ancestors of Çatal Hüyük.

6

How Large Cities
Generate Exports

We shall now turn back to the subject of how new exports and new exporting organizations arise in cities. In this chapter we shall be concerned with how this process occurs in cities that have already grown explosively and whose local economies are thus already large.

If one leafs through the pages of a classified telephone directory in a large city, one of course encounters a vast variety of producers' goods and services. A sampling from the beginning of the P's in the index to the New York City directory conveys the idea: Packing and filling services; Packers' (meat) equipment and supplies; Paging and signaling systems; Paint brush cleaning; Painters (smokestack); Pajama trimmings; Pallet racks; Pamphlet preparation; Pancake machines; Panel coils; Panic exit devices; Pantographic engraving; Papaya products; Paper bag machinery; Paper cones; Paper drilling machines·

Parking area maintenance; Patent development; Pavement marking; Payroll preparation; Pearl dipping equipment; Perforated metals. . . .

In cities with many organizations supplying so many bits and pieces of work, it is possible to start a new exporting organization while depending upon others for many of the goods and services one needs. Henry Ford did so when he started the Ford Motor Company. He bought his wheels from one supplier, his engines from another, parts of the car bodies from others, lamps from another, and so on. Later on, his company became unusually self-sufficient but at first it depended heavily on work done by other producers in Detroit.

An acquaintance of mine who makes instrumentation amplifiers and amplifier supplies in a Long Island suburb of New York and who sells these tools all over the country had unusual freedom a few years ago to choose a location. To understand why, it is necessary to go into his history a little. Some ten years earlier, he had broken away from his job at Hughes Aircraft in Los Angeles and with two partners had started a company in the Los Angeles local economy; they supplied aircraft manufacturers with electronic transducers for wing de-icers. The company built up its work successfully, and in time it was coveted by a large but infertile corporation. The partners agreed to sell their company for a good price but, since the purchaser wanted to minimize competition, part of the agreement of sale was that the three partners—who dissolved their partnership upon selling—each agreed not to start another company like the old one anywhere, nor to start in business again in California.

So my acquaintance could start another company producing something different, anywhere but in California. He had capital from his part of the sale price. He decided to produce the amplifiers, and to sell them nationally from the first. Thus he did not have to be concerned with a local market for his product and he could choose any location that struck his fancy as long as it provided the goods and services his new company would need to get started. During a three-month scouting trip he visited more than twenty cities with the result that he found his choices more limited than he had anticipated. Besides Los Angeles and San Francisco which were off-limits, only Chicago, Baltimore, Boston and New York afforded the goods and services—some of them highly technical—that he required. But in addition he needed local goods and services that were more ordinary. He had to be in a place, he told me, where there are competent businesses to prepare sales catalogs and leaflets. He needed a service to supply temporary office help when he enjoyed a rush of inquiries. He needed a service supplying traveling salesmen to supplement his own sales efforts and help follow them up until he was well enough established to have built up his own sales force.

We might say of this way of launching a new exporting enterprise that the exporter adds an export to other people's local work. The relevant local work consists of pre-existing divisions of labor. To be sure, the new export work proliferates subsequent new divisions of labor of its own. But to begin with, it ordinarily depends heavily on local producers' goods and services. Sometimes after only a first growth explosion—if it has been a large and prolonged one—new exports can be generated in this way. But ordinarily a city must have had several growth explosions, and must already have produced many other exporting businesses by other means before its local producers' goods and services are sufficiently varied and numerous for new exports to depend heavily upon them.

In medieval cities, the process of adding new exports to other people's local work does not seem to have come significantly into play until the fifteenth century and then only in large and varied cities as London, Antwerp and Frankfurt. In those cities, the first organizations to arise in this way seem to have been new trading services which were to increase the number of long-distance merchants. The city merchants of the Middle Ages, before this new process came into play, were successors to the vagabond traders of tenth-century Europe; but as their work had grown in subsequent centuries, their divisions of labor had multiplied and they became men with large organizations of their own. They had warehouses, counting houses, resident agents, traveling agents, and financial shares in ships or in individual voyages. They financed craftsmen who supplied them with various wares until the craftsmen, when they became well established themselves, took to finding other customers or exporting on their own behalf, or adding new and different work to their old. Then the merchants financed more craftsmen. Unless one became an exporting craftsman—a merchant craftsman—or else came of a merchant family or married into one, it was increasingly difficult in medieval Europe to set oneself up *de novo* as a merchant. In most small cities it continued to be difficult—or impossible—through Renaissance times.

But abruptly in the early or mid-fifteenth century this seems to have changed in such cities as London, Antwerp and Frankfurt. These cities had developed, by that time, enough independent organizations in their local economies so that one could become a merchant by drawing upon the goods and services of those same local organizations, instead of supplying them for oneself or financing organizations to create the goods and services one needed. That is, one could buy from already established, independent craftsmen on credit and pay them when the goods were sold; one could contract for warehouse space in other people's buildings and cargo space in other people's ships; one could use colleagues in other cities as agents and serve as their agents in return.

A treatise written at the beginning of the sixteenth century by an Englishman who deplored these parvenu merchants is quoted by Unwin. "The breeding of so many merchants in London, risen out of poor men's sons, hath been a marvelous destruction to the whole realm," he complained. "About fifty years ago such young merchants began to increase in number. . . ." What the writer of the treatise especially disliked was that owing to the competition of the new, young merchants, many of the "rich old merchants" had stopped trading during the latter half of the fifteenth century, and instead had concentrated upon one of the activities they had formerly added to their trading work: financing other enterprises. Instead of just financing craftsmen, now they were financing, increasingly, the new class of merchants. As the complaining treatise put it, the old merchants "occupy their money by exchange . . . which is plain usury." Thus the old merchants, withdrawing from trade, had become merchant bankers, the indirect economic ancestors of the investment bankers and commercial bankers of our own day, and the direct economic ancestors of today's merchant bankers. From the viewpoint of the new merchant class, "risen out of poor men's sons," this meant that another kind of autonomous enterprise was available in the local economies of their cities: the counting house. Now a merchant need not have a counting house of his own; he could use a bank. And in the cities there were now independent lawyers upon whom to draw. How contract making and litigation flourished. And with them flourished higher education for these secular purposes, added to what had begun as clerical education in the religious sense.

Nowadays, the more local enterprises in a city, the greater the inherent opportunity for exports of many different kinds to arise there. In Baltimore, as in New York, certain science-based exports can be added in this way. But in Baltimore it is hard to start a new magazine for export, while in New York such an enterprise can be started, and frequently is, in the editor's living room, because of all the relevant divisions of labor readily available outside that living room.

While all but the largest enterprises in a modern city are apt to use local producers' goods and services, new exporters depend especially heavily, for a reason, upon this local supply. To produce something for a city's own local market, and at the same time build up a reasonably complete organization to do the work, without extreme dependence upon other local suppliers, is not necessarily difficult. Even small towns, where few producers' goods and services are locally available, can and do have their own drugstores selling within the town, sometimes their own newspapers, and so on. But to export something from its place of production adds many difficulties. It is not as easy to find distant customers and distribute to them as it is to find local customers—or to be found by the local customers—and to serve them.

When somebody plans to start a new organization that will export its work from the start, think what an inherently difficult task he is attempting. He must start production (with all the trial and error it implies) and at the same time arrange to export the work produced. If, also at the same time, he has to build up a relatively self-sufficient organization—as far as its local needs are concerned—he is taking on a superhuman task. At least, we can assume it to be superhuman, for it is almost never successfully accomplished. The task is tailored to human capabilities only by leaving as much as possible of the organization's work to be done by already experienced outsiders within quick and easy reach. Ford's organization could not master the upholstery business, the lamp business, the wheel business and the engine business at the same moment it was trying to find distant customers for its cars and distribute to those distant customers. This heavy dependence on other people's local work when one tries to become an exporter *de novo* reduces the amount of capital required. But it is not just a way of managing with relatively small capitalization. The need for those local goods and services is inherent in the practical difficulty of the process. This is evidently not well understood by people with great command of capital. And one can understand that they are apt to discount the need for the local goods and services because so often these are obscure and are produced by small and obscure organizations. Yet even when the local organizations are only filling little chinks in new export work, they are indispensable.

A recent experience of the Rockefellers in India illustrates this point. The Rockefellers, early in the 1960s, decided to build a factory in India to produce plastic intrauterine loops for birth control. At the same time they were undertaking to combat the Indian birth rate,* they also wanted to curb the migration of rural Indians to cities. A way to do this, they thought, was to set an example of village industry, placing new industry in small settlements instead of cities. The location they chose for the factory, then, was a small town named Etawah in highly rural Uttar state. It seemed plausible that the factory could as well be located one place in India as another. The machinery had to be imported anyway and the loops were to be exported throughout India. The factory was to be small, for with modern machinery even a small factory could begin by turning out 14,000 loops a day. The work had been rationalized into simple, easily taught tasks; no pre-existing, trained labor pool was required. The problem of hooking up to electric power had been explored and judged feasible. Capital was sufficient, and the scheme enjoyed the cooperation of the government of Uttar.

But as soon as the project was started everything went wrong, culminating in what the *New York Times* called "a fiasco." No single problem seems to have been horrendous. Instead, endless small difficulties arose: delays in getting the right tools, in repairing things that broke, in correcting work that had not been done to specifications,

---

*In the belief, one gathers from their public statements, that poor people perpetuate their poverty by multiplying excessively.

in sending off for a bit of missing material. Hooking up to the power did not go as smoothly as expected, and when it was accomplished the power was insufficient. Worse, the difficulties did not diminish as the work progressed. New ones cropped up. It became clear that—even in the increasingly doubtful event the plant could get into operation—keeping it in operating condition thereafter would probably be impractical. So after most of a year and considerable money had been wasted, Etawah was abandoned and a new site was chosen at Kanpur, a city of some 1,200,000 persons, the largest in Uttar, where industry and commerce had, by Indian standards, been growing rapidly. Space in two unused rooms in an electroplating plant was quickly found. The machinery was installed, the workers hired, and the plant was producing within six weeks. Kanpur possessed not only the space and the electric power, but also repairmen, tools, electricians, bits of needed material, and relatively swift and direct transportation service to other major Indian cities if what was required was not to be found in Kanpur.

I think the little fiasco of Etawah casts light on the great fiasco of Chinese economic planning in 1957–58, so hopefully called The Great Leap Forward. The planners of this program shared with the Rockefellers the belief that village industry would be more wholesome for a predominantly rural country than city industry. In part, for reasons to be mentioned later in this book, the policy seems to have been a defense measure. But it was also, in part, evidently based upon the conventional belief that cities are superficial economically while rural production and rural life are "basic." At any rate, as China was about to launch The Great Leap Forward, the official press agency of the country reported, with alarm, that whereas in 1950 the country had had only five cities with populations of more than a million, it now had thirteen of this size or larger; people inadvisedly kept flocking from the villages to cities where they tended to engage in "unproductive" pursuits, if any. The Great Leap was designed to counter the movement to the cities, as well as to industrialize China rapidly. According to plans, the Chinese economy was to expand at the stupendous rate of forty percent annually by a combination of industrial and agricultural development.

In industry, the growth was to be achieved by building hundreds of thousands of factories each year, scattered, for the most part, among the half million Chinese villages and local market towns. Some of these factories were to produce goods for people in their immediate vicinities. Many were to export to other settlements in their provinces. And some, among them thousands of projected small blast furnaces, were to export to existing industrial centers. Most factories were to be small. In spite of heroic efforts, few of these factories ever got into production; the program was abandoned after two years. The economic corpses of the attempt dot China. The Great Leap was the fiasco of Etawah multiplied by the hundreds of thousands.

It is understandable that in underdeveloped countries like China and India, where communication and transportation are somewhat cumbersome, new exporting industries must depend upon locally available producers' goods and services if they depend (as they must) upon producers' goods and services at all. But why the need for local availability of such things in more highly advanced economies? After all, thousands upon thousands of different kinds of producers' goods and services have become exports from the cities of highly advanced economies. If they had not done so, the cities could not have grown, nor their economies developed or expanded. Doesn't this also mean that those same producers' goods and services are easily imported wherever they are not produced?

The arrangements worked out by a young physicist of my acquaintance may help answer this question. He recently undertook in New York some research work for an organization outside the city. He had no market for the work in New York. To explain why he was working in the city nonetheless, he showed me his shopping list for the preceding month and was kind enough to organize it under the sources of supply.

From an electronics supply store: one voltage reference diode, five precision resistors of three different sizes, ten alligator clips, one ordinary resistor, a published collection of electronic industrial circuits, a quantity of insulated copper wire, a dry cell, a small potentiometer;

From a store selling surplus electronics equipment: two precision resistors of still other sizes, and a double-pole, double-throw switch;

From a laboratory supplier: a quantity of aluminum sulphate, a specimen jar for crystal growing, glass rod, glass capillary tubing, vacuum grease, epoxy glue;

From a surplus tool store: a screw-threading die;

From a hardware store: two drill bits, a quantity of braided steel wire, silicone sealing cement, screw eyes, two dry cells;

From another hardware store: brass bolts and turnbuckles;

From an industrial hardware store: a drill bit, a hacksaw blade, two fine-threaded large steel bolts and a stainless-steel machinist's rule;

From a plastics supply house: plexiglass sheets of two different thicknesses;

From the factory of a small manufacturer of specialty wire: a two-foot length of extra-fine stainless-steel wire;

From a machine shop: a soft-iron cone, made to order;

From a scientific supply house: two first-surface mirrors and a special lens;

From an aircraft supply house: rubber O rings of three different sizes.

The last two sources of supply were outside the city; in buying from them, my friend acted as his own importer. Finding one of these sources and getting precisely what he wanted turned out to be more than twice as time consuming as obtaining all the other items on the list put together. The machinist who made the iron cone and the manufacturer who made the extra-fine wire, both in the city, were the producers of the goods they supplied him.* What of the other eight suppliers, all of whom were concentrated conveniently in lower Manhattan? They were providing him with goods made in many different places; some made in the city but most made outside it. Those suppliers were his importers—his purchasing department, if you will, or his "prime contractors." To be sure, they were at his service only because he was one among many who bought from them. But their services are indispensable precisely because so many of these goods are imported into the city.

To return for the moment to the fiasco at Etawah—if the economy of India develops appreciably in years to come, the day will arrive when there will be some industries that can be transplanted, from the cities where they developed, to Etawah or to other inert little towns. The transplanted industries will be going concerns, however, their production and distribution problems already solved. They will have repair and maintenance departments with easy and practiced access to what they need, and probably a home office in a city to see that they get their needs. But by then, still newer exporting organizations arising in India will need local city economies for their work. They will need them, in fact, for producers' goods and services that exist nowhere in India today but will sometime be found—

*The machinist, incidentally, although he was a brilliant mechanic, was almost illiterate. He could work from drawings, but not from written words. Making out the receipt, in laborious writing, he spelled cone "come" and he abbreviated physics as "Fi."

if the country develops—in producing organizations and in stores within the local economies of large cities.

Adding Exports to One's Own Local Work

Mrs. Rosenthal, you will remember, was a custom dressmaker in the local economy of New York. She added to that work something she exported: manufactured brassieres. The Dodge Brothers of Detroit made transmissions and automobile engines for Olds and Ford, among others, before they added automobiles which they exported. In both these cases, a product for export was added to a different product made for the local market. Drab little scraps of local work can, and often do, serve as parent work for different export products. The nucleus of what is today the largest American producer of paper and thin plastic tableware and packaging began as an obscure maker of paper milk-bottle caps in Chicago for local dairies. To this the proprietors added manufacture of meat wrappers which they sold to packers outside Chicago as well as within. Philco and Motorola, large manufacturers of many kinds of communications equipment, started in the local economies of their home cities, Philadelphia and Chicago. Both produced batteries for other manufacturers, thoroughly humdrum producers' goods. Philco added ordinary radios for export; Motorola car radios.

In all the cases so far mentioned, the export work not only arose upon the different local work; it was suggested by the local work. The producers, when they began their local work, had no foreknowledge of the export work they were eventually to create. But sometimes the sequence of suggestion is reversed. That is, a person planning to create an exporting organization, and well aware from the first of what he wants it to produce and export, may nevertheless begin by producing some other goods or service in the local economy of a city.

Allen Loughhead, founder of Lockheed Aircraft, knew

he wanted to design and build planes and sell them everywhere. But to go about this, he first established himself in the local economy of Los Angeles, selling sight-seeing flights and doing exhibition flying. Meanwhile, he designed his first plane and started building up his organization. Leroy Grumman planned to manufacture airplanes, but first he established himself in the local economy of New York—in a Long Island suburb of the city—repairing damaged amphibian planes as a subcontractor to their manufacturer, and making aluminum trailer bodies for local truckers. His first export contract was for pontoons for U.S. Navy planes. When Andrew Carnegie started the organization in Pittsburgh that was to become the nucleus of U.S. Steel, he first bought a forge that made steel axles for local railway-car builders and he added his new export work to that. A manufacturer of earth-moving equipment in Dallas began by making electric rabbits for the local greyhound racing track, then took on contracts to manufacture parts for people who exported oil-drilling machinery from Dallas, but all the time he knew what *he* intended to export. The founders of Ampex, makers of recording devices, originally tried to start as exporters in a San Francisco suburb, but part way through their preparatory work they ran out of capital. One of their expedients in this crisis was to take on a contract to make 25,000 small electric motors for a manufacturer of furnaces, and this work helped hold their organization together. They thus found local work—although a little belatedly.

The process of adding different export work to one's own local work affords a variety of advantages to the people using it. Even when the local work does not suggest the export work, it performs other functions. It provides an organizational foothold, as well as income, while the export work itself is being developed and the organization is building up. Even when people deliberately select local work as a foothold for intended export work, and then successfully grow into the export economy, they proceed as if they were adding the export logically to local parent work. That is, the local work sought is always something that uses skills necessary to the export work. In either of the two ways the process occurs—whether creatively or expediently—it is a means by which an organization can be productive locally at the time that it is developing different work for wider distribution.

Exporting Local Work

Of course people who have an enterprise in the local economy of a city and then become exporters do not necessarily become exporters of something different. More commonly they export exactly what they first provided in the local economy. We are already familiar with this process, because when a city first starts growing, people who supply producers' goods and services to already existing exporters then become, in their turn, exporters of the same things they first provided locally, as was explained in Chapter Four.

The difference, once a city has grown explosively, is that its local economy contains so many more kinds of exportable goods and services than it did when the city was small and young and its local economy meager. The larger a city's local economy grows, the more it contains that is immediately or potentially exportable. We are most aware of this fact where consumer goods and services are concerned. "Everything's up to date in Kansas City, they've gone about as fur as they kin go," runs the song in *Oklahoma* describing the city's indoor plumbing and burlesque shows to the folks back on the farm. First comes news of what people have in this city or that. Then, in time, come some of the things themselves. Others you always have to go to the city to get.

"Hospitals and medical organizations in Peking and major provincial cities," says a 1964 Reuters dispatch from Peking, "have formed mobile medical teams to work in the countryside." The measure makes better sense than the policy adopted in The Great Leap Forward when the countryside was expected to originate its own new goods and services. The dispatch continues, "The program, which the Chinese press described as 'a revolutionary measure in our health work' brings specialists to remote village clinics and dispensaries and to larger medical centers in peoples' communes." What we have here is local work developed in cities now being exported from them.

Consumer goods and services in a large city may not be exported themselves, and yet local organizations serving them may become exporters nevertheless. For instance, not many New York dentists export dental work. But some of their suppliers of goods and services—enterprises that make dental instruments or do specialized dental laboratory work, as well as the schools that began by training local dentists but now train students coming from other places too—commonly do export their work. Just so, the public school system of Chicago is not exported. But at least one of its suppliers—an enterprise started by a former Chicago superintendent of schools who went into business to provide the local school system with diplomas and then added scientific wall charts, then other science and laboratory equipment—has become a supplier of scientific equipment and materials for classrooms in many cities. Los Angeles exports few houses, but it exports many components for builders of houses which were first supplied to local builders. I do not get my eyes examined or my spectacle lenses in London, but lots of people do. Evidently some local suppliers of that work have become exporters for I notice that my spectacle frames are made in London, by a firm with the charming name of Oliver Goldsmith. Thus, among the exportable goods and services in a large city's economy are not only some producers' goods and services for existing exporters, but some consumer goods and services, and also some producers' goods for nonexports.

There is still another major group of goods and services in the local economies of large cities that contain many exports and potential exports. These are goods and services used in common by all, or almost all, segments of a city's economy. Graphics consultants, stationery engravers and designers, specialists in the ventilation of buildings, lighting consultants and advertising agents are examples. They simultaneously serve other local organizations providing producers' goods and services, exporters, and enterprises supplying consumer goods and services to local people.

In medieval times, some of the local craftsmen who served many segments of their cities' markets were painters who specialized in adorning buildings or in decorating chests and other furniture; wood joiners who specialized in cabinetwork or in carpentry; and metal forgers who specialized in hardware. All three of these activities—decorative painting, wood joining and metal forging—seem to have begun in medieval cities as divisions of labor in saddlery. But by adding different and new specialties of various kinds to their old work for saddlers, many painters, joiners and lorimers were soon doing other kinds of painting, joining and metalwork for other kinds of city customers. And because they drew upon the whole market of the city for their customers—not merely upon one craft—they were able to multiply into various specialties for that large local market. Work done for customers throughout the whole market of a large city is apt to become unusually specialized in itself.

Many future transportation devices and services will be in this group. So will future goods and services to process and recycle wastes. The fragmentary recycling services that do exist have already found opportunity in serving many different segments of big-city markets. Chicago is now the world headquarters of trade in used machinery and this work began with the local services of scavengers who bought discarded machinery from Chicago manufacturers and resold what was usable to other Chicago manufacturers. Both the scavengers' suppliers and their customers were in all parts of Chicago's economy: exporters, makers of local consumer goods, makers of local producers' goods. At the end of World War II, when thousands of Chicago factories were trying to retool at the same time, the machine scavengers started combing junkyards and factories in Cleveland, Detroit and Indianapolis for their Chicago customers. In the course of doing so, they also found customers in those cities for machines and parts that were surplus in Chicago. They extended their range farther. By the mid-fifties they were matching up supplies in Atlanta with demand in Madrid, and supplies in Milan with demand in Bombay. Now that they deal nationally and internationally, they are known as brokers, not junkmen and scavengers; but the work is the same work exported and the men who do it are the same men who once did it only locally.

There is one exception to the rule that it is more difficult to export work than to provide something for the local market: it is not more difficult when customers take the initiative by importing. Customers, of course, come to large cities from other places for shopping, entertainment, special medical services, financial services, legal services, to receive professional training in schools, and so on. They are drawing on local goods and services. Many enterprises that export the same things they provide locally sell only a small fraction of their goods or services to outsiders, but in a large and diverse city these fractional exports become enormous in the aggregate.

To export local work, especially when customers take the initiative, might seem the simplest way to generate a new export in a city. It is often the most practical way. But it seems as simple as it does only because all the complications, except the act of exporting itself, have been worked out first within the city's local economy. In fact, this is the way the most complex and influential exports of cities are generated. The scrolls that went from Athens to the great library of the ancients in Alexandria, the complex work of Roman surveyors and engineers who mapped out aqueducts in the Iberian Peninsula and Gaul, the treatises on agriculture and fossils and the musical instruments that went forth from Paris to Thomas Jefferson in Monticello, the periodicals sent from London to Benjamin Franklin in Philadelphia, the medical work being done by the teams of specialists sent forth from present-day Peking—these are not what one could call simple exports. What we abstractly call the dissemination of cultures consists of many exports, some of them amazingly complex, that were first developed within the local economies of cities.

The Limited Number of the Export-Generating Processes

Once a new exporting organization has been developed in a city, the organization can, of course, add further exports to its initial ones. This is what the Ford company did when it added tractors to automobiles, or Minnesota Mining and Manufacturing when it added all those other products to its unsuccessful sandpaper and its successful abrasive sand and masking tape. This is also what is happening when a store in Dublin that sells handwoven blankets to tourists adds hand-knit sweaters. But by definition, an organization does not add new exports to older exports unless it is already exporting something. First, it has to become an exporter.

We have been considering three different processes by which organizations can first become exporters:

- They can add the export work to other people's *local* work.
- They can add the export work to different *local* work of their own.
- They can export their own *local* work.

The significant fact about these processes is that they all depend directly on local economies. (This is shown diagrammatically in Section III of the Appendix.) The fact might not be so important if there were other ways for cities to generate new exporting organizations, but there seem to be none. At any rate, these are the only ways I have been able to discover after reasonably diligent searching; certainly no other export-generating processes occur often, if they exist at all. Indeed, it soon becomes exceedingly tiresome to read the business histories of exporting organizations because their narrative plots are so few. One might be reading the same three novels over and over again.

It follows that if these are the ways cities generate new exporting organizations, these processes have to be revitalized in cities which have become economically stagnant, for unless they are, nothing else can halt the city's economic decay. The real world is full of evidence that tells us exactly this: nothing serves but the generating of new exporting organizations, and plenty of them. Pittsburgh is a good illustration because so many irrelevant things have been tried there, so ambitiously.

About 1910, the economy of Pittsburgh began to stagnate. The city was then specializing ever more heavily, to the neglect of adding new work, on a few of its most successful types of export work—mostly steelmaking and the manufacturing of various construction materials. Pittsburgh had become an efficient city for a few well-established companies. In the following years, Pittsburgh's economy expanded only very slowly, then halted, and finally began to contract. Poverty and unemployment grew. Unemployment would have grown faster except that so many people of working age, especially if they were ambitious, emigrated; indeed, they left in such numbers that the age composition of the population in the Pittsburgh metropolitan area has gradually become ever more heavily weighted with people too young or too old to work. During World

War II, the rulers of Pittsburgh took stock of the city and its long-gathering troubles and decided that the city was not "attractive" enough to hold its young people or to attract new industries. In the twenty years since, one measure after another has been tried, much as if the economic problems of Pittsburgh were the problems of a young lady with insufficient grooming, manners, breeding and popularity.

Richard K. Mellon, current chief of the family that has dominated Pittsburgh throughout its decline and for a few years before the decline began, has caused to be employed, and to minister to Pittsburgh, thousands of economic consultants, industrial analysts, regional planners, city planners, highway planners, parking planners, cultural planners, educational planners, planning coordinators, urban designers, housers, social engineers, civic organizers, sociologists, statisticians, political scientists, home economists, citizen-liaison experts, municipal-service experts, retail-trade experts, antipollution experts, publicity experts, development experts, redevelopment experts, dispensers of birth-control pills to the poor, and of course experts at "attracting" industry. They have industriously documented, studied, analyzed, psychoanalyzed, measured, manipulated, cleaned, face-lifted, rebuilt, cajoled, exhorted and publicized Pittsburgh. But nobody has done anything effective about generating new exports from Pittsburgh's local economy. Capital that might have been available for young enterprises has been devoted to manipulating the people of Pittsburgh and to immensely expensive urban-renewal and highway programs that have not helped the economy at all. Indeed, their chief effect has been negative, since they have reduced and rooted out much of the potentially valuable local economy the city still had, simply because it was physically in the way. By 1967, Pittsburgh's economy was worse off than it had been twenty years before. Its population of working age had further declined and, even so, rates of unemployment and underemployment were high. Nor is there sign of economic improvement at this writing, in 1968. How can there be? Artificial symptoms of prosperity or a "good image" do not revitalize a city, but only explicit economic growth processes for which there are no substitutes.

Pittsburgh's local economy may be too humdrum and meager now to contain anything much that is exportable, either of producers' or consumer goods and services. If such a ruined city is ever to be revitalized, its development processes may have to begin over again, much as if it were an embryonic city. That is, it may have to seek new "initial" exports. But since Pittsburgh actually does have a good deal more of an economic foundation than an embryonic city does, these new initial exports might derive from adding different export work logically to the humdrum local work. If, but only if, such new export work supports a growing complement of new producers' goods and services (some of which, in turn, can become new exports), then the city's economic growth might get under way again. Certainly, before Pittsburgh once more has much of a local economy that is directly exportable, the city must have a new episode of import replacing and explosive local economic growth. But it will not have that until after it has earned more imports by generating new exports.

Even an episode of import replacing does not necessarily guarantee a local economy from which plentiful new exports will come. The replacement of imports must, itself, be reasonably creative to provide a foundation for vigorous future growth. In short, mere receptivity to branch plants, transplanted from other places, is not enough. A few years ago, the president of the Carling Brewery of Cleveland announced that his company was establishing a branch plant in Atlanta because consumption there warranted it. The plant was not only to supply Atlanta itself, the biggest single market in that part of the country, it would also brew Carling beer for the Southeast generally. From Atlanta's point of view, therefore, not only was an import being replaced but the city was getting, at the same time, an instant export. However, Atlanta is never going to export Carling beer to Cleveland; indeed, Atlanta is never going to export Carling beer any farther than the territory allotted to its branch plant. If Japan had replaced its imports of sewing machines merely by receiving branch plants of the Singer Sewing Machine Co., Japan would not now be a great exporter of sewing machines, nor of producers' goods and services that started by serving local sewing machine manufacturers. Locally originated production of former imports is often a slower way for a city to acquire new exports from the replacement work itself, but it is potentially productive of greater and more various export work.

Between about 1910 and 1920, San Francisco had an episode of import replacing. The replacements were overwhelmingly made by former exporters to San Francisco who moved their work to the market. Relatively few local replacements seem to have been made during this particular episode. Probably this local sterility was a symptom that banks and others who controlled capital in San Francisco were not at this time financing development of local work. In any case, the episode of import replacing brought to the city a great array of branch plants. Oakland, an industrial suburb of San Francisco, was built up rapidly at this time; its economic base was formed of these branch plants. They produced hundreds of things, from light bulbs to corsets and from fruit jars to shoes. The future exports from these branch plants were inherently limited. Furthermore, Oakland, whose economy was built from them, has generated almost nothing more from that economy except a single large exporting organization, the Kaiser enterprises, which began with construction work. Oakland, in economic decline almost from the time it built up, stands as continuing evidence of the economic sterility of that episode of import replacing in San Francisco.

Streams of new exports and new exporting organizations are necessary to a city but they are derivative and secondary. Their source is in a creative, developing local city economy. This relationship, which begins with the very beginning of a settlement's growth as a city, continues no matter how old, how large and how complex the city's economy becomes.

7

Capital for City Economic Development

In the nineteenth century, saws and axes made in New England cleared the forests of Ohio; New England ploughs broke the prairie sod; New England scales weighed wheat and meat in Texas; New England serge clothed businessmen in San Francisco; New England cutlery skinned hides to be tanned in Milwaukee and sliced apples to be dried in Missouri; New England whale oil lit lamps across the continent; New England blankets warmed children by night and New England textbooks preached at them by day; New England guns armed the troops; and New England dies, lathes, looms, forges, presses and screwdrivers outfitted factories far and wide. But by the twentieth century, New England plants were closing up and laying off workers. To most New Englanders the cause of the region's economic decline seemed obvious—loss of industry. They brooded upon reasons for this loss:

cheaper labor in the South, obsolescence of the old brick factories along the rivers and beside the waterfalls, the decay of Boston's docks, imports from Switzerland and Japan. They tried to think of ways to surmount these disadvantages and to hold to what they still had.

But at least one New Englander had a different idea. Ralph Flanders—later a U.S. senator—had spent most of his adult life as president of a machine-tool company in Vermont. During World War II he served as president of the Federal Reserve Bank of Boston and from this vantage point he enjoyed an excellent view of the region's banking and other financial activities. Flanders concluded that the region's trouble was not the loss of old industries, but the lack of new ones. Furthermore he thought the trouble was localized in the region's metropolis, Boston, which was not incubating new work for itself or for the region. As he put it, Boston's birth rate of new enterprises was too low. He concluded that this low birth rate was due to lack of capital for new enterprises there. Not that Boston lacked capital, but that it was used unproductively. Much of it was tied up in ancient trusts where it was routinely invested in tax-exempt government bonds and in the stocks and bonds of venerable enterprises; some of it was exported to other places; some was poured into old and moribund mills, watch factories and railroads that were being run aground by incompetents or milked by respectable scoundrels.

A less practical man than Flanders might have worn himself out exhorting Boston's banks to wake up and take a chance on the young people of Boston but Flanders was not one to depend on the dead to breed new life. What Boston needed, he thought, was a new financial organization, unencumbered by tradition and dedicated specifically to financing new enterprises in Boston. He persuaded two or three Boston capitalists to experiment and together in 1946 they organized a company called American Research and Development, capitalized, to begin with, at less than five million dollars. Perhaps Flanders' most unorthodox and creative move was to establish the policy that American Research and Development would not take over control of the enterprises in which it invested. Control was to be left in the hands of their present proprietors. Although this practice had once been common in the United States, it had become almost unheard-of in 1946 and indeed remains exceptional today. No policy was adopted concerning the kinds of enterprises to be financed; the company would invest in any kind of young and promising Boston business.

The first customer of American Research and Development was Tracerlab, the first of the city's postwar science-based industries. (It had one prewar predecessor, Polaroid, which had yet to add its work of making cameras.) Tracerlab had been started late in 1945 by three young scientists at Harvard who had pooled a few thousand dollars from savings out of their salaries and from personal loans and had set themselves up in business in a decrepit but, for their purposes, marvelously cheap old building in downtown Boston. Later they told a *Fortune* reporter that if they had not found cheap space in a central and convenient location, they could not have started at all. Their business was buying radioactive isotopes from Oak Ridge, Tennessee, and packaging them for Boston's numerous hospitals and medical centers where they were used for diagnostic and treatment work. This soon led to new work. Tracerlab built a machine for counting the radiations from the isotopes and began to sell copies of the machine outside of Boston as well as locally. It had orders for more than fifty, and to the proprietors of Tracerlab it seemed clear that this was only a small fraction of the market. But to pursue this new work the company had to expand rapidly which required capital far larger than the personal resources of the proprietors and their families and friends.

First the proprietors of Tracerlab visited bankers and

other investors in Boston but could not raise a dollar. Next they tried bankers in New York, with whom they had an equal lack of success. But on Wall Street they found several investors willing to advance the necessary capital in return for fifty-one percent of the voting stock of the company, that is, in return for control of the company. This the proprietors declined, although it appeared that they must now go out of business or else loaf along with the isotope-packaging work. At this point American Research and Development came into existence and was immediately approached by Tracerlab's proprietors. American Research and Development, after a swift study of the company and its plans, decided Tracerlab needed $150,000 for its expansion, somewhat more than the proprietors had requested. The investment was made, and Tracerlab went on to prosper.

The transaction not only rescued Tracerlab from being one more stillbirth in Boston's business statistics; it profoundly affected American Research and Development's own development. In those days, although it is hard to credit now, scientists, professors and others of the academy were considered by bankers, investors and indeed by the business community generally, to be persons congenitally incapable of meeting a payroll. The success of Tracerlab's proprietors caused American Research and Development to look with favor upon people who had hitherto been presumed to live in ivory towers. The organization made investment after investment in other science-based industries primarily doing work based on electronics, organic chemistry and physics. Soon there were breakaways from these enterprises in which to invest too. By no means were they all exporters of products or services from Boston. Many, especially at the time they started, supplied goods or services to the science-based industries that had already been started and to those just starting.

To be sure, American Research and Development made

some loans to other than science-based enterprises. At one point, indeed, it had so far forgotten its original reasons for coming into existence in Boston that it financed a tuna-fishing scheme in the South Pacific. According to *Fortune*, it had been persuaded into this venture on the strength of a study by the Rockefeller Brothers Fund. The scheme failed—the tuna would not bite, it is believed, because they found too much food other than the bait—and American Research and Development went back to concentrating upon loans in Boston. There it continued to have its most gratifying successes with science-based industries.

But now a very interesting thing began to happen. By the early 1950s, American Research and Development was exporting capital, not for random enterprises, but for the same kinds of enterprises it was financing most successfully in Boston. Some of the early electronics manufacturers in Long Island, for example, got their capital from American Research and Development. Through its investments, American Research and Development was not only supplying goods and services to other producers in Boston but, after having established its work locally, it began exporting the same goods and services.

The answer to the question of where capital for economic development comes from is that it comes from the same places, and by the same processes, that other producers' goods and services come. Development capital implies the work of dispensing capital. This work arises, originally, in the local economies of specific cities. The organizations that do this work begin either as breakaways from other organizations dealing in capital and money, which in effect is how American Research and Development was formed, or else they add the work of dispensing development capital to older work, as the merchant bankers had done. An organization successful at supplying development capital may eventually be widely imitated, like any other successful activity.

Capital as Producers' Goods

Since development capital is a form of producers' goods, organizations that provide it can arise only where other kinds of producers are also arising. The relationship is symbiotic, like that between the Detroit marine-engine manufacturers and the Detroit shipbuilders. Thus cities that grow into great industrial and commercial centers also grow into important financial centers. Their local economies contain unusually large numbers and varieties of financial goods and services, many of which become exports, just as other kinds of producers' goods and services often become exports. The work of a large city's various suppliers of capital is inherently exportable, because neither the variety nor volume of their work is duplicated in smaller cities nor, of course, in the rural world. Thus a young city commonly imports capital from larger cities. But if it is growing, it replaces many of these imports; new banks are started, for example, along with insurance companies, factoring companies, acceptance corporations and so on. Explosively growing cities often add financial goods and services that they previously neither imported nor produced locally.

The commonest way in which organizations providing capital become exporters is the way American Research and Development did when it began investing in science-based industries outside Boston. That is, they export the same work they have first done locally. Thus New York became the financial capital of the United States only well after it had supplanted Philadelphia, the former financial capital, as a center of commerce and industry. Antwerp, in medieval times, was the financial capital of Northwest Europe, probably because it was also the largest center of the cloth industry and of transactions in wool, flax and cloth; Antwerp exported financial services to London. But after London surpassed Antwerp as a center of commerce and industry in Renaissance times, it went on to surpass Antwerp as a financial center as well.

Los Angeles, having already surpassed San Francisco as the chief industrial and commercial center of the West Coast, is now in process of becoming the financial capital of the West Coast. Tokyo, having become one of the world's great industrial and commercial centers, has rapidly become one of the world's major financial centers. Even if Moscow were not the political capital of the Soviet Union, it would be the financial capital simply because the government must undertake more capital transactions of more different kinds there than in any other single place.

Theoretically, there is no reason why governments cannot devise new ways of dispensing capital and new means of closing "credit gaps" so that new and unprecedented, as well as old and well-established, kinds of work can be supplied with capital and other financial goods and services. But governments—Communist as well as capitalist—imitate financial work that originated in city economies. Government central banks; agricultural credit corporations; agencies insuring crops, bank deposits or bank loans; government agencies that issue bonds for their own work or bonds to finance the work of still other government agencies; government-sponsored producers' cooperatives that dispense credit to their members; government agencies and development banks that dispense long-term development capital; government agencies that dispense working capital to approved enterprises; government acceptance corporations—all these have been copied, sometimes with minor adaptations to be sure, from work that began locally in cities.

Why governments should be so imitative, rather than innovative, in their work of dispensing capital I do not know. Perhaps it is because people who run government activities, the world over, tend to seek sweeping answers to problems; that is, answers capable of being applied wholesale the instant they are adopted. People in government work—with an exception I shall soon touch on—do not seem to bring their minds to bear on a particular and often seemingly small problem in one particular place. And yet that is how innovations of any sort are apt to begin, including financial ones. Furthermore, when new financial goods and services are first added into economic life, they are commonly added, like other innovations, to different older work. For instance, modern banking began as an addition to trading. Transactions in futures began as an addition to warehousing; factoring as an addition to cloth making; sales of shares as an addition to trading; premium investment as an addition to insuring risks to ships; acceptance corporations as an addition to automobile manufacturing; and, as mentioned in an earlier chapter, general equipment leasing—now a standard way of supplying medium-term capital—as an addition to food processing.

Banks often start by serving particular kinds of customers. Sometimes their quaint names tell us so: Boatmen's National, Merchants & Traders, Planters National, Emigrant Savings & Loan. A few years ago two New York banks named the Corn Exchange Bank and Chemical Bank & Trust merged, and for a time (until another merger) rejoiced in the name Chemical Corn Bank. But behind many a colorless bank name, too, is a history of particularized work. According to *Fortune*, there was "only one place of welcome" in the banking world for the early garment manufacturers of Los Angeles, the people who in the 1920s and 1930s got the industry started and supported the obscure but vital little collections of local producers' goods and services that helped make practicable the great growth of the garment industry there during the 1940s and 1950s. The singular place of welcome was Union Bank & Trust, which was very small too. Had its name described its actual function, it would have been called Los Angeles Garment Makers' Bank & Trust.

As a rule, the more kinds of customers a bank serves, the less apt it is to be much involved in development of new work. Senator Flanders' original idea was that American Research and Development would invest in all types of enterprises. As we have seen, it did not fulfill that aim. But the point is not that it should have; had its directors, in fact, tried to finance all manner of new businesses, they almost certainly would not have done a good job with any. The point, rather, is that to fulfill Senator Flanders' purpose would have required several new investing organizations and, in the course of time, multiplication of those by breakaways from them. As it is, while the Boston birth rate of science-based industries has risen dramatically and has included much innovative work, the birth rate of other kinds of enterprises remains low and innovations few.

Banks that provide almost all kinds of financial services to all kinds of customers have usually become generalized with age; they have added new work to old, like other organizations. They tend, if their work has become generalized, to become bureaucratized and to routinize their many functions. They extend astounding amounts of money to tired old enterprises and sometimes, too—as scandals like the Billie Sol Estes, Kreuger and Insull cases periodically demonstrate—to charlatans who have the plausible and reassuring look of big, solid success. But old, well-established, generalized banks tend to dismiss out of hand ideas for genuinely new and unproved goods and services.

As economically underdeveloped countries revive their economies, most of the new work they at first require is not, in fact, new and unproved. Nobody in a currently underdeveloped nation has to prove that tractors, cameras, automatic pin-making machines or chest X-ray clinics will work and are useful. Such goods and services can be financed by bureaucrats who need seldom make judgments about truly unprecedented goods and services. But bureaucratized financing can work, if at all, only up to a point. Unless a currently underdeveloped country is always to be in the position of "catching up" to other economies, and is to halt its own development when advanced countries whose goods and services it imitates become stagnant, it follows that sooner or later the currently underdeveloped country must itself become a vigorous innovator of unprecedented goods and services. For this, the country must create new financial organizations, and must continue to create them. It would seem, from past experience in developing economies, that the way to create these organizations might be for the government to establish considerable numbers of small and decentralized lending agencies in the local economies of various cities— more of them in the larger cities—and to encourage them to specialize by seeking out promising new goods and services being added to older work in their cities. They would have failures, but they would also finance unprecedented industries. The new, creative financial organizations that became successful locally could then export their services too, and could become organizations working nationwide.

Innovations for War

As has often been observed, war has spectacularly stimulated advances in metallurgy, mechanics, civil engineering, chemistry, physics, transportation, footgear and other clothing, communications, literacy, surgery, epidemiology and sanitation. New work produced to wage war or to prepare for it is often later applied to more merciful and constructive purposes. But war is plainly not the "secret" of economic development. Societies that have concentrated furiously upon military strength and conquest, and very successfully too, have nevertheless often stagnated economically and collapsed behind their legions. Furthermore, economically stagnant countries have as much difficulty developing military goods and services as they do in developing other kinds of goods and services, no matter how much their rulers or their people may want to be militarily strong.

War depends on "peace work," directly and literally. The bicycle shop of the Wright brothers was not a war plant. When American Research and Development began financing science-based industries in Boston, those new industries had neither war contracts nor prospects of them. Rather, work was being created into which, seven or eight years later, the U.S. government could pour immense sums for war goods and war-related research.

The solid fuel now being employed in the United States for ballistic missiles and space shots has a history that began in 1926 when two Kansas City chemists formed a little company to try to make a new kind of antifreeze. By mistake, they made a rather poor type of synthetic rubber which they decided to improve and develop instead. They had to buy their way out of a contract with an oil company which had advanced them capital to develop the antifreeze. A Kansas City salt merchant and a few other small investors put up $75,000: $50,000 of it to break the contract and $25,000 for working capital to develop the rubber. At this point Boss Prendergast, who controlled Kansas City, told Thiokol, as the little company was called, to get out of town. According to *Fortune*, the moonshiners and wine makers of Kansas City, who were working clandestinely during Prohibition, had complained to Prendergast that the smell from Thiokol's plant was tainting their products.

So Thiokol moved to Trenton, New Jersey. During the next ten years "its only really important accomplishment was a notable lessening in the odor of its product," *Fortune* reports. It is rather a wonder the company survived at all. Most of its sales were to other chemical companies who tried this or that with the strange product, then gave up. At one point Dow Chemical bought a third of the stock and rights to the manufacturing process; but Dow could make nothing usable from the concoction, resold the stock, and dropped the manufacturing. In the meantime, du Pont had developed a good synthetic rubber.

Then in 1946, Thiokol began to receive small but repeated orders from time to time from the California Institute of Technology's Jet Propulsion Laboratory. The proprietors of Thiokol inquired why the laboratory was interested in the material and they were told that some of the people at C.I.T. seemed to think it was the best substance for fueling rockets. But it was a solid fuel and at this time both the U.S. space program and the Department of Defense were committed to liquid fuels for rockets. No rocket engines existed, at least in the United States, that could use solid fuels. Therefore, Thiokol attempted to get from the Department of Defense a contract to develop such engines. The department was not interested for several years, according to *Fortune*, because the ranking savant of U.S. rocketry, Wernher von Braun, opposed the development of solid-fueled rockets and so did his Army colleagues working on rocket missiles. Nevertheless, Thiokol persisted and meanwhile word filtered into the United States that the Russians were developing solid-fueled rockets. In 1953, Thiokol was awarded a contract for development work on the engines and their fuel, and the work proved to be successful. In 1958, the Department of Defense announced publicly that it had shifted from liquid- to solid-fueled missiles and rockets and that the change represented a major advance in the art of rocketry. The change also turned Thiokol into a rather big business, with numerous factories spun off into the rural world and small towns.

Now consider an interesting remark made at a subcommittee hearing of the House of Representatives in 1966, as reported in the *New York Times*. The congressmen were questioning Donald F. Hornig, the director of the government's Office of Science and Technology. They wanted to know why that office was putting so much (ninety percent) of its resources into development of war goods and war-related research and so little into development of solutions to city transportation, housing and pollution problems. Dr. Hornig said his office could not find promising proposals in these fields to invest in. "We cannot buy and create progress," he said, "in a field which is not ready to progress." It is likely that Dr. Hornig and his colleagues did not know what to look for. Nevertheless, in principle, he was quite right. Capital, by itself, can create nothing; and there is nothing in which to invest development capital of any magnitude until there are already in existence various starting points, however small, like Thiokol or the young electronics companies that arose in Boston and Los Angeles in the late 1940s. To use capital purposefully and knowledgeably for development is impossible unless small sums have first gone—most likely for quite different purposes—into a multiplicity of small new departures.

War ministries seem to do rather little to create these vital starting points that, after the fact, become so important to them. What they do excel at—if they are successful in promoting innovations at all—is at "buying progress" in "fields that are ready to progress." That is, they do seize upon relevant goods, services and organizations that have been cast up by the general processes of economic development, and then pour development capital intensively into further development and production. This, I think, is the salient connection between war and economic development generally, and between war goods and the innovations that are so often developed in war goods and war services. This observation does not "explain" war any more than the large local economies of great cities "explain" the artists who find places in those economies, but I do think it casts light on how war work is responsible for so many innovations.

The way capital is used for development of war goods is rather different from the way capital is ordinarily used. For war goods, development capital is apt to be employed strictly as if it were producers' goods: it is fed to producers so they can produce, much as shirting is supplied to shirt-makers or leather to shoemakers. And it is effective. This approach does result in the creation and production of new goods and services.

Capital is not used this way by most agencies of govern-ment, especially those presiding over services for "the gen-eral welfare." Those agencies tend to use capital, for the most part, as if money itself were capable of solving problems and promoting the general good. Is an educa-tion system, a housing program, a health system collaps-ing? More money, for more of the same, is the common prescription. But without creativity, as Dr. Hornig testified, there is really very little, if any, "progress" that money can buy. Nor, for that matter, with few exceptions (like American Research and Development or the old Union Bank & Trust that served the Los Angeles garment makers), do many nongovernmental financial organizations use de-velopment capital as if it were mere producers' goods. Rather, they try to use it as if its multiplication were an end in itself. War ministries the world over, whether in Marxist or in capitalist countries, have their own ideology about capital.

Much of the creative effort that goes into war work, perhaps even most of it, has little to do with the passions of war. The advertisements of developers and producers of war goods are a case in point. One in *Scientific Ameri-can* says, "The catapult that 'slings' a jet fighter into the air within the limits of a 1,000-ft. runway requires a super braking system to stop the steel launch cable after the jet is airborne," and then goes on to express, not a passion for war, but a passion for finding and serving customers who want this company to "create [other] problem-solving products" in its métier, which it describes as work with asbestos, rubber, sintered metal and specialized plastics. Another developer and producer of war and space goods, this time advertising for employees (chemists, engineers, analysts of various kinds, also mechanics), appeals to them thus: "There's more to us than buildings. There's activity, enthusiasm, professionalism, people. In this environment you can find it easy to make things happen."

At first thought, it is difficult to understand how intelligent and humane people can devote themselves, as many do nowadays, to creating not only missiles and bombers, but gases and poisons, and even to breeding mutated bacteria that can be loosed on plants, animals and people. Certainly neither patriotic fervor nor bellicosity seems to have much to do with people's participation in such evil. They are not necessarily proud of their work, as patriots would be. Indeed, they tend to hide their revolting occupations, as executioners do. Or when, like the inventor of napalm, they are identified and put on the defensive, they like to protest that they have only been contributing to knowledge, possibly useful knowledge; and, far from indicating a fever for war, they are apt to disassociate themselves and their work from it. They say the uses to which their work is put are not their responsibility. I suspect that the sheer purposefulness and interest of the work, as a quality apart from its uses, exerts an immense attraction. The purposeful and intense work on a device that will brake that launching cable; the purposeful trial and error directed at creating a gas difficult to make and unusual in its properties: these can be absorbing problems. It is hard to work without purposefulness. It is agonizing to be capable of solving problems and have no opportunities to do so. It may be that many people prefer involvement in bad purposes and wicked creations to aimlessness and boredom in their occupation. The impulse to work where "you can find it easy to make things happen," especially new and difficult things, is certainly not in itself unhealthy. Or, let us say, it is no more unhealthy than willingness to work for a repair shop where one must cheat the customers instead of using honest craftsmanship, or than working in a hopelessly rotten welfare system or school system, accomplishing nothing. As Paul Goodman has pointed out, people can find that most kinds of work open to them have become absurd.

Almost anyone who is trying to invent or develop a new product or service, of any kind for any purpose, invests the work with tremendous importance, an attitude that may be necessary for innovators. But it is rare to find a corresponding respect for the importance of the work on the part of those whom one must depend upon for capital. So I think there may be much that is practical, and possibly adaptable, to be learned from the way capital is used to buy progress of war goods in "fields that are ready to progress."

But the other effects of war upon economic development are changing from those of the past. In spite of its destructiveness, war used not to be inherently at cross-purposes with the processes of economic development. War was not inherently incompatible with city growth and with concentration of work in cities. Indeed, cities were usually the safest places for people, property and work in time of war; the countryside and villages were more vulnerable. This is no longer true. The arts of war have now reached the point where international war and the existence of cities are incompatible. That change seems to be one reason why the Chinese are so determined—although futilely —to try to develop their economy without developing great, productive cities. The policy is a defense measure. Under the circumstances, it may be well reasoned and sane, but as a defense measure only.

What Is "Basic" Capital?

The orthodox notion that a country's "basic" capital is the land and the labor poured into the land is obviously incorrect. If it were true, then predominately agricultural countries would nowadays be exporting capital and other financial services to highly industrialized and urbanized countries rather than the reverse. And within industrialized and urbanized countries rural areas would be exporting capital to cities, probably through tax subsidies from country to city. Henry George, reasoning from the premise that land is basic capital and basic wealth, asserted that all profits made in cities derive from the value of city land. Of course the peculiarly high value of city land does not derive from anything inherent in the land, but from the concentrations of work upon city land.

A country's basic wealth is its productive capacity, created by the practical opportunities people have had to add new work to older work. But to speak of basic capital is to invoke a rather platonic concept in any case. It is a little like saying, "Yes, I understand about those people who make shirting for shirtmakers, but what is basic shirting?"

In the real world, capital originates much as any other city goods do, and rural development is financed by exports of capital from cities. All developing economies generate capital. Thus, to say that underdeveloped countries must be financed from abroad is equivalent to saying that they are to be "developed" as inert colonial dependencies, not self-generating economies. If economic development is actually occurring within an aided country or region, outside help is only briefly necessary at most.

Inescapably, a country's economic development depends upon its own work. The relevant assistance that a highly developed and prospering country can extend to an underdeveloped country is to buy from it: give its embryonic or stagnated cities an opportunity to serve expanding export work, earn imports, and replace imports. No form of financing, however lavish, can help an economy develop if people within its own cities are not adding new kinds of work to old, and if organizations are not being created there to finance the process. But the same rule applies to highly developed economies too: if they do not continually create organizations to supply capital for new work in their cities, they too must stagnate and then their wealth must inevitably begin to dwindle, even though slowly.

Discriminatory Use of Capital

People at the bottom of a society customarily find it difficult to get capital for development work. Even if they can get it, they may not be permitted to use it. In societies that are supposedly economically "free," social discrimination and unequal protection of people and their rights by the law (in actual fact, as opposed to theoretical equality of people under law) can effectively prevent many persons from developing their work, no matter what their inherent capacities for doing so may be. In Socialist societies, those who have worked their way up in the bureaucracies have much better access to development capital than others. Whether good use, or any use, is made of such a privilege is another matter.

Considered purely as an economic matter—quite apart from the inherent brutality of social discrimination—the effects of discrimination are not serious in the rural world; an economy can develop in spite of rural caste systems, as happened in medieval Europe and in many other times and places.* But discrimination in cities is a serious economic

*Rural caste systems often disintegrate as economies develop because rural people migrate to cities where they change their social standing. This kind of event was expressed in medieval Europe in the doctrine, "city air makes free," which was applied to serfs who managed to migrate to cities;

matter. It creates profound economic blocks and flaws. Lowly work has often been the parent work of important new goods and services, as we may expect it will continue to be. It is no economic accident that in societies where virtually all women, including those in cities, have been effectively kept in the position of chattels, the potential development of goods and services based on despised women's work—food processing, garment making, laundering—remains stultified. It is no accident that the work of slaves, even when it has been done in cities, has developed very little. Furthermore, acute practical problems in cities often bear most heavily upon people lowest in the social hierarchies, and thus are noticed, and also often understood, by these people long before they are taken seriously by those who lead more sheltered lives. If people who do lowly work cannot add new work to it, not only does that work itself become an economic dead end, but also many serious practical problems that will ultimately affect everyone are apt to remain unsolved.

In developing economies, parvenus are constantly emerging. Historically, we are apt to see these movements as accumulations: the rise of a merchant class with whom an aristocracy is forced to share power, and the rise of a manufacturing class with whom the merchants have to share power. But in stagnant economies the same people—and those whom they choose to admit into their ranks—hold onto power indefinitely. When they are overthrown violently and abruptly, we hear of janitors who suddenly become factory managers, coal miners hailed as efficiency experts, universities suddenly filled with sons and daughters of poor workers, cold and hungry guerrillas who live to negotiate international trade pacts, peasants who become premiers. Such changes do not necessarily bring about

---

also, when subsistence farms take on cash crops in developing economies, or farms with cash crops replace manual labor with machines, the old rural social order disintegrates.

economic development, because they may amount only to a turnover of personnel rather than revival of the processes we have been investigating. But in any case, the radical social changes become symbols of the revival of economic growth. People the world over understand (and the more downtrodden, the better they understand) that juggling social hierarchies and economic improvement go hand in hand.

People who are economically submerged are shut off in two ways from access to development capital. First, access to development capital may be hard to come by, but once acquired it is usable. In American cities, new immigrant groups other than those coming from Protestant North Europe have always found it hard to get initial capital for enterprises of their own. One way of breaking through this obstacle has been to develop sources of capital other than banks and the various other organizations selling financial goods and services. But alternate sources have frequently been either illegal or disreputable. That is to say, capital has been derived from extortionate slum landlordship (building very little money into considerable money), organized crime, and profits derived from political graft. Many a respectable American citizen of today got his education, and many a legitimate and constructive enterprise got its initial capital, from precisely these activities. Without them, the education would not have been possible, nor the laudable enterprises. This is one reason, I think—perhaps even the principal reason—for the extraordinary tolerance of organized crime and graft in American society. Certainly it is often the direct reason for covert cooperation with crime on the part of persons who are industrious and, in most things, law abiding.

These observations do not mean that crime, graft, bribery and slum exploitation have been either proper or inherently necessary ways of financing legitimate aims. On the contrary, they have had vicious consequences of many kinds. They have also been thoroughly gratuitous because legal capital, had it been less discriminatory, could have done the same constructive work—and made a profit too. But it is no use saying that because illegally derived capital was improper, an alternative would have been for immigrants who were discriminated against to build up capital by sheer thrift, self-denial and hard work at whatever menial tasks came to their hands. The Japanese and Chinese immigrants in America tried that strategy and were judged an intolerable economic threat. Their reward for economic puritanism was the Oriental Exclusion Acts.

One could argue that if immigrants had derived no capital from these sources—organized crime, machine politics and systematic slum exploitation—the economic development of the United States would have halted. Without alternate initial sources of capital, many a group of immigrants in many an American city, together with their descendants, would have been unable to create economic enterprises. They would eventually have become economically redundant—an unproductive burden upon the rest of society. They would be in much the same position that black Americans are in today. Problems of discrimination that are only now destroying the United States would have become dangerous long since. After the initial block was overcome, people from immigrant groups found access to orthodox capital easier. For by then, many of them had already become successes in business and the professions.

Now let us consider the fact that some people are prevented from developing their work even if they can get the capital to do so. Back in the 1830s, some of the many free Negroes in Washington, D.C., had begun to make solid economic gains. They owned quite a number of business enterprises that served the local economy in many ways. In particular, they were doing well in the tavern and restaurant businesses. But the city was controlled by whites, and in 1835 a city ordinance was passed prohibiting shop licenses to be issued to blacks thereafter.

The one exception permitted was carting and hackney work. To this day, one finds black owners of taxicabs in Washington, but of little else.

All over the United States, wherever and whenever blacks got access to capital and attempted to use it, they were generally prevented from doing so. The means to prevent them were often oblique (the more northern the city, the more oblique). McKelvey, in his history of Rochester, New York, cites an occurrence at the turn of the century: "Economic and social obstacles everywhere obstructed [the Negroes'] progress, and in Rochester, when several enterprising Negroes, accepting the fact that no decent hotel in the city would admit them, sought to erect one of their own, no suitable site could be found."* Blacks in the United States have been kept in economic subjection not by their suppression in the rural world where, in any case, they could have added no new jobs to the economy. They have been kept in their economic subjection by discrimination in cities.

Long ago, W.E.B. DuBois compared the condition of blacks in the United States to people imprisoned behind "some thick sheet of invisible but horribly tangible plate glass" through which they can see and be seen but through which they cannot be heard. He wrote of the people behind the glass that, at first, "one talks on evenly and logically . . . but notices that the passing throng does not even turn its head, or if it does, glances curiously and

*But political progress was being made! This also from McKelvey about Rochester: "A local branch of the Colored Voters League was formed in 1895, a Republican club that created a new but healthy division within Negro ranks and assured them an occasional appointment. Thus one of their number . . . held the post of secretary to the local board of civil service examiners that year. Although the efforts of several Negroes to secure equal treatment in restaurants and shoeshine parlors failed when the courts managed to dodge the question, the press carried many strong editorials condemning lynchings in Southern states."

walks on. . . . [The prisoners] get excited; they talk louder; they gesticulate. Some of the passing world stop in curiosity; these gesticulations seem so pointless; they laugh and pass on. They still either do not hear at all, or hear but dimly, and even what they hear, they do not understand. Then the people within may become hysterical. They may scream and hurl themselves against the barriers, hardly realizing in their bewilderment that they are screaming in a vacuum unheard and that their antics may actually seem funny to those outside looking in. They may even, here and there, break through in blood and disfigurement, and find themselves faced by a horrified, implacable and quite overwhelming mob of people frightened for their own very existence."

But the situation is worse than even this picture suggests. For if whites in the United States really were to ignore what blacks do, if they really were unaware of what goes on in black communities in American cities, blacks would, in fact, actually have a chance to develop work and add new work to old. But black people in their ghettos are regulated absolutely by whites. A black neurosurgeon, Dr. Thomas Matthew (about whom I shall have more to say shortly), replied when he was asked by a white government official how city agencies might help Negro self-help projects, "Get out of our way, and let us try something." Among well-meaning whites, the latest fad is to give tax exemptions to white corporations to build new housing for blacks and grants of millions to white-owned public utilities and other large corporations to train blacks. This is much like foreign aid to a colony that is not allowed to develop its own work. Along the same lines, a few years ago New York City and the Federal government undertook, with fanfare, to rehabilitate a group of thirty-seven buildings in Harlem. Black-owned construction firms were theoretically free to bid for the work, but there was a booby trap. All thirty-seven buildings were put into one "package." Therefore, only firms able to get bonding (required by city and Federal regulations) for so large a job could bid for it, and the only firms that could get the bonding were firms that were already doing big jobs, which meant that they were white contracting firms. Of course the work went to a large, white-owned company. If the contracts had been awarded for each building individually—an eminently practical procedure and customary in cases where buildings are being rehabilitated privately in white areas—black contractors could have competed for the jobs. An association of black construction and contracting organizations in New York, struggling to establish a foothold for their work, had begged the city to put the buildings out to bid separately, to no avail. The association, again to no avail, then asked the House of Representatives to investigate this situation and find out why the city was freezing them out of work they were capable of undertaking.

In 1966, the Small Business Administration of the Federal government proudly announced a program for encouraging new businesses owned by blacks. But the agency placed certain restrictions on its loans, of which the first was that any person receiving such a loan must be "at the poverty level," which in practice means being virtually a pauper. This, of course, eliminated in one neat stroke a great many potentially fine loan prospects. In December of 1966 the New York administrator made still another strange rule. All persons in the ghettos seeking loans "must prove a real need in their community for the type of business they want to start." It had to be shown that the work would fill an existing, recognizable "economic void." The administrator, of course, was to be the judge. Any possibility of innovations was nullified.

But in other cases, the excuse for continued suppression is that the ghettos are not different and must be subject to the same rules that apply elsewhere. Consider the experience of Dr. Matthew who is the organizer and director of an interracial community hospital in the largely black section of Jamaica, Queens, at the outskirts of New York City. Though he got no encouragement from the city, and some interference, the hospital managed not only to survive but to flourish. Its success gave rise to a problem. Public transportation in the neighborhood was so poor that the hospital's workers and many of its patients were inconvenienced going back and forth. To solve this problem, Dr. Matthew organized a "free" bus service. Under his plan, riders who could afford to pay bought, with each ride, a twenty-five-cent bus company bond. Those who could not, paid nothing. This novel arrangement was a brilliant solution to a number of difficulties. Those who could not pay, but who needed the transportation, got it. Bonds, instead of fares, afforded advantages. For one thing, they made a proud statement: that here was a service that really belonged to the black community. For another, the bonds were not technically fares. Transportation services charging a fare need a franchise to operate, and that is hard to come by. Dr. Matthew had invented a loophole. Franchises, when they were first instituted, were useful in promoting development of transportation because they afforded protection, rather like a patent or copyright, for transportation innovators. Later, they were a bulwark of city corruption; they were something that people who controlled political machinery could sell. Now the only usefulness of franchises is that they protect obsolete monopolies. These monopolies are, for the most part, publicly owned, which means there is no recourse against them no matter how badly they perform.

Dr. Matthew's bus service flourished, so much so that he soon organized a second bus line in Harlem where people have long complained about the public surface transportation and have engaged in numerous but futile little campaigns to persuade the city to improve it. Up to this point, what had been occurring was a classic illustration

of some of the development principles I have been discussing in this book. New work had been logically added to
older work, to solve a peripheral problem. The new work
was being expanded in its own right. It was not a slavish
imitation of existing methods, but was adapted creatively
to the real and concrete situation. Pause to consider where
this kind of innovation might lead. Suppose scores—or
better, hundreds—of small new transportation services
were started in the city to meet this or that difficulty.
Transportation in New York might actually begin to improve—even to develop.

But early in 1968, as soon as Dr. Matthew's second bus
line had started, the city government went to court and obtained an injunction against both lines, which were forced
to close. That was the end of that. People who are prevented from solving their own problems cannot solve problems for their cities either.

Excess Capital

One of the most expensive things an economy can buy is
economic trial, error and development. What makes the
process expensive are the great numbers of enterprises
that must find initial capital—which must include those
that will not succeed—and the great numbers that must
then find relatively large sums of expansion capital as they
do begin to succeed. "Expensive," of course, does not
mean "wasteful." Development work pays; indeed an economy does not continue to pay its way without development
work, unless by a gradually declining standard of living
among many of its people. Nevertheless, economic development is expensive and when development work is skimped
or obstructed, large amounts of capital thus become available for other uses instead.

Consider, for a moment, how much investment in new
and young enterprises might be bought with $300,000,000.
For example:

5,000 loans of $10,000 each	($ 50 million)
4,000 loans of $25,000 each	($100 million)
1,200 loans of $50,000 each	($ 60 million)
200 loans of $150,000 each	($ 30 million)
100 loans of $500,000 each	($ 50 million)
10 loans of $1,000,000 each	($ 10 million)

I mention the sum of $300,000,000 because it happens to be the amount of money that was spent in the 1950s upon public housing and related public construction in one district of New York, East Harlem, which has a population of about 200,000 persons. The economic problems of East Harlem are now worse, if anything, than before this expenditure was made. The rates of unemployment, underemployment, welfare—and even the deterioration of housing—have increased, not declined. All kinds of acute practical problems have become more acute.* No money to speak of goes into East Harlem for people there to use producing goods and services, developing new work, and becoming economically self-supporting. But this is obviously not owing to lack of capital, per se; witness the $300,000,000 made available to the housing projects.

Consider the welfare costs of New York City which, as I write this, have reached a rate of $1,400,000,000 annually. Suppose ten percent of that were invested annually in new and young enterprises; consider how many such investments could be bought with $140,000,000 in one city in each year. Does ten percent of the welfare budget seem a lot? But welfare costs have doubled in only a few years, which means that much more than an annual ten percent increment has been available for a thoroughly unproductive type of expenditure. Lack of capital, per se, has obviously not been the reason for lack of a relatively modest investment in development of new work. Con-

*Incidentally, more than 1,300 commercial enterprises, of which a large proportion belonged to Puerto Ricans, and more than 500 noncommercial enterprises were destroyed, because they were physically in the way of the housing projects.

sider the billions of dollars available for highways, many of which are pure makework for powerful construction unions.* One is reminded of Mohenjo-daro and Harappā where the mass-produced pottery multiplied while nothing new was developed, until the people must have had more cups than they knew what to do with.

In sum, when the development of a formerly strong economy is neglected, so much capital becomes available for unproductive purposes that it is almost an embarrassment. People are hard put to devise ways to use it. The society seems extraordinarily affluent for a time, and in a way it is. For the society is economizing on one of the most expensive things it might otherwise buy. All sorts of philanthropies, extravangances and displays of vainglory become possible. One reason Manchester impressed Disraeli so favorably was that large amounts of capital generated in Manchester were *not* going into further development of the Manchester economy. Thus they were available in great plenty for other uses, including unusual civic adornment.

To cope with an embarrassment of riches, a city may export capital. To be sure, developing and growing cities are normally exporters of capital, but when they stop developing their own local economies—stop generating new exports and replacing imports—they become extraordinary exporters of capital. Charleston, South Carolina, was just such before the Civil War. It was unable to use the capital it generated locally—probably because almost half its people were slaves. When everyone within so large

*Just one stretch of such highway in New York City, less than two miles long—which will solve nothing and indeed will only compound present traffic and pollution problems—will destroy or dislocate some 800 businesses employing about ten thousand persons, and will cost close to $200,000,000. It is being pushed by an alliance of the construction labor unions, one of the city's two largest banks, and a number of government agencies whose own growth depends upon this and similar projects.

a proportion of a city's population is forestalled from engaging in development work, there is relatively little use locally for capital after a certain amount has been spent upon luxury and display. Extraordinary exports of capital from a city are invariably, I think, associated with discriminatory use of capital in that city. Most of Charleston's exported money seems to have gone to Boston. But it is doubtful that much of it was spent upon development work in Boston itself, for Boston, beginning in the 1820s, was exporting capital also—though closer to home. Boston capitalists were beginning to build up the stagnant company towns of New England. Charleston money joined Boston money in these enterprises. And soon Boston itself was to contain a large population, its Irish immigrants, who were discriminated against by Boston's capitalists and hampered from developing much new work of their own.

Almost no capital is used in Detroit now for developing new goods, services, enterprises or industries there, while Detroit exports extraordinary amounts of the capital it generates. Some is exported in the form of the immense philanthropies of the Ford Foundation, dispensed from its headquarters in New York throughout the world. Among other things, the Foundation has financed many studies of the "causes" of poverty, and of what is wrong with the poor in stagnant cities.

When most of the cities in a country neglect their development of new kinds of work, especially by those low in the social hierarchies (whose numbers must either grow in such a situation, or be drained off by emigration to countries with expanding economies), there is nowhere to export the embarrassing superfluity of capital except abroad. The immense exports of capital by the United States during the past quarter century are, in large part, money that was *not* spent in the expensive business of economic trial, error and development by blacks—and others too—in American cities; money that was *not* spent on development of new goods and services to solve acute practical problems in those cities as those problems began to pile up. The embarrassment of riches in an economy that is economizing on development of new work is temporary. It is a prelude to stagnation.

8

Some Patterns of
Future Development

We now have in hand all the major processes at work in a
growing city economy. First, the city finds in an older
city or cities an expanding market for its initial export
work, and it builds up a collection of numerous local businesses to supply producers' goods and services to the initial
export work. Second, some of the local suppliers of producers' goods and services export their own work. The
city builds up an additional collection of local businesses
to supply producers' goods and services to the new export
work. Some of these new local suppliers take to exporting
their own work. The city builds up more local businesses
to supply producers' goods and services to them, and so
on. The city earns a growing volume and growing diversity
of imports.

Third, many of the imports the city has been earning
are replaced by goods and services produced locally,

a process that causes explosive city growth. The city, at the same time, shifts the composition of its imports. Its local economy grows large (and diverse) in proportion to the volume of the city's exports and imports. Owing to the powerful multiplier effect of the replacement process, the local economy contains room for entirely new kinds of goods and services, that is, goods and services formerly neither imported nor locally produced. Among these can be unprecedented goods and services. The replacement of imports causes total economic activity to expand rapidly.

Fourth, the city's greatly enlarged and greatly diversified local economy becomes a potential source of numerous and diversified exports, including many consumer goods and services as well as producers' goods and services, and still other exports built upon local goods and services. The city's exporting organizations arise by a) adding the export work to other people's local work; b) adding the export work to different local work of their own; and c) exporting their own local work. By generating new exports, the city earns more imports. But many of the new exports merely compensate for older exports the city loses through obsolescence of older exports, transplants of some exporting organizations into the rural world, and replacement of its exports by local production in former customer cities.

Fifth, from this time on, the city continues to generate new exports and earn imports; replace imports with local production; generate new exports and earn imports; replace imports with local production, and so on.

All of these processes, taken together, compose two interlocking reciprocating systems; the first triggers off the second. (A diagram correlating the two reciprocating systems appears in Section IV of the Appendix.) If any one process fails, the entire system fails and the city stagnates economically.

Among the producers' goods and services that form in the course of these events are those that supply capital to new goods and services that are forming and growing, as well as to older goods and services. The root process is the adding of new work to older divisions of labor, thus multiplying the divisions of labor, to some of which still newer activities can be added. This underlying process, which I have symbolized as $D + A \longrightarrow nD$, makes possible all the others.

The Emergence of Differentiated Production

These processes and the systems they compose are old and predictable, though the goods and services they cast up change and are not necessarily predictable. As the new goods and services emerge, certain dominant patterns of economic organization also change. These are large, gradual and cumulative movements. For example, the dominant form of manufacturing used to be craftwork. This has been succeeded in currently advanced economies by mass production, a sequence, incidentally, which occurs in ancient as well as modern times. Mohenjo-daro and Harappā had their mass-production industries, and cities of the Roman Empire developed mass-produced lamps, pottery and other utensils. Machines developed in the industrial revolution of the nineteenth century have been strikingly successful means of carrying out mass production, but the concept and practice are older. Is mass production the ultimate type of manufacturing? Or is there a more advanced type?

Before touching on that question, let us notice another large pattern that has changed over time: organizational work. Merchants used to organize manufacturing; in the main, the type of manufacturing they organized was craftwork. Trade was not only the work of arranging exchanges of goods, it was also the activity that organized other economic activities. Manufacturers used to aspire to become merchants because merchants were the organizers. But now we do not find automobile manufacturers, say, aspiring to become dealers. Manufacturing now tends to be the economic activity around which other activities center, including many forms of trade and services. Manufacturing has become not only the work of making things, but also an activity that organizes other economic activities. This change has corresponded, in time, with the rise of mass-production manufacturing. For those who would like to see these movements shown schematically, a little diagram appears in Section V of the Appendix.

When Adam Smith looked at England, the most advanced economy of the eighteenth century, he found clues to future patterns of economic development. Mass production was not then the dominant form of manufacturing, but nevertheless Smith saw it as a coming thing. I think, from the symptoms to be observed, that the economy of the United States is in process of stagnating.* Nevertheless, it is still the most advanced economy to be found. Therefore, no matter what its own future may be, it is a suitable economy in which to look for clues to patterns that may be found in more highly developed economies of the future—wherever those economies may prove to be.

Garment making, I think, affords an interesting clue to future manufacturing because it exemplifies manufacturing of three distinctly different kinds. The oldest is craftwork, the method of hand tailors and seamstresses. It persists to this day in fine custom tailoring and in the work of couturiers. The second is mass production. This is the method used for making overalls, army uniforms, men's popularly priced shirts, most socks, nylon stockings, and many

*I would not venture to prophesy how decisive this stagnation is. If it proves to be profound and unremitting, it could be comparable to that of the later Roman Empire or to that of many another economy in which revitalization, if it has occurred at all, has followed only upon revolution. If stagnation is still reversible in the United States, then by definition vigorous city-development processes not only can, but will, start into motion again.

standard items of underclothing. Mass-production manufacturing of garments in the United States began in the 1860s. At that time, it would have appeared that garment manufacturing was to be done in a few very large organizations turning out highly standardized products. One of the first successes, described by Ishbel Ross in *Crusades and Crinolines*, was a small hoop skirt turned out in the factory of Ellen Demorest, a remarkable innovator of many developments in garment manufacturing, pattern manufacturing, and fashion journalism. The skirt she mass-produced was "one of the wonders of the crinoline age and achieved immense popularity and distribution." A writer of the time, quoted by Miss Ross, said, "Madame Demorest deserves grateful remembrance for being the first to introduce a really excellent, cheap hoop skirt; and so popular did they immediately become, that other manufacturers were compelled to reduce their prices, although none have ever pretended to vie with these in cost, quality of material used, and amount of labor expended upon them." It was these skirts to which *Fortune* was referring in a survey of the New York garment industry almost a century later, when it noted that one-third of all those employed in the industry in New York in the 1860s worked in one establishment that made hoop skirts, "certainly the closest approach that there has ever been to a General Motors in the [women's] clothing trade." While no one organization did come to dominate the mass-production clothing industry, the greatest successes in mass-produced garments were made by firms that concentrated upon finding large common denominators in the clothing market.

The third method of garment manufacturing has arisen chiefly during this century, has grown much more rapidly than the other two, and has become the dominant form. For lack of any present generic name, let us call it differentiated production. This method produces relatively modest amounts of each item as compared with mass production, yet it is not craft manufacturing either. In some ways it resembles mass-production work more than it resembles craftwork. Thanks to this third kind of garment making, one can look at a crowd of thousands of persons in a large city park on a fine day or gathered to watch a parade, and be hard put to find two women or two children dressed in identical outfits. One also sees in the same crowd more variety in men's clothing than one would have found a generation ago. This is the kind of garment manufacturing that used to amaze visiting Europeans; they took back the extraordinary news that even shopgirls and factory girls in the United States were fashionably clothed in a dazzling variety of dresses. Europeans now use this kind of manufacturing themselves. In America it is this manufacturing that renders the poor deceptively invisible, as Michael Harrington has pointed out. They do not wear a uniform of the poor, nor do they dress in rags. Because of their clothing, they look more prosperous than they are, an amazing economic achievement on the part of the garment industry.

The salient distinction between mass production and differentiated production is in the way the manufacturers look at the market—or, if one prefers, at the need for garments. A mass-production manufacturer seeks common denominators in the market; he exploits similar needs. A differentiated-production manufacturer depends on differences to be found in the market. He deliberately exploits the fact that people have differing tastes in styles, fabrics and colors, differing clothing budgets and, as individuals, reasons for needing diverse clothing (e.g., garments for going to parties, lounging, sports, work, city activities, country activities). The two different approaches to the market give rise to other distinctions between mass production and differentiated production. Mass production churns out far greater numbers of identical items than does differentiated production. Much more design and development work goes into differentiated production than into mass production, in proportion to the volume of output.

Mass-production manufacturing introduces variations into total output only if great expansion in volume justifies variations which can also be produced in large volumes. A producer of black socks may devote part of his expanding volume to production of brown socks, much as automobile makers have introduced new models when their markets expanded. But the variations thus introduced in mass production are almost invariably superficial and they too are calculated to satisfy major common denominators in the potential market. The variations created through differentiated production are precisely what permit this production at all; *variations are not a result of expanded volume in differentiated production*, they are primary.

Consider, in this light, what has been happening to newspapers in the United States. The mass-production city dailies, aimed at common denominators in the market for newspapers, seem to have passed their heyday. They have declined steeply in number; many of those remaining have declined in circulation. In the meantime, city and suburban weekly newspapers have been growing rapidly both in number and circulation. The new weeklies aim at differences within the city newspaper markets. They carry news and features which are of vital importance or of interest to people in this or that district, but may be of little importance or interest elsewhere. Some cut across geography to aim at special communities of interest. These weeklies are not a return to the old-fashioned country and small-town weeklies run off on hand presses by their editors. In their production methods, the new papers are more like the mass-production newspapers. Nor are they, as a rule, culturally backward. Some make the mass-production newspapers seem old-fashioned in their writing, layouts, photography and subject matter. The weeklies are doing a job that was left undone, and that must inherently be left undone, in mass production. The reason the mass-production dailies are declining is not, however, that there are no significant similarities in a city's total market for news, but that the job once done by mass-production newspapers has been largely duplicated by television and radio news and feature programs, and by the mass-production weekly news magazines.

Also, there is a market for standard agricultural tractors and their accessories which are aimed at widespread similarities of needs among farmers, though this is no longer the kind of farm-equipment business that is growing appreciably. As far back as 1961, *Fortune* reported that the giant, mass-production farm-equipment manufacturers were in economic trouble. Their business was static or declining, and they were saddled with huge factories working below capacity and numerous retail outlets that no longer paid their way. The rapidly growing farm-equipment business was going disproportionately to more than a thousand small manufacturers who were aiming precisely at differences within the market. The big companies had stayed too long with "the mass concept," *Fortune* commented. "Less of [the farmers'] equipment money goes for the standard items. . . . Today a small company can manufacture a highly specialized item of equipment just as easily as a large firm, and often at a better profit." Again, the relatively small-scale differentiated equipment production is not a return to craft methods.

In *The Silent Spring*, Rachel Carson attacked the practice of applying chemical pesticides wholesale—the mass-production approach to pest infestations. Instead, she advocated differentiated production based upon sophisticated biological controls of varying kinds, according to circumstances. This is a far cry from depending on the barnyard cat and the fly swatter, and resigning oneself to watching the locusts consume the year's work. It is a far more advanced approach than indiscriminate, wholesale use of chemicals. Miss Carson also advocated differentiation of crops within geographical localities, pointing out that mass production in farming itself—great factory farms devoted to one kind of cash crop—leads inherently to drastic imbalances of natural life and tends to increase the potential ravages of plant diseases and pests. (It also, I might add, can be economically disastrous to a rural region and often has been. A rural economy with all its eggs in one basket is bound to lose out from changes in markets.) As we might expect, Miss Carson's point has been heeded first in cities. Not many years ago, for instance, New York City was using the mass-production approach to street-tree planting. All the trees planted were London planes which were raised in great mass-production tree nurseries. As Robert Nichols, a landscape architect, had been pointing out, some twenty different varieties of trees do quite as well as London planes on the city streets; but the city had been committed, under a powerful administrator, Robert Moses, to mass production in this as in all things affecting parks or supervised by the parks department. Now, realizing the wholesale disaster that a London plane tree blight would bring, the city has begun differentiated planting of street trees.

I have brought trees and agricultural equipment into this discussion not only because they illustrate that there is more reason to produce for differences than variations of whims or tastes, but also to show that differentiated production is not a luxury and another term for "custom made." Differentiated production, in spite of its disproportionate requirements for design and development work, is not an extravagance. In real life, real and important differences abound, whether in nature or in a market, whether in the resistance of trees to diseases or in the information about current events needed by people in differing districts. And with economic development all kinds of differentiations increase; they do not diminish.

For some economic needs, mass production is superb.

The common denominators are valid and enduring. Mass production is well suited, for example, to brick manufacturing, making screwdrivers, bed sheets, paper, electric light bulbs and telephones. I am not proposing that mass production will disappear from economic life. Farmers still need their standard tractors; people still need standard denim pants or their equivalents. The point is that for some goods, mass production is a makeshift. It represents only an early stage of development and is valid only as an inadequate expedient until more advanced differentiated production has been developed. Consider transportation. The automobile is overdepended upon as an expedient for replacing the still less adequate horse; it is largely a makeshift in lieu of still undeveloped types of vehicles and methods of surface transportation for short and long distance. Still, it is unlikely that the automobile will be supplanted by some other mass-produced vehicle. Rather, it will be supplanted by many different kinds of vehicles and many new kinds of transportation services based not upon crude common denominators of moving people and goods, but on differentiations. Nor will the automobile be wholly supplanted. It will be valid for some of these needs, although no doubt it will be radically changed and also more differentiated. Other vehicles will be completely different from automobiles. New forms of swift and smooth water travel will almost surely be developed, possibly making use of hydrofoils of many designs and sizes. These will first be used on waterways for express transportation within cities and between cities. Their manufacture will most likely begin in cities where they are used first.

In still other kinds of manufacturing, mass production is so unsuitable that it cannot be used even as an expedient. In such cases, if the industry is to develop at all, it must be based on differentiated production from the beginning. The electronics industries are an illustration of this kind of manufacturing. Many business analysts have pointed out that electronics manufacturing has developed differently from automobile manufacturing in which hundreds of enterprises were reduced to very few as the industry grew. The hundreds of early electronics enterprises did not reduce to a few huge mass-production companies. Instead, the hundreds increased to thousands and most have remained relatively small. The radical difference is not accidental. Electronics manufacturing is based only slightly on similarities of needs for electronic devices; it must satisfy immense numbers of diverse needs within the total market.

The construction industries have emerged only rather recently from the craft-manufacturing stage, of which many vestiges linger. As mass production became predominant in many other types of manufacturing, construction was a case of arrested development. Now construction seems to be arrested in the mass-production stage, although mass-production building is clearly a makeshift. For example, back in 1961 New York City proposed rebuilding the neighborhood in which I lived. The idea was to wipe out virtually every structure that occupied the land and mass-produce a new "neighborhood," formed for the most part of large, identical buildings. Even if the plan had been to construct identical small buildings it would have been the same approach in essence. The idea was to build for similarities of need, similarities of use and, by means of clearance, to impose similarities of sites that could accommodate mass-production construction. The project was to have cost an estimated $35,000,000. Because of the wholesale destruction of more than seven hundred already existing dwellings, the expenditure would have resulted in a net gain of about 300 dwelling units and a net loss of 156 businesses that employed about 2,500 persons. Some of these businesses might have relocated elsewhere, at additional economic costs not included in the $35,000,000, but most would have represented a total loss. They would have disappeared from the economy.

This scheme was defeated. Residents and property owners in the neighborhood, through their civic organization, the West Village Committee, then hired a firm of architects and planners and instructed them to work out a wholly different scheme. New buildings, gardens and public sidewalk plazas were to be added in already vacant sites, abandoned plots and makeshift parking lots, without destroying a single existing dwelling or requiring the removal of any business, other than the random and usually illegal parking. The architects met these requirements by working out designs for three different sizes of relatively small buildings (most, of ten apartments each) that could be fitted into existing vacant and abandoned sites individually and in combinations. The buildings themselves were capable of many differentiations, not only into apartments of differing sizes, but also of differing uses such as retail stores and workshops. This scheme, costing an estimated $8,700,000 instead of $35,000,000 (both at 1964 prices), provided a net increase of 475 dwelling units, instead of 300, and destroyed no businesses. This second plan was a far cry from the old craft manufacturing of dwellings; indeed, it was designed to use a number of building techniques and materials more advanced than those being currently employed by mass-production builders. But it is a long way from mass-producing a neighborhood.*

---

*Apparently it was too advanced. Although the differentiated-production plan was prepared in 1962, and building could have begun that year, the city bureaucracies—whose philosophy and also rules and regulations were all shaped by the mass-production approach to construction and planning—opposed it adamantly until 1967, when they at last permitted it to begin inching its way through red tape, a process still under way as this is written. In the meantime, mass-production construction has continued, and vast amounts of money have of course been spent for an amazingly small yield of improved housing accommodations; the shortage of habitable housing has thus been increasing, not diminishing, as deterioration has outrun net construction.

With growth of differentiated production in developing economies of the future, we may expect to find other changes in economic life. The average size of manufacturing enterprises will be smaller than at present. But the numbers of manufacturing enterprises will greatly increase and so will the total volume of manufactured goods. Most mass-production enterprises that have not been made obsolete by differentiated production—and many will remain—will have been transplanted to the countryside and into inert towns. There, with their low requirements of labor, their large requirements of space, and their relative self-sufficiency, these industries can operate more efficiently than in cities. Mass-production manufacturing will no longer be regarded as city work. Cities will manufacture even more goods than they do today, but these will be almost wholly differentiated production goods, made in relatively small, or very small, organizations.

Manufacturing work will, I think, no longer be the chief activity around which other economic activities are organized, as it is today and as the work of merchants once was. Instead, services will become the predominant organizational work, the instigators of other economic activities, including manufacturing. For an obvious example, consider what has been happening in the case of office machines. The older sorts—typewriters, dictating machines, adding machines and so on—are bought simply as machines. If a service is also bought along with them, it is a minor appendage: maintenance checking and repair, brief instructions to users of the machines, a trade-in service when a new machine is bought to replace an old one. But some of the new kinds of office machines are not bought in this way. Rather, what is bought is first and foremost a service: the service of analyzing and programming the work of an office, such as billing, payroll preparation, and sales and inventory analyzing. The machines are bought as an appendage to accommodate the system prescribed by the analytical service. Sometimes the machines are not even bought. Instead, an office may buy services from a computer or data-processing center, and it will be the service organization that buys or leases the necessary machines. In either case, service work is the organizing activity for the other work, including the manufacturing of the machines.

It is not likely that manufacturers of vehicles will organize the transportation of the future, as they do now, to a considerable extent. The organizing forces, rather, will be transportation services, including even the services of renting differentiated automobiles for different purposes to individual users. The manufacturing will be done specifically to meet needs of these various services. When I was conjecturing, in Chapter Three, how waste recycling systems might be organized in developing economies of the future, I suggested that services would be the key work in such industries, and that the service organizations would be customers for many kinds of waste-collecting equipment. This conjecture was based upon the logic of the work, but it corresponds to what I suspect is the coming trend in economic organization generally. Service organizations in developing economies of the future are likely to draw upon products made by many different manufacturers, and are likely to be larger than manufacturing organizations. Even so, they will begin as small businesses and expand as they add innovations.

No doubt, to English-speaking people of the future, especially if they happen to live in developing and highly advanced economies, it will seem quaint that "service" carries a connotation of servants' work, and even quainter that these economically important and awesomely large organizations should, in many cases, have sprung from such menial work as cleaning, minor maintenance or chauffeuring. The case will seem, no doubt, as quaint as it seems to us that manufacturing arose upon servants' work, or that merchants originated from vagabonds and beggars who were even lowlier than the manorial servants of their time.

Economic Conflict

There is no point in pretending that economic development is in everyone's interest. Development of petroleum for lamp fuel was not good for the American whaling industry nor for those whose economic and social power were bound up with that industry. Development of new forms of public transit would not be good for today's petroleum industry or highway builders or automobile manufacturers, nor for anyone whose economic or social power is bound up with those industries. Development of economically important new goods and services by blacks would not be to the interests, as they see them, of white racists, including unconscious racists and paternalists.

In developing economies, even the well-established activities that are not directly affected adversely by new goods and services are indirectly affected, and so are the people whose economic and social power are tied up with those established activities. It is a question of sharing power. As an economy grows, its older, well-established economic interests grow less important and less powerful as a part of the whole. Furthermore, the most meteoric rises (starting at almost nothing) occur in new activities. The older activities do not necessarily decline in absolute size and wealth—indeed, they or their changing derivatives often expand in response to the general expansion—but they suffer at least a relative decline. And so do the people who derive their social and economic power from them. In Çatal Hüyük it is unlikely that the huntsmen ruled the roost as they must have at an earlier, remote time when there was no trading in the ancestral society and no way of getting food and craft materials other than hunting. The malapportioned state legislatures of the United

States, elected by votes disproportionately weighted in favor of rural areas, small towns and little stagnant cities, were an anachronism. But they were an accurate picture of political, social and economic power at the time apportionments were first made. And then they were clung to by precisely the groups in American life—the farmers, the people in inert towns—whose importance in the whole had declined as the rest of the economy developed more swiftly. In short, economic development, no matter when or where it occurs, is profoundly subversive of the status quo.

Marx thought that the principal conflict to be found in economic life, at any rate in industrialized countries, was the deep disparity of interests between owners and employees, but this is a secondary kind of conflict. If one accepts Marx's conception, then revolutions should occur (as indeed he expected) in the most industrialized societies, rather than in economically backward and stagnant countries. Also, if one accepts his conception, much of the behavior of labor unions becomes impossible to understand. In real life, unions, once they have become institutionalized, can successfully deal with employers; and the interests of the two, to a large extent, then coincide. It is to the interests of construction workers that a great deal of construction be undertaken, and if this hurts other workers by wiping out the businesses to which their jobs are attached, so much the worse for them. It is also in the interests of labor unions that their industries should not change technologically; this, of course, often puts unions in conflict with employers—but even more so, in conflict with the interests of industries (and workers in those industries) that produce new technological devices. The inherent solidarity of the working class is an economic fiction.

Nor do the interests of already well-organized workers inherently correspond with the interests of those who have no well-established work to pursue, who are "redundant" in a stagnant economy, and thus short-changed on the goods and services they receive. Should the creativity of such people be allowed to flourish, it must change things as they are, upset the status quo, make some well-established activities obsolete and reduce the relative importance of others. Of course, the creativity of "redundant" people would make the economy develop, prosper and expand; but it is also a threat to all those workers and employers attached to activities potentially threatened by development. It is no accident that demands by blacks for control of ghetto education are desperately opposed not only by school boards (employers) but also by associations of school principals and by teachers' unions (employees); if anything, more implacably by the latter than the former. That the change may be to the benefit of children, and might result in significant development of education, is beside the point to those threatened. To be sure, when almost no workers in an economy believe they are becoming better off, and almost all are coming to hate the status quo, they may join in an attack upon it. But an economy must already have become profoundly flawed before this occurs, especially if the assault is to succeed.

The primary economic conflict, I think, is between people whose interests are with already well-established economic activities, and those whose interests are with the emergence of new economic activities. This is a conflict that can never be put to rest except by economic stagnation. For the new economic activities of today are the well-established activities of tomorrow which will be threatened in turn by further economic development. In this conflict, other things being equal, the well-established activities and those whose interests are attached to them, must win. They are, by definition, the stronger. The only possible way to keep open the economic opportunities for new activities is for a "third force" to protect their weak and still incipient interests. Only governments can play this economic role. And sometimes, for pitifully brief intervals, they do. But because development subverts the status quo, the status quo soon subverts governments. When development has proceeded for a bit, and has cast up strong new activities, governments come to derive their power from those already well-established interests, and not from still incipient organizations, activities and interests.

In human history, most people in most places most of the time have existed miserably in stagnant economies. Developing economies have been the exceptions, and their histories, as developing economies, have been brief. Now here, now there, a group of cities grows vigorously by the processes I have been describing in this book and then lapses into stagnation for the benefit of people who have already become powerful. I am not one who believes that flying saucers carry creatures from other solar systems who poke curiously into our earthly affairs. But if such beings were to arrive, with their marvelously advanced contrivances, we may be sure we would be agog to learn how their technology worked. The important question however, would be something quite different: What kinds of governments had they invented which had succeeded in keeping open the opportunities for economic and technological development instead of closing them off? Without helpful advice from outer space, this remains one of the most pressing and least regarded problems.

Provided that some groups on earth continue either muddling or revolutionizing themselves into periods of economic development, we can be absolutely sure of a few things about future cities. The cities will not be smaller, simpler or more specialized than cities of today. Rather, they will be more intricate, comprehensive, diversified, and larger than today's, and will have even more complicated jumbles of old and new things than ours do. The bureaucratized, simplified cities, so dear to present-day city planners and urban designers, and familiar also to readers of science fiction and utopian proposals, run counter to the processes of city growth and economic development. Conformity and monotony, even when they are embellished with a froth of novelty, are not attributes of developing and economically vigorous cities. They are attributes of stagnant settlements. To some people, the vision of a future in which life is simpler than it is now, and work has become so routine as to be scarcely noticeable, is an exhilarating vision. To other people, it is depressing. But no matter. The vision is irrelevant for developing and influential economies of the future. In highly developed future economies, there will be more kinds of work to do than today, not fewer. And many people in great, growing cities of the future will be engaged in the unroutine business of economic trial and error. They will be faced with acute practical problems which we cannot now imagine. They will add new work to older work.

Appendix

I *The Simple Export-Generating Process, Diagramed*

As explained in Chapter Four, an embryonic city begins its growth because local suppliers of goods and services to the city's initial exporters become exporters of their own goods and services. This is a diagram of the embryonic city's economy before the process of export generating starts. That economy consists of four "blocks" of goods and services:

> the settlement's original export work (E);
> the imports earned by that work (I);
> local goods and services for producers (P);
> local goods and services for consumers (C).

The last two blocks, together, compose the local economy.

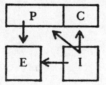

Some imports are directly incorporated into the city's export work, e.g., raw materials and machines for the export work, bought from other places by exporters. The rest of the city's earned imports go into the local economy where they are incorporated into locally produced or locally handled goods and services for producers and consumers. The arrows attached to the import block indicate these destinations.

Now let us suppose that a local supplier of goods and services to the initial export work begins to export his own work. This adds to the variety and also to the quantity of the city's exports:

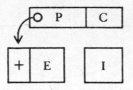

The imports earned by the embryonic city also increase. Some are likely to be preempted directly by the new export work, but the rest feed into the city's local economy, which is growing. Local producers' goods and services can grow and diversify owing to the growth of export work to be served; consumer goods and services can grow and diversify owing to the increase in the city's population of workers and their families. This local growth is the "export-multiplier effect," and is designated "+ EM":

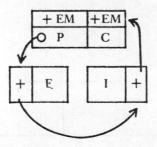

Because of the increased numbers and diversity of organizations supplying goods and services to the city's already increased export work, the same process is even more likely to happen again. More local suppliers of producers' goods and services take to exporting their own work:

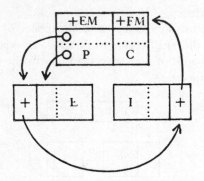

If this process continues vigorously, the net effect (subtracting any losses of older exports) is a consistent growth in both the volume and the variety of the young city's exports, accompanied by great growth in the variety and numbers of local suppliers of producers' goods and services and also growth of local consumer goods and services.

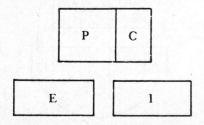

II *The Import-Replacing Process, Diagramed*

As explained in Chapter Five, after a city has built up a considerable volume and variety of imports, it becomes capable of replacing many of those imports, that is, producing them locally. For the sake of simplicity, let us assume that the city's volume of exports remains the same while an episode of import replacing is occurring. Let us use, as our diagrammatic example, the young city previously pictured, which is now earning a sizable quantity and diversity of imports and is about to replace half of this volume of imports with the same things, locally produced. We can think of this replacement work as a transferal of goods and services from the import block into the two blocks of the local economy. What is added to the local economy is subtracted from the imports:

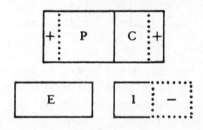

The part of the import block that had previously been occupied by those goods and services is now indicated by a dotted line. But of course the city is still earning as many imports as it would have, had this transferal not occurred. It is thus able to import other things, in place of those now locally produced. It has only shifted the composition of its imports. Therefore, beside the portion of the import block we have left vacant, let us add a new block of shifted imports (SI):

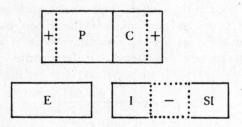

Some of these new, shifted imports must be incorporated into the locally made goods and services that were formerly imported. So let us cross out (X) that portion of shifted imports. The rest are, in effect, "extra" imports. They consist of increased quantities of things the city has continued to import (has not replaced), and also things the city did not previously import at all. These extra imports feed into the city's local economy:

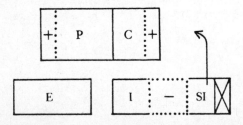

Due to those extra imports, the city's local economy can grow. This local growth is the "import-replacing multiplier effect" (+IM).

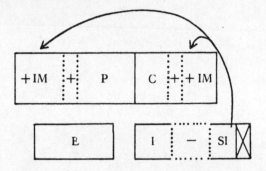

Now let us remove the empty space in the import block, that is, reconnect the two parts of the block. And let us compare the composition of the city economy now with its composition when import replacing was about to begin:

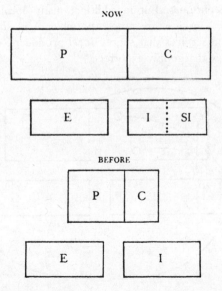

The volumes of exports and imports remain the same, although the imports have shifted in composition. The local economy of the city has grown. Therefore, the proportions of the local work and export work have changed.

III *Export Generating in a Large City, Diagramed*

As set forth in Chapter Six, after a city has developed a large local economy, it has also acquired a large reservoir of potential new exports. The simple export-generating process continues. But in addition, many local consumer goods and services are now exportable. And so are many goods and services that supply *local* producers, quite apart from those that supply exporters:

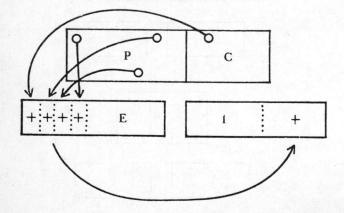

And in addition to these exports from the local economy, others are made possible by the local producers'
goods and services on which they can draw. We can show these
exports connected by dotted line to the local producers'
goods and services on which they depend:

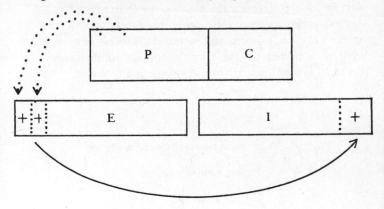

Of course, the city is also losing older exports while
it is generating new ones. But to the degree that new
exports overcompensate for losses of old ones, the city's
volume of imports grows. And the local economy grows
too, owing to the export-multiplier effect, just as happened
in the case of simple export generating.

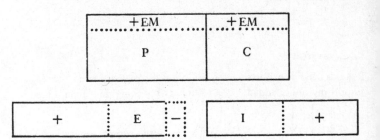

Conditions are thus prepared for another episode of the
import-replacing process.

IV *The Two Reciprocating Systems of City Growth*

The various processes that have been diagramed operate as two major reciprocating systems. The first system is the process of simple export generating in a young city. Producers' goods and services become exports. The export multiplier increases the numbers and varieties of producers' goods and services. More producers' goods and services become exports, and so on, the process sustaining itself as indicated by the curved arrows. Simultaneously, the city's earned imports grow in volume and variety:

SYSTEM 1

(((P goods become exports   )))
↙ ↙ ↙   Export multiplier added   )))

↓ ↓ ↓

Imports grow

The second system is set in motion. Imports, having grown, are replaced. The versatile export generating of a large city becomes possible. So do subsequent episodes of import replacing:

SYSTEM 1

P goods become exports
Export multiplier added

↓ ↓ ↓

Imports grow

SYSTEM 2

Imports replaced and shifted
Import-replacing multiplier added

↘ ↘ ↘

Versatile export generating
Export multiplier added

↓ ↓ ↓

Imports grow

V *Changing Patterns of Economic Activities*

As suggested in Chapter Eight, the predominant methods of manufacturing change as an economy develops. So do the kinds of activities around which—and also by which—other economic activities are organized. Let us correlate these changes, and also relate them to the situation in currently highly developed economies:

PAST	PRESENT	FUTURE?
craft production →	mass production →	differentiated production
organized by merchants ⟶	organized by manufacturers ⟶	organized by suppliers of services

VI *A Brief List of Some Ordinary Definitions*

Our ordinary vocabulary does not take account of the differences between the nature of cities and the nature of other settlements; e.g., "town" and "city" are often used interchangeably, as if cities were larger towns. We do not need new words to express the differences, but rather a little more precision in the use of old words. I suggest the following:

City—A settlement that consistently generates its economic growth from its own local economy.

Stagnant city—A settlement that formerly grew as a city, but has stopped doing so.

Metropolitan area—Economically, it means the same as "city." Politically, it means a city that has physically expanded beyond its formal boundaries, in the process engulfing former towns and, in some instances, coalescing with other, formerly separate, cities.

Town—A settlement that does not generate its growth from its own local economy and has never done so. The occasional export a town may have generated for itself has produced no consistent self-generating growth thereafter.

Village—A smaller town.

Urban—Pertaining only to cities and stagnant cities, not to towns.

National economy—While its accepted meaning, the sum of a nation's production of goods and services, is useful, the connotation of an amorphous sum is not. Owing to Leontief's analyses, it is now becoming widely appreciated that a nation's production is composed of "output" items for ultimate consumers and of "input" items going into that production. However, we need to add the further understanding that changes within a national economy arise from changes within city economies. A national economy is the sum of a nation's city economies and the past and current secondary effects of city economies upon the economies of towns, villages, countrysides and wildernesses.

Index

The page numbers indicate major references; they do not include all minor references.

JANE JACOBS was born in Scranton, Pennsylvania, and now lives in Toronto. From 1952 to 1962 Mrs. Jacobs was an associate editor of *Architectural Forum* in New York. She is married to an architect and they have two sons and a daughter. Her book *The Death and Life of Great American Cities* is also available in Vintage Books.